Galbraith
Harrington
Heilbroner

Economics and
Dissent in an
Age of Optimism

Galbraith Harrington Heilbroner

Economics and Dissent in an Age of Optimism

PRINCETON
UNIVERSITY
PRESS

By Loren J. Okroi

Copyright © 1988 by Princeton University Press
Published by Princeton University Press,
41 William Street, Princeton, New Jersey 08540
In the United Kingdom: Princeton University Press,
Guildford, Surrey

All Rights Reserved
Library of Congress Cataloging-in-Publication data will
be found on the last printed page of this book

ISBN 0-691-07771-1

Publication of this book has been aided by the
Whitney Darrow Fund of Princeton University Press

This book has been composed in Linotron Times Roman

Clothbound editions of Princeton University Press books
are printed on acid-free paper, and binding materials
are chosen for strength and durability. Paperbacks,
although satisfactory for personal collections, are not
usually suitable for library rebinding

Printed in the United States of America by
Princeton University Press,
Princeton, New Jersey

For my parents, Ann and Bernard Okroi

Alexis de Tocqueville

Towards the middle of the eighteenth century a group of writers known as the "Physiocrats" or "Economists," who made the problems of public administration their special study, came on the scene. Though the Economists figure less prominently than our philosophers in histories of the period and perhaps did less than they towards bringing about the Revolution, I am inclined to think it is from their writings that we learn most of its true character. In dealing with the problems of government the philosophers confined themselves for the most part to general ideas and purely abstract theories; Economists, while never losing sight of theory, paid more heed to practical politics. Whereas the philosophers depicted imaginary utopias, the Economists sometimes pointed out what could and should be done in the existing world.

Contents

Acknowledgments

I am indebted to all of my teachers in the Department of History at the University of California, Irvine, and to the department in general for the benefits I derived from its innovative and interdisciplinary approach to historical studies and for its financial support and confidence in my work. Most especially, I am grateful to my adivser and mentor, John Diggins, who encouraged me and taught me always to ask the hard questions and never to expect easy answers. Peter Clecak also provided helpful remarks concerning an early version of the manuscript. Of particular help in turning my dissertation into a book were Spencer Olin, whose criticisms of an earlier draft led me to rethink some of my views on corporate capitalism and who introduced me to the large and growing literature on participatory democracy, and Aida Donald of Harvard University Press, who introduced me to an indispensable process all authors must learn—editing down a manuscript to a lean and efficient form so that its chief function is explaining something to the reader and not, as in all preliminary expository writing, explaining something to oneself. I also wish to express my gratitude to Allan Gruchy and Robert Lekachman for their comments on a later draft of my work, to my editor at Princeton University Press, Sanford Thatcher, for persuading me to make some of the changes that were suggested and for other helpful advice, to copyeditor Andrew Mytelka for catching stylistic flaws I had overlooked, and to manuscript editor Charles Ault for his final editing and his help in moving the book through to publication. Finally, I wish to thank Michael Harrington for his kind permission to quote from his autobiographical work *Fragments of the Century*.

Introduction   *Ideas, Institutions, and Intellectuals*

"Government is not the solution," President Reagan proclaimed in his first inaugural address, "it's the problem." With this statement, summing up his essential philosophy of economics, society, and politics, Ronald Reagan set the tone for an administration that attempted to drastically alter the policies and programs of the previous half century. The extent and durability of the changes Reagan and his followers have set in motion are as yet uncertain; yet the direction and overall thrust of their efforts are unmistakable. They aim at nothing less than the drastic curtailment, if not the eradication, of the institutional legacy of the New Deal—that is, the American counterpart of the European welfare state. Moreover, just as striking as Reagan's proposed revolution has been the apparent public response. Less than two decades before, Americans had seemed willing not only to maintain their allegiance to the reformist ideals of the Democratic party, but even to expand the legislative embodiment of those ideals in the Great Society programs of President Johnson. Yet by 1980 they had seemingly become more than happy to "get government off their backs" and appeared to acquiesce in the dismantling of much of Lyndon Johnson's—and indeed even some of Franklin Roosevelt's—legislative work. FDR's birthday centennial in 1982, originally expected to be an approving glance backward and to some extent a celebration of the policies and programs of Roosevelt and his followers, instead turned out to be a strangely somber affair. Television and newspaper commentators used the occasion not to praise a once revered political leader, but rather to present melancholy retrospectives on the history of welfare capitalism in America. Portrayed as the misbegotten creation of well-intentioned but misguided idealists, it was now an inefficient and unwieldy luxury that, like an expensive, exotic pet, Americans could no longer afford to keep.

How had things come to such a pass in such a relatively short period of time? The answer is not simple or obvious. What *is* obvious however, is that one consequence of the events that had been set in motion during the previous decade was the apparent rejection not merely of the specific policies of Democratic politicians, but—much more significantly—the ideological and philosophical *rationales* for those policies. Those that had been formerly proclaimed and at least passively accepted, as well as the policies and programs that issued from them, can be broadly termed "social democratic." In general outline, they mimicked many of those common to other postwar-era Western democracies that had been governed by social democratic parties or coalitions. Why had social democratic ideology—the philosophy that underlay the modern welfare state—become largely discredited since the days of Roosevelt, Truman, Kennedy, and Johnson? In order to understand this, one must first come to terms with the role of ideas, their originators, and their popularizers in the realms of economics, society, and politics.

It is the underlying assumption of this essay that ideas, values, ideologies, and theories do not arise or exist in isolation from the institutions, historical events, processes, and forces that form their enveloping milieu. Ideas, whether influential or not, do not appear except in response to events, issues, problems, or to other ideas that are themselves responses to the concerns of real people living in a real world. Moreover, the only way that ideas can become influential and remain so in the long run is by becoming part of a nexus of socially sanctioned and legally protected roles and relationships that are called institutions. But just as it is a mistake to say, as John Maynard Keynes once did (although he perhaps did not intend this hyperbole to be taken literally), that the world is ruled by ideas and by little else, it is also an error to see them only as reflections of an underlying social reality. The best approach, I believe, is one that sees ideas as neither determined by their environment nor the reverse, but rather sees both as being in a constant state of mutual interaction.

Indeed, I see no a priori reason to suppose that the single group whose concern for ideas is its chosen vocation—intellectuals—has had less impact on history and social evolution than other groups (although, like many groups, they do not always have the impact they believe they have or wish to have). On the contrary, there is good reason to believe that, if anything, they have been more influential than many others, at least in modern societies. This is especially true if one broadens one's view of the intellectual community to encompass the larger intelligentsia: the writers, editors, publicists, journalists, and other educated professionals who are influenced by, and who sometimes influence, the academic establishment proper. Most of the figures in this study *are* academics—economists and social theorists—but many, including the central ones, have moved rather freely back and forth through the concentric circles that emanate from the university. Their ideas, moreover, have had significant and occasionally great influence both within the intelligentsia and in society at large, while mirroring the concerns, hopes, and dilemmas of Americans during the second half of the twentieth century. In practical terms, the broadest and most powerful impact of intellectuals is clearly related, as Peter Steinfels has noted, to their role in legitimizing ideas, values, and policies among the mass public, politicians, and other, wider segments of the intelligentsia.[1]

The ideas that form the core structure around which this essay revolves are those of three individuals who have written—and spoken—extensively to legitimize and, in many cases, to *de*legitimize ideas and beliefs in American economic and social thought since World War II. Their interests and even their perceptions have to a significant degree overlapped; however, what unites them is not any nearly perfect congruence of their theories, but rather their steadfast refusal to consider economic issues in isolation from the social world in which they exist and out of which they have arisen and, of equal and related importance, their awareness of economic events as phenomena enmeshed in the flux of historical change. In short, they have examined modern American capitalism not simply, or even primarily, from an economic standpoint, but instead with a fundamental regard for the social and historical contexts in which it operates. Indeed, they have shown convincingly that it is the failure of conventional economic analysis to take these issues into account that has contributed in large part to the dismal performance it has exhibited in its attempts to explain the economic currents of our time.

Another part of the unique bond these writers share is their special concern for the social impact of capitalism in America and, conversely, for the effects of social change on capitalism itself. That is, they have sought to explain not only how and why the American economic system has come to be what it is, but also what it has meant to the lives of those who live under it. They have thus surveyed a wide variety of changes in postwar America in all their multifaceted complexity, but always with a main focus on the institutional evolution of modern American capitalism and a concern for the possible attainment of what each of them perceives as a democratic and just society, to be achieved through the evolution of some form of social democracy.

Reform has been out of fashion in America for several years, but there

---

[1] Peter Steinfels, *The Neoconservatives: The Men Who Are Changing America's Politics* (New York: Touchstone, 1980), p. 6.

are unmistakable signs that this is rapidly changing. In the past (as will be seen in the following pages), periods of conservatism have invariably given way to periods of political activism and change. It is already clear that the movements and issues emerging to shape the next period bear the distinctive marks of a new age imprinted by the forces of a constantly moving historical reality. Yet the main concerns that have risen to the fore are strongly related to the ones that have been raised by the three thinkers presented in these pages, for they have arisen from common problems faced by all industrial civilizations. It is out of a conviction that the perceptions of the critical intelligentsia are essential in understanding the political agenda of contemporary America that this study is written.

THE BACKGROUND

Abraham Lincoln,
1859

The prudent, penniless beginner in the world, labors for wages awhile, saves a surplus with which to buy tools or land, for himself; then labors on his own account another while, and at length hires another new beginner to help him. This, say its advocates, is *free* labor—the just and generous, and prosperous system, which opens the way for all—gives hope to all, and energy, and progress, and improvement of condition to all. If any continue through life in the condition of the hired laborer, it is not the fault of the system, but because of either a dependent nature which prefers it, or improvidence, folly, or singular misfortune.

Franklin D. Roosevelt,
1944

We have come to a clear realization of the fact that true individual freedom cannot exist without economic security and independence. "Necessitous men are not free men." People who are hungry and out of a job are the stuff of which dictatorships are made.

Chapter 1

The Great Transformation: American Economic Thought, 1865–1945

A modern novelist once wrote that history is like grass growing: one cannot see it happening. Whatever might be the general validity of this proposition, it is certainly true when applied to virtually all mid-nineteenth-century observers of American economic development. When Abraham Lincoln called upon his countrymen to save the Union from the illiberal philosophy and institutions of a patriarchal, elitist Southern society, he was asking a nation composed of numerous farmers, many small-town dwellers and small businessmen, and some self-employed professionals to join in a crusade that he believed would, among other things, ensure the growth of a liberal, essentially small-scale, and virtually classless market society.

"By some it is assumed," Lincoln told a farmers' organization the year before he was elected president, "that labor is available only in connection with capital—that nobody labors, unless somebody else, owning capital, somehow, by the use of that capital, induces him to do it." But this theory was, he said, false. Indeed, he made it clear that he agreed with those who proposed that "labor is prior to, and independent of, capital; that, in fact, capital is the fruit of labor, and could never have existed if labor had not *first* existed—that labor can exist without capital, but that capital could never have existed without labor," and that "labor is the superior—greatly the superior—of capital." "There is, and probably always will be, a relation between labor and capital," he admitted. "A few men own capital," Lincoln acknowledged, and thus were able to hire—and in the South even buy—others to work for them. But he went on to emphasize, undoubtedly with some exaggeration, what his audience already knew: namely, that "A large majority belong to neither class—neither work for others, nor have others working for them." In America, he proudly pointed out, "Men, with their families—wives, sons and daughters—work for themselves, on their farms, in their houses and in their shops, taking the whole product to themselves, and asking no favors of capital on the one hand, nor of hirelings or slaves on the other." And, while "a considerable number of persons mingle their own labor with capital," he argued that "this is only a *mixed*, and not a *distinct* class.''[1] America, in others words, was not like, and would not become like, Europe. Just as importantly, for Lincoln as for the vast majority of Americans, expectations involved a rather straightforward extrapolation of past economic and social trends into the indefinite future.

Lincoln and other Americans expected to see the continued push of westward expansion and its concomitant agricultural development, the growth of some old, and many new, small towns and even some large cities, and the erection of a number of small- to medium-sized factories, mainly on their outlying fringes, to offer employment to a few hundred, or perhaps a few thousand, of their inhabitants.[2] None of this, they believed, would involve any substantial change in American institutions or ideology. Things would change in quantity, of course, but not in kind. Lincoln therefore saw no reason to question the relevance of classical liberal economic, social, and political philosophy to the postwar America he expected to see after the South was defeated, and his death in 1865 guaranteed that he would never have to face the searching reexamination of his simple liberal faith that would almost certainly have been necessary for such a sensitive man had he lived another twenty-five years. In fact, the grass had already been growing under Lincoln's feet for at least a score of years, but he cannot be blamed for not noticing it. And, even if he had, the natural tendency would have been to interpret the new phenomena through the liberal ideological lens that had shaped Americans' perceptions of their society and its development as it had since the early eighteenth century, and therefore to find refuge in the only philosophy he knew.

What neither Lincoln nor his contemporaries could foresee was the rapid emergence of an industrial and urban society to replace the commercial and rural society whose way of life they were fighting to protect. Instead of maintaining the decentralized structure and balanced growth of small towns, family farms, and factories coexisting in a relatively harmonious, mutually symbiotic relationship between vast rural expanses and small, isolated islands of economic development, America in the fourth quarter of the nineteenth century was rocked by the explosive growth of huge industrial complexes within great, sprawling, interconnected urban centers

[1] Abraham Lincoln, ''Address Before the Wisconsin State Agricultural Society At Milwaukee,'' in T. Harry Williams, ed., *Abraham Lincoln: Selected Speeches, Messages, and Letters* (New York: Holt, Rinehart, and Winston, 1957), pp. 114-116.

[2] See Eric Foner, *Free Soil, Free Labor, Free Men: The Ideology of the Republican Party before the Civil War* (Oxford: Oxford University Press, 1976), especially chapters 1 and 2.

that increasingly dotted the land. The newly expanded rail system forged an iron grid whose nodes and linkages would remake the face of the nation. Between 1865 and 1900 the United States moved from the position of a second-rate industrial power to that of the greatest economic juggernaut on earth, and the economic, social, and political consequences as well as the perplexing social problems and political issues that arose during that era are still with us today.

Lincoln's America had by no means been the idyllic land enshrined in popular mythology; nonetheless, it was a nation that believed it knew itself and where it stood. In a freely competitive, decentralized market society—the kind that had previously existed in the minds of Americans and to a considerable degree in reality—the ultimate source of legitimacy in the social and economic sphere was largely the market itself. Did it not allocate land, labor, capital, and goods and also determine wages and prices in an entirely impersonal, yet efficient manner, unfailingly rewarding the clever, thrifty, and industrious, damning the dull, imprudent, and slothful, and thus objectively determining the status and function of all who participated in its workings? And, although it was not always adhered to, did not the policy of free trade among nations make optimum use of those resources and capacities unique to each nation, thus maximizing the benefits to all mankind and so reproducing on a global scale the salutary effects of the free market? The answers to these questions seemed obvious to Americans in 1865.

To be sure, the system had flaws. There were periodic slowdowns of production and financial crises; but these were minor and even *necessary* setbacks. They were, in fact, an essential part of the remarkable, self-adjusting mechanism that provided employment and opportunity. The workings of the market, like the more general laws governing the universe, were simple and immutable: men naturally sought their own self-interest and, by so doing, furthered the interests and well-being of all. Prominent economists, sociologists, and writers of the immediate post–Civil War period heartily endorsed this view, and they proclaimed the universal benefits of economic growth and the perfect balance of market forces.

But this balance of forces seemed to be increasingly precarious as the nation moved toward the twentieth century. The clockwork mechanism of Adam Smith was still used as the model of the American economy by business, the public, and the vast majority of the intelligentsia, but its explanatory power was becoming far less impressive for many observers of the American scene. And for good reason.

What happened was that the decades of the 1880s and 1890s witnessed a fundamental transformation of the economic system Americans had come to know, as new technologies, rapid economic growth, industrial concentration, and the resulting economic and social disruptions and dislocations seemed to threaten the very fabric of American society. New urban metropolises drew in from surrounding agricultural regions large numbers of displaced persons needed to run the machinery of the expanding factory system, while many of those left on farms gradually lost control of their lands (close to 40 percent no longer owned their own farms by the 1880s) and their economic destinies. The new America was urban by the 1890s—not in a quantitative sense, but in the sense that urban institutions, especially the large corporation, had by this time come to be the decisive and representative institutions of American civilization. As the situation worsened for farmers, as work environments and living conditions deteriorated for large numbers of urban inhabitants, and as economic depressions (caused by rapid technological change, industrial overproduction, great maldistributions of wealth, the end of huge investments in railroad construction, and the ripple effects of European economic downturns) grew more severe, the nation was convulsed by social tensions, industrial violence, and seemingly by the very kind of class conflict that Lincoln believed the nation would permanently avoid.

A well-known scholar has noted that American farmers and workers never challenged the social order in a fundamental way, and in retrospect this is clearly true.[3] But in the last two decades of the nineteenth century this was not so obvious. Farmers, squeezed by tight money and by the economic power of distant manufacturers, bankers, and businessmen, were often forced into desperate financial straits. Disoriented by their loss of political influence, they eventually sought redress through a mass political movement that shook the American party system and for a while

[3] See Louis Hartz, *The Liberal Tradition in America: An Interpretation of American Political Thought since the Revolution* (New York: Harcourt, Brace & World, 1955). I have never quite understood why Hartz has been berated by Marxists and radical historians for his simple contention—buried beneath unnecessarily flowery and stilted prose—that Americans have long possessed a powerful and largely unconscious liberal ideology. The history of American labor is among the bloodiest in modern Western civilization, and nothing Hartz has written calls this into question. Indeed, as Hartz writes, "one cannot say of the liberal society analysis that by concentrating on national unities it rules out the meaning of domestic conflict. Actually it discovers that meaning, which is obscured by the very . . . analysis that presumably concentrates on conflict. You do not get closer to the significance of an earthquake by ignoring the terrain on which it takes place" (p. 20).

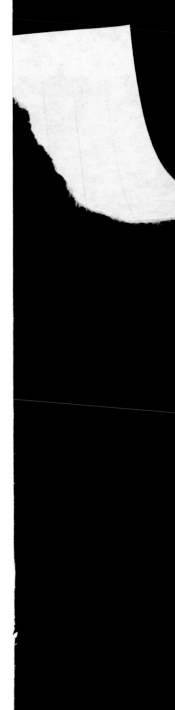

seemed on the verge of gaining national power. As one historian has written of these disgruntled agriculturalists, "they saw the coming society and they did not like it."[4] Urban workers evidently were also displeased, since between 1881 and 1900 there were 2,378 strikes, which involved more than 6 million of them and which began to give the National Guard its long-enduring (and largely well-deserved) reputation for repression, bias, and ruthlessness. Great armories sprang up across the land as government prepared to deal with the social unrest that seemed to have become a permanent part of American life.

Given these developments, it would be astonishing if one were not to find rumblings in the intellectual community to parallel the explosive forces let loose in the society at large. Indeed, the social, economic, and political implications of rapid industrialization and urbanization were profound, and intellectuals predictably began to grapple with them. Perhaps the most central of these issues was the problem of power.

Economic power in a free market system theoretically did not exist, since any single producer's influence on the market was, relative to that of numerous other producers, infinitesimally small. Also, although some people were undoubtedly much better off and more influential than others, it had been the common (though, in reality, not entirely justified) belief that anyone could, through diligence, frugality, and hard work attain equal or even greater status. But as enterprises and the scale of production grew steadily larger and the concentrated industrial power of a relatively few individual companies began to exert a palpable force on the entire market structure, making it far less plausible that average citizens could themselves become capitalists, Americans were presented with an obvious dilemma. If economic activity was no longer regulated by an impersonal market mechanism, but was instead dominated by a relatively few identifiable groups and organizations, the following questions arose: How did they obtain this power? By what right did they exercise it? If the market was no longer "free," how could one justify the results it produced, especially if some of them were widely judged to be undesirable?

The intellectual reaction to the turmoil engulfing the new Age of Industry was varied. Social Darwinists such as William Graham Sumner saw the newly emerging society in positive terms, as a beneficent, evolutionary cultural form, while reformists such as Edward Bellamy in his portrait of

[4] Lawrence Goodwyn, *The Populist Moment: A Short History of the Agrarian Revolt in America* (Oxford: Oxford University Press, 1978), p. 320.

the new urban masses in *Looking Backward* and Lester Ward in his exposé of the misapplication of Darwinian principles to human society were dismayed by the social ills they saw in abundance around them. But of particular interest are those theorists who focused their attention on the economic changes of this era, and their impact on the structure of American capitalism. Several of them comprise what has been called the "New School" of political economy, whose members included John Bates Clark, Richard Ely, and Simon Patten—men who questioned in varying degrees many of the fundamental assumptions of laissez-faire capitalism and advocated increased state intervention in the economy. Indeed, the American Economic Association, founded in 1885 by young, reform-minded economists, included a call for such reforms in a statement proclaiming the principles on which the organization was established. Although these men espoused no unified program, each of them proposed new ways of perceiving a rapidly changing America and put forth new ideas for remedying the economic and social problems these changes entailed, ideas that ranged from moderate, ameliorative measures to radical, utopian schemes for a planned economy.

No, this burst of unorthodox thinking was not a freak event. In fact, it eventually gave rise to a new current of economic thought whose founder was a Norwegian immigrant's son from rural Minnesota, a strange man named Thorstein Veblen. One of John Bates Clark's students, Veblen went beyond the New School in a literally radical sense: he did not stop (or even begin) with moral condemnations or reformist proposals, attempting instead to locate and analyze the very roots of America's social and economic condition at the turn of the century.

The flaunting of wealth and the seemingly rapacious behavior exhibited by American businessmen and the upper class suggested to Veblen a link between their psychology and that of the "big men" and plunderers of primitive cultures with their unending quest for wealth, power, and prestige. This explained why the economic institutions of modern America seemed to contradict Max Weber's association of capitalism with rational modes of thought. The forces underlying institutional behavior were thus not necessarily rational desires: they were most often irrational drives that were little understood, while the institutions themselves were merely more highly developed forms of archaic roles and practices that had modern structures superimposed on them through an evolutionary process of accretion. Thus, the American economy was not a maximally efficient, rational machine that produced an abundance of socially useful goods and diffused power widely throughout society; it was instead, Veblen believed, an unstable, contradictory mixture of rational industrial organization and massive economic waste, and an arena of competition for power among rival groups and interests.

His conclusions aside, the important point to note is that Veblen rejected many of the basic axioms of classical economics and eschewed its narrow technical analysis of static economic relationships, concentrating instead on broader issues concerning the structure, dynamics, and historical evolution of economic institutions themselves. Those scholars who, following his lead, investigated economic behavior within the context of entire social systems and habitually ignored disciplinary boundaries in an effort to obtain a holistic view of the modern American economy became known as "institutionalists," and their advent is significant. Whenever a substantial proportion of thinkers in any field become so disenchanted with the explanatory power of a prevailing theory that they seek alternative theories and methodologies, it is a sign of the disintegration of a dominant theoretical framework.[5] It was in the institutionalist tradition that John R. Commons examined the legal structure of capitalism, the role of tradition in economic affairs, and the nature of exchange relationships. In the same tradition, Wesley Clair Mitchell urged a more rational and comprehensive collection of economic statistics, evincing an institutionalist concern for ascertaining the practical workings and actual aggregate outputs of the economy, as distinct from what classical theory might predict.

It was in such an intellectual and historical milieu that progressivism—a reform movement that, like the intellectual rebellion that accompanied it, was multifaceted, rather amorphous, and, to a certain degree, self-contradictory—was born in the early twentieth century. Both progressivism and Progressive thought, although seemingly amoeba-like in their general lack of sharply defined direction and purpose, can and must be seen as reactions to the new demands and problems created by an industrializing and urbanizing nation. Progressivism, to the extent that it had any unified goals, sought to mitigate the disruptive effects of industrialization and generally to impose rational administrative control on a highly decentralized and fragmented political structure; the associated intellectual movement was an attempt to adapt the quasi-Jeffersonian liberal political and social theory still dominant in America to the stark new realities of industrial life

[5] See Thomas S. Kuhn, *The Structure of Scientific Revolutions*, 2d ed. (Chicago: The University of Chicago Press, 1970).

and to deal with crucial questions that an earlier generation had ignored, failed to recognize, or simply could not resolve.

Perhaps the most important and influential intellectual effort to establish a "new liberalism" was Herbert Croly's *The Promise of American Life*, published in 1909. Croly, who together with Walter Lippmann and Walter Weyl had founded the new liberal journal *The New Republic*, saw no possibility of salvaging the individualistic liberalism of old and advocated an increase in the active regulatory power of the state in economic and social affairs.[6] The nation, he believed, was now facing its greatest crisis since the Civil War—an opinion shared by one of Croly's admirers, the ebullient Theodore Roosevelt.

It was Roosevelt's administration that had ushered in the new century in America, both literally and figuratively. Roosevelt's political instincts and intuitive grasp of the forces that underlay America's economic transformation had led him to renounce classical liberalism years before Croly and others had provided the philosophical justification for doing so. Indeed, he was the first national leader to recognize the economic and political implications of the decline of small-scale entrepreneurial capitalism as the dominant force in the American economy. Roosevelt accepted the new economic order because he could not accept the only obvious alternatives: the breaking up of large corporations or the substitution of socialist institutions for capitalist ones. Regulation, he believed, was the only feasible solution to the problems posed by the growth of great concentrations of economic power.

But Roosevelt, Croly, Lippmann, and Weyl remained in the minority. Aside from a small socialist party, few American politicians and intellectuals recognized these economic and political developments and trends for what they were: harbingers of a new order shaped by the inherent realities of modern corporate capitalism. Even many Progressive reformers limited their perspective to a concern for clean and efficient government, moral rehabilitation, or the enforcement of antitrust legislation, thus displaying an implicit appreciation of social change, but no new, comprehensive theoretical framework that could serve as an alternative point of reference or as a guide to political action. The dominant view was held by those who, like Woodrow Wilson, Robert La Follette, and William Jennings Bryan, still embraced, in principle or at least in public, the old liberal creed and looked to the rejuvenation of small-scale entrepreneurial capitalism. This

---

[6] See Herbert Croly, *The Promise of American Life* [1909] (n.p. Archon, 1963).

attitude was summed up by Wilson's vice-president, Thomas R. Marshall, who declared in 1913: "The people were told in the last campaign that trusts were a natural evolution, and that the only way to deal with them was to regulate them. The people are tired of being told such things. What they want is the kind of opportunity that formerly existed in this country."[7]

Yet in practice Wilson and his followers did not succeed in implementing their ideology, which became increasingly compromised and irrelevant. The Sherman Anti-Trust Act—passed in 1890 and itself extraordinary testimony to the influence of American liberal philosophy and its fear of concentrated power—was enforced no more strenuously during the Wilson administration than before. Indeed, these men presided over the further concentration of corporate power as well as the extension of state intervention in the economy. Significantly, Wilson himself was once forced to concede that "we shall never return to the old order of individual competition" and that "the organization of business upon a grand scale of co-operation is, up to a certain point, itself normal and inevitable."[8] Corporate capitalism thus continued to develop for two decades while Americans, including an entire generation of muckrakers, writers, journalists, economists, sociologists, and other intellectuals tended to accept the phenomenon willy-nilly, without any satisfactory effort to come to terms with it, its underlying causes, its philosophical implications, or even its long-term practical consequences.

Theoretical revolutions are a response to external pressure and result from demands for a clearer, more comprehensible picture of a changing reality. Nothing tends to squelch innovative social thought as much as periods of relative social and economic stability. With this basic assumption in mind, it is not difficult to understand why, after the Progressive movement largely died out during World War I and the 1920s witnessed a wave of marked, though uneven, prosperity, there was little incentive to reformulate established theories of American business, economic structure, and society, and even less incentive to accept such reformulations.

Of course, dissent from the majority view was not totally silenced in the age of Harding and Coolidge. In fact, by the end of World War I economic and social theory was effectively bifurcated regarding the fundamental nature of American capitalism. Adherents of the old school, such as the economist Frank Knight at the University of Chicago, continued to support the

---

[7] Quoted in Richard Hofstadter, *The Age of Reform: From Bryan to FDR* (New York: Vintage, 1955), pp. 248-249.

[8] Quoted in ibid., pp. 249-250.

classical view, while the "realists," institutionalists, and many of the remaining Progressive theorists persisted in denying the relevance of old principles and assumptions to the new world of mammoth business enterprises and imperfect markets no longer guided by the constraints of free competition. But it was only with the coming of the Great Depression that the tide turned in favor of the realists and that the most talented social theorists of this era were intensely motivated, as were their counterparts a generation before, to ask the crucial questions: What kind of industrial organization now existed in America? How should Americans deal with it?

The depression of the 1930s was in many ways not unique; there had been several in the United States during the previous one hundred years. The main differences were three. First, it lasted longer than any prior crisis. Second, because of the highly integrated structure of modern America's economy and society coupled with the urban circumstances of most Americans by this time, it posed an unprecedented economic and psychological burden for more people and also for a larger proportion of the citizenry than ever before. Third, it shattered the general belief that the fundamental problems of industrial society in America had been solved. These problems were now placed in high relief as the Great Depression—one of the most calamitous events in US history—produced a national trauma destined to leave a livid scar on the consciousness of Americans for over half a century. It predictably sparked a revival of interest in the structure and behavior of large firms and of the economy as a whole.

One of the most significant intellectual events of these years was the publication of *The Modern Corporation and Private Property* by Adolf Berle and Gardiner Means. While the major empirical findings in their study were not particularly novel or startling (most had been posited decades before by the Progressives), their book vigorously and systematically attacked many of the most cherished assumptions of microeconomics (the theory of the business firm). In addition, the statistical evidence they amassed displayed for the first time—in literally graphic terms—facts that previously had often been based on impression or simply assumed on the grounds of theoretical logic.

As a nation mired in economic stagnation was asking itself what had gone wrong with its market system, Berle and Means had a few questions of their own. What, the authors asked, did "ownership" mean when most large corporations were gradually passing into the effective control of managerial personnel, while stockholders, theoretically the "real" owners but usually possessing only small, scattered blocks of shares, owned merely what amounted to tokens representing a "bundle of ill-protected rights and expectations"? What did "private property" mean when the functions of management and the legal status of ownership were increasingly divorced? What did "competition" mean when business enterprise in America was so concentrated that the largest (in terms of gross assets) two hundred non-banking corporations received more than 40 percent of the income of all non-banking corporations? Berle and Means argued that, if these terms meant anything at all, they certainly did not mean what they had meant in the days when a "business" referred to a small shop personally owned and operated by an individual. Assessing the consequences of the changes they were analyzing, the authors were not at all hesitant to conclude that the economics of small and large corporations were "essentially different," that in the latter "the interests of owner and of ultimate manager may, and often do, diverge," that many checks on corporate power had now been eroded, and that their very size "tends to give these giant corporations a social significance not attached to the smaller units of private enterprise." Furthermore, given the "new responsibilities" of the managers and the "new relationships" engendered by these conditions, these new organizations had caused a "revolution" whereby they had "changed the nature of profit-seeking enterprise."[9]

This concern with institutional change was not confined to analyses of structural differences between small business firms and large corporations. In point of fact, the area of most general interest in the early 1930s, especially in the works of economists, tended to be the impact of industrial concentration and the resulting market power on competition and price behavior. It was in this field of study that the most significant breakthroughs were made in the first half of the decade, when three economists—one Briton and two Americans—wrote seminal works on the problems of monopoly and oligopoly (the domination of an industry or market by one or a few large firms, respectively).

The mere existence of oligopolistic markets was not, of course, a new or particularly disturbing revelation. This much had long since been conceded by classical theorists. What Joan Robinson, Edward Chamberlin, and Arthur R. Burns demonstrated was not simply that oligopoly existed, but that the phenomenon that classicists viewed as an aberration was no

---

[9] Adolf A. Berle, Jr. and Gardiner C. Means, *The Modern Corporation and Private Property* (New York: Macmillan, 1932), pp. 6-7.

such thing. As Chamberlin pointed out, the classical school had in its analysis carefully separated the phenomena of competition and monopoly, something available data did not justify.[10] Perfectly monopolistic markets were indeed rare, if not nonexistent; but semi-monopolistic markets were not. Actual competition had little to do with "pure" competition, and Chamberlin noted that "This association of the theory of competition with facts which it does not fit has not only led to false conclusions about the facts; it has obscured theory as well. This is the more serious because the mixture of the two forces is a chemical process and not merely a matter of addition."[11]

Thus, Chamberlin and his colleagues proposed that the assumed dichotomy between competition and monopoly still prevalent (though not unchallenged) was in large part simplistic, artificial, and unrealistic. *Real* markets and firms in advanced capitalist economies were, they contended, neither purely competitive nor purely monopolistic: they were an intricate combination of competitive, oligopolistic, and monopolistic elements, each lying somewhere along a continuum between the two extremes of free competition and unfree monopoly. Large firms, although still adversaries, no longer competed with one another through an impersonal, objective process determined by the laws of classical economics, but rather in a politicized, conscious manner as each powerful enterprise calculated the probable effects of its actions on those of other powerful enterprises and on the market as a whole. This acknowledged extinction of the free market also meant, among other things, that prices could no longer be expected to move as freely up and down as they had in the heyday of entrepreneurial capitalism, tending instead to become "sticky" and hence upsetting the self-adjusting mechanism that quickly filled and flushed out markets according to the law of supply and demand.

Many of these ideas and conclusions were, again, not entirely new. But they were now fully developed, stated with analytical rigor, and backed up with empirical evidence. Another blow had been struck against classical theory. However, even as its architects labored on their new models of business organization and market behavior, a more extensive assault was being prepared at another level. It would shake classical economics to its very foundations.

Indeed, the fascination of American scholars with outlining and inves-

[10] Edward Chamberlin, *The Theory of Monopolistic Competition* (Cambridge: Harvard University Press, 1935), p. 3.

[11] Ibid.

tigating the structure of large corporations and the phenomenon of "imperfect competition"—in fact, the entire field of microeconomic analysis—was soon to be eclipsed by a new development in *macro*economic theory (the theory of aggregate output, employment, and spending on national and international levels) that sent shock waves through economics. In 1936—the seventh year of the Great Depression—the British economist John Maynard Keynes unleashed a brilliant attack on orthodox theory comparable to Einstein's earlier reformulation of Newtonian mechanics, and an entire generation of American economists and social theorists were to be occupied for a long while testing its validity and speculating on its implications. Keynes argued in his book *The General Theory of Employment, Interest, and Money* that one of the most fundamental assumptions of classical macroeconomic theory was fallacious. There was, he maintained, no reason to assume that a modern capitalist economy always tended toward the full employment of its human and material resources. This directly challenged the orthodox view that the market was a nearly perfect machine that automatically balanced demand and supply orders and maximized economic output.

The orthodox faith in the almost flawless workings of the market was based on the classical axiom known as Say's Law, which was composed of two seemingly unassailable propositions. First, Say's Law stated that the very process of producing economic goods and services automatically generated the income and therefore the consumer demand and capital spending necessary to buy them back. Keynes saw this as a virtually tautological proposition and accepted it completely. Further, Say's Law asserted that the income thus generated would be spent and reinvested at a rate that would guarantee full employment. This he denied.

Keynes admitted that Say's Law might indeed be valid, but only under certain circumstances: its principles were acceptable, he proposed, only as a special case among many possible outcomes in a market system. Eighteenth-century capitalism may well have been a nearly self-regulating system with an inner gyroscopic device to keep it steady and balanced, but a modern economy was something quite different. As one of his chief American interpreters has pointed out, Keynes saw that savings from income in such an economy need not be immediately or rapidly reinvested and that the old formulation of economic theory

> was cast in terms of a society that has largely passed away—a society in
> which most producers were typically self-employed individual proprie-

tors, whether peasant farmers or master craftsmen. Either they raised farm produce or else they ''manufactured'' products, and their income consisted of the sale of those products. To be ''employed'' meant simply to operate a farm or to set up a shop and to sell one's own output in the market. The proceeds were spent directly on tools, on farm and home buildings, and on consumers' goods. Saving *was* investment, not a distinct and separate process. The producer sold his *product*, not his *labor*. The greater the number of producers, the greater the size of the market. Products exchanged against products; supply created its own demand.[12]

.Keynes thus perceived that in a complex monetary economy based on wage labor and the investment of social savings by specialized institutions Say's Law could not be expected to hold. Modern businessmen based their investment plans not on the amount of income they received during their last business period, but instead on what they expected *consumer demand* would be in the *next* period. Keynes argued that for a variety of economic, social, and psychological reasons it was impossible to know how much savings businessmen might be willing to invest and therefore how much employment and income would be forthcoming when that time came. These savings would eventually be reinvested, but not necessarily rapidly enough to ensure full employment and to prevent economic slowdowns.

The meaning of Keynes's theory for the world's market societies was seemingly ominous. Classicists had long been willing to concede that temporary imbalances or market imperfections could lead to cyclical crises and readjustments, but these were seen to be short-lived and not damaging to the market mechanism itself. Indeed, Say's Law allowed for such occurrences. What both they and it disallowed was the possibility of a *general, prolonged glut* in a free market economy. Keynes, however, maintained that even a free market could fall victim to just such a glut and to a long-term economic depression. Moreover, such a depression could feed on itself and drastically reduce industrial output and national wealth. This, he proposed, was precisely what had now occurred in Western economies.

Yet Keynes offered a solution to this specter of stagnation and crisis. His theory implied not that capitalism per se was not viable, but merely that *laissez-faire* capitalism was not stable in a modern economy. Further-

---

[12] Alvin H. Hansen, *A Guide to Keynes* (New York: McGraw-Hill, 1953), p. 17. Indispensable for an understanding of Keynesian theory and its historical context are: Robert Lekachman, *The Age of Keynes* (New York: McGraw-Hill, 1975) and Guy Routh, *The Origin of Economic Ideas* (New York: Vintage, 1977), chapters 3-5.

more, the theory itself provided a way out of the dilemma. The crux of the problem was, according to Keynes, an insufficiency of spending: specifically, capital investment had withered because it was not profitable for any individual proprietor or corporation to risk capital during a period of depressed prices and greatly decreased consumer demand. But consumer demand was itself low because of high unemployment and low income caused by inadequate business investment. The only remaining agency with the resources needed to escape from this predicament was *government*, since it did not operate under the constraints faced by business and the public. It alone, Keynes argued, could break the self-perpetuating cycle of depression and take up the slack in consumer and investment spending until the economy regained momentum. Government, Keynes believed, needed only to spend sufficient funds from either taxes or public borrowing, which would then, through a tiered process of successive respending throughout the economy, stimulate economic activity by an amount much greater than the initial sum spent. With this remedy, effective action could be taken quickly, since it required no drastic changes in the basic structure of the economy or the organization of the firm, leaving the useful and benign mechanisms at the core of the market economy untouched.

So were laid the theoretical foundations of the Keynesian Revolution, and nowhere did it excite more interest than in America. It was, after all, no secret that many American thinkers of the early twentieth century (Thorstein Veblen for example) had become disillusioned or at least dissatisfied with neoclassical equilibrium theory. Indeed, one of the most notable precursors of Keynes was the American economist John Maurice Clark. Clark, essentially an institutionalist, questioned the orthodox concept of inevitable equilibrium in a series of writings, among these his book *Strategic Factors in Business Cycles*, published in 1935. Although Clark was clearly skeptical of received doctrine, developed cogent, ad hoc criticisms of the neoclassical school, and recognized as early as 1931 the multiplied effect of increased spending in creating jobs, income, and further investment in a depressed economy, he did not construct a comprehensive, *general* theory to account for the anomalies to which he called attention. Keynes did develop such a theory and, as a result, American scholars— mainly those of the younger generation—largely ignored Clark and instead flocked to the Keynesian banner.

But the triumph of Keynesianism would have to await a number of developments, among which the first was the collapse of the Hoover administration. Its chief executive was, to be sure, no proponent of laissez-faire capitalism. Indeed, Herbert Hoover had repeatedly broken with economic orthodoxy to an unprecedented degree throughout his career in government and especially during the first two years of the Depression. Nevertheless, he was sufficiently wedded to his vision of a decentralized and cooperatively managed market economy stubbornly to resist the use of powerful, direct, and immediate federal action to deal with the mounting crisis. In the end, his self-destructive refusal to abandon his principles by greatly increasing centralized control over the economy led to an action that to many came to symbolize this tragic presidency: Hoover's call for a tax increase in December 1931 in a futile attempt to preserve a domestic and international financial system that was rapidly disintegrating—this at a time when the American economy was itself plummeting deeper into depression. Hoover's policy was to change as a consequence of continued failure toward still greater innovations, but they were undertaken too late and without the general reformulation of basic assumptions necessary to reinvigorate the economy. For these and other reasons he was unable to inspire the public confidence that could have preserved his political power and saved his reputation from irreparable damage.

It was thus left to the administration of Franklin Roosevelt to deal with the economic disaster that had crippled the nation. An Eastern aristocrat and a reformer by personal inclination as well as philosophical conviction, FDR, like his relative Theodore, was convinced that basic changes were needed regarding the role of the state in economic and social life. Unsophisticated in his view of the business crash, uncertain of the consequences of his own proposals, he knew only that the federal government could no longer avoid extensive, continuous, and direct intervention in the economic activities of a modern industrial society. The state, he also believed, would itself be required to assume ultimate responsibility for social welfare. An experimentalist almost to the point of incoherence, Roosevelt wanted to make as many changes as necessary, but as few as possible, to save American capitalism. For this purpose he brought to Washington during his first term a large corps of economists, social scientists, journalists, social workers, and other scholars and professionals from almost every major sector of the American intelligentsia. Not since the Revolutionary Era had intellectuals entered American political life in such large numbers or with such determination to reshape the course of the nation's history. An urgent task lay before them.[13]

[13] Thomas A. Krueger and William Glidden, ''The New Deal Intellectual Elite: A Collective

Roosevelt and his main advisers saw four basic options available to them to fight the Depression. They could: (1) revert to the old policies of government economy, balanced budgets, and a generally pro-business posture; (2) adopt some form of corporatism—close, cooperative planning among government, private corporations, and other major interest groups; (3) resort to radical antitrust action to break up large concentrations of economic power in the hope of jarring loose blocked flows of production and income; or (4) increase government spending by large amounts. Each option had a group of supporters in the administration; all were eventually tried, occasionally in overlapping and confusing ways in the flurry of activity that characterized Roosevelt's first two terms in office. Yet there was a roughly logical and somewhat distinct temporal progression from one course of action to another.

The first and second options were tried simultaneously during Roosevelt's first term. The first, aside from being too closely associated with the Hoover administration, turned out to be patently ineffective and did not enlist the expected business support. The second, enacted in the form of the National Recovery Administration, was initially successful but was soon marred by distrust and eventual animosity between government officials and business groups. It was, in addition, contrary to American traditions and values in its implicit acceptance of large, oligopolistic corporations and concentrated economic power. The *coup de grâce* was the Supreme Court's declaration in 1935 that the program was unconstitutional. The third plan, a wave of antitrust action, was carried out from 1938 to 1941 in the hope of restoring fluidity to markets and price structures. The results were mixed and included a further embitterment of relations between the administration and business interests. Antitrust activity virtually came to a halt with the advent of World War II and the need for business cooperation and for the efficiencies of scale and simplicities of coordination in the production of huge amounts of war materiel by giant firms.[14]

The final option—the acceleration of government spending and the acceptance of budget deficits for an indefinite period—was tried in varying degrees throughout FDR's first two terms, but had never been pursued con-

Portrait," in Frederic Cople Jaher, ed., *The Rich, the Well Born, and the Powerful: Elites and Upper Classes in History* (Secaucus, New Jersey: Citadel, 1975), pp. 338-374.

[14] Ellis W. Hawley, *The New Deal and the Problem of Monopoly: A Study in Economic Ambivalence* (Princeton: Princeton University Press, 1966); Herbert Stein, *The Fiscal Revolution in America* (Chicago: University of Chicago Press, 1969), chapters 6 and 7.

sistently or vigorously. Old beliefs concerning fiscal policy were still influential in America; nor were they to be totally discredited for many years.
Roosevelt himself, apprehensive about budget deficits and cognizant of the
opposition they aroused among conservative politicians and the business
community, had always been personally uncomfortable with their seeming
threat to the nation's financial stability. Interestingly, Roosevelt had met
with Keynes in 1934, a mutually disillusioning encounter that evidently
had little direct impact on the course of the New Deal during the next few
years. (Roosevelt, it seems, understood little of what Keynes had said.) In
any case, as an astute politician, FDR could hardly have wholeheartedly
embraced a Keynesian solution to the Depression despite periodic advice
and warnings from Keynes himself as well as the persistent urging of presidential advisers Harry Hopkins and Marriner Eccles and administration
economists. His ear always to the ground, Roosevelt was well aware of
public opinion surveys that indicated that Americans were overwhelmingly
opposed to the idea of deficits and increased government spending. He
therefore felt, with some justification, that any radical or prolonged departure from traditional fiscal policy would be a reckless and unwarrantable
flirtation with political suicide. Furthermore, neither he nor his economic
advisers realized the magnitude of expenditures that would be necessary in
order for them to be effective. The amount of government spending during
most of the New Deal was therefore usually just large enough to frighten
business interests and stir up serious opposition, while being at the same
time too small to have a substantial beneficial impact.

A critical turning point was reached in the period 1937–1938. By 1936,
when the worst effects of the Depression seemed to have passed and as the
economy began slowly and sluggishly to expand, the administration tight-
ened credit and cut back relief and public-works projects. The consequences of these actions were severe. A sharp recession beginning in the
summer of 1937 resulted in the loss of two million jobs, widespread declines in income, and large numbers of people being thrown onto relief
programs. These were precisely the results Keynesian theory had predicted, and the lesson of these events was not lost on the president. By
April of 1938 he had reversed government monetary and fiscal policy, and,
by the time he gave his budget message to Congress in 1940, he had formally accepted Keynesian doctrine. Still, Keynesian theory had not been
given a decisive test. Federal expenditures in 1940 amounted only to about
$9 billion, while unemployment hovered at a disheartening 14.6 percent.

It was unquestionably World War II that finally ended the Great Depression and also proved Keynes's theory of economic recovery. As government expenditures doubled, tripled, quadrupled, and eventually reached a figure more than ten times that of 1940, unemployment decreased to a practically insignificant level and the economy boomed for the first time in more than a dozen years. As Robert Lekachman has written in his definitive study of the Keynesian Era, "The Second World War was an incomparable laboratory demonstration that deficits do cause prosperity."[15]

Keynesian theory had at last triumphed, and young Keynesian economists and intellectuals became the dominant faction of the Washington intelligentsia that had managed the myriad agencies established during the New Deal and that now began to mobilize the nation's resources for a world war. Many of them were in future years to assume positions of increasing influence either as government personnel, as formal or informal advisers to politicians, or as social analysts and critics outside of government. Three such people were Alvin Hansen, Seymour Harris, and Paul Samuelson, Harvard economists who had helped to launch the Keynesian movement in America and who became regular contributors to *The New Republic*. Like the triad that had founded this journal for liberal activists, they were convinced, as were the many other Keynesian scholars and new liberals who wrote for the publication, that they were standing at a crossroads of economic, social, and political change in America. Unlike Croly, Lippmann, and Weyl, however, they had had direct influence in government, not only as bureaucratic functionaries, but as counselors and advisers to those in the innermost circles of political power. As these intellectuals surveyed the accomplishments of the administration they had served, they could justly feel a good deal of satisfaction. The American economy had apparently been revitalized, badly needed social reforms had been enacted, and liberal institutions had been preserved.

But what of the future? Keynesians knew (or at least strongly *believed*) that cyclical economic crises could be averted through state monetary and fiscal policy. But Keynesian theory had only been tested during wartime. The war had temporarily taken up the slack from the Depression years, but what would happen when the war ended, the troops came home and needed jobs, and war production screeched to a halt? The general belief among the public was clearly expressed in a series of Gallup Polls taken during the war years. Americans consistently listed postwar unemployment and economic troubles as the most important problems they expected to face

[15] Lekachman, *The Age of Keynes*, p. 143.

once the fighting ended, and a majority predicted the return of high rates of joblessness and lower wages. Even more significantly, most economists, intellectuals, and public officials agreed with this pessimistic prognosis.

Symptomatic of this anxiety was a collection of essays published in 1943 under the title *Postwar Economic Problems*. Edited by Seymour Harris, it contained an appraisal, mainly by leading liberal economists, of the nation's probable economic future. Most of the contributing writers, including Paul Samuelson, expressed apprehension regarding the transition to a peacetime economy. "All our findings," Samuelson warned, "lead to the conclusion that there is serious danger of underestimating the magnitude of the problem of maintaining continuing full employment in the postwar period."[16] Alvin Hansen, though less pessimistic concerning short-term economic developments (he anticipated a postwar boom and inflation), saw America on the threshold of a basic and permanent change with respect to national economic policy. "One lesson stands out with great clarity," he wrote, "from the experiences of the last two decades. It is no longer possible to accept the thesis that cycles of prosperity and depression may be complacently regarded as a characteristic of a system of free enterprise and private property. In the modern world no system can survive which permits the continued recurrence of serious depressions." If it were indeed true that depressions were inevitable, then the system was "doomed." But he did not believe this. If a "substantial approximation to full employment" could be achieved, the system could be saved.[17] In the next section of his article, Hansen called for "democratic planning," the institutionalization of Keynesian economic policies to ensure continued production and full employment, the rebuilding of American industry, the renovation of both urban and rural areas, the expansion of social services, and international cooperation to further the goal of full employment, aid underdeveloped countries, and "promote world trade and the effective worldwide use of productive resources." Given such policies, neither Hansen nor the majority of his colleagues doubted that American capitalism was salvageable.

Many government officials held the same view, and it is no mere coincidence that in March of that same year the National Resources Planning Board published its famous final project before being dismantled under

[16] Paul A. Samuelson, "Full Employment after the War," in Seymour E. Harris, ed., *Postwar Economic Problems* (New York: McGraw-Hill, 1943), p. 53.

[17] Alvin H. Hansen, "The Postwar Economy," in ibid., pp. 9-10.

pressure from conservatives, business groups, and rival bureaucratic agencies. Entitled *Security, Work and Relief Policies*, the report set off a wave of interest and excitement in liberal circles. Like its British counterpart the Beveridge Report, it called for guaranteed employment, universal health care, and the establishment of minimum standards of living for all citizens and represented the culmination of liberal Keynesian proposals for unfinished social reforms.

But liberals knew that, although their basic reforms could not be undone, their active power in government to promote positive change was, at least temporarily, on the wane. Even as they carried out their wartime duties, they saw the resurgence of corporate and conservative influence in political affairs, and many of them correctly perceived that their time was limited. Indeed, time was even shorter than they realized, for Roosevelt's death was soon to deprive all liberals—especially the New Deal intelligentsia—of effective leadership and an intimate access to political power that they were not to regain for almost two decades. The high-water mark of post–New Deal reformist activism during the last part of the Roosevelt Era was reached in January of 1945, with the introduction of a Full Employment Bill in Congress. Eventually enacted, albeit in greatly diluted form, as the Employment Act of 1946, it created a Council of Economic Advisers who were yearly to assess economic conditions and make a report to the president recommending national policies to "foster and promote free competitive enterprise and the general welfare, conditions under which there will be afforded useful employment, for those able, willing, and seeking to work, and to promote maximum employment, production, and purchasing power." Never again would the government allow a national economic collapse and mass unemployment. Keynesian economic policy had been enacted into law.

Yet by the time the Employment Act was signed by President Harry S. Truman it seemed rather superfluous, for, contrary to the expectations of economists, intellectuals, politicians, and the general public, the US economy did not collapse or stagnate when the war ended. An economic boom stimulated by (1) the massive savings accumulated by workers during the war years that were now being spent by a nation whose pent up consumer demand from both the Depression and war period was now finally unleashed and (2) the huge investments required to replenish America's depleted capital stock and to rebuild the war-shattered economies of Europe (in the latter case, through US loans recycled back to purchase American exports) upset the predictions of those who had foreseen, at a minimum, the need for a slow, carefully guided transition in order to head off economic disaster. With dizzying speed in a period of several months (not the *years* predicted by many economists) war industries were converted to the production of consumer goods, wage and price controls were abolished, and the remnants of the New Deal—largely dismantled during the war—became part of what has been called the "Broker State," that is, "a government intervening in an ad hoc and piecemeal fashion on behalf of those groups with sufficient political or economic power to obtain assistance."[18]

And so, by the end of the first half of the twentieth century, it appeared that the economy had been sufficiently restructured so that the economic disorders and social crises that had plagued the American industrial system since its traumatic birth in the late nineteenth century were no more. Keynesian policy would prevent cyclical slumps in production, while the Broker State mediated the residual conflicts that might arise among various groups and interests. The country therefore embarked upon a cautious and conservative course, as it invariably does after a period of crisis, reform, and war. American intellectuals, once the spearhead of progressive social thought, now recoiled from an overly skeptical or critical examination of American society and culture. Most historians, economists, and sociologists, no longer profoundly disturbed by questions of economic stability, concentrated power, and social justice, turned now to other pursuits. Many were now fascinated, not by the long period of turmoil, uncertainty, and unrest since the dawn of the Age of Industry, but instead by the sources of America's present institutional stability. Within this vein, the historian Daniel Boorstin was, within a few years, to write of the "genius" of American politics, while his colleague Arthur Schlesinger, Jr., in *The Vital Center* warned against any actions that might threaten the sensible, middle course Americans had managed to steer, avoiding the treacherous reefs of fascism and communism.

And yet there was a distinct feeling among some observers that all was not well and that much was being covered up or ignored. Perhaps the historian Richard Hofstadter expressed this feeling best when, in a study of American political history appearing in 1948, he sought to locate the origins of the self-satisfaction and the simultaneous, though paradoxical, coexistence of a wave of "national nostalgia" during these years. Hofstadter admitted—indeed emphasized—that there had been "a common

<hr>

[18] Otis L. Graham, Jr., *Toward a Planned Society: From Roosevelt to Nixon* (Oxford: Oxford University Press, 1976), p. 65.

ground, a unity of cultural and poltical tradition, upon which American civilization has stood.'' He warned, however, that American culture ''has been intensely nationalistic and for the most part isolationist; it has been fiercely individualistic and capitalistic. In a corporate and consolidated society demanding international responsibility, cohesion, centralization, and planning, the traditional ground is shifting under our feet.''[19] Hofstadter explained that the reaction of Americans to these new realities was perfectly understandable, but also disturbing: ''In American politics the development of a retrospective and nostalgic cast of mind has gone hand in hand with the slow decline of a traditional faith. When competition and enterprise were rising, men thought of the future; when they were flourishing, of the present. Now—in an age of concentration, bigness, and corporate monopoly—when competition and opportunity have gone into decline, men look wistfully back toward a golden age.''[20] What Hofstadter was clearly saying was that the great transformation of American society in the twentieth century had not been faced squarely. A number of America's most perceptive social thinkers recognized this and continued their critical examination of what the nation had become after five decades of incredibly rapid and unprecedented change.

The most commonly expressed fear—reinforced by the experience of the New Deal, wartime controls, and the shocking experience of fascism and Stalinism—was that a market economy could not survive after the war or that it could do so only through state-directed economic planning. Although this particular anxiety receded somewhat as the war ended and comprehensive governmental constraints on the economy were rapidly lifted, the long-term impact of state intervention as well as the very process of corporate concentration and economic change—spurred by war production from which large-scale enterprise had benefitted in a greatly disproportionate manner—attracted the attention and interest of those who saw in these developments an acceleration of statist and bureaucratic forces that would reinforce already existing trends. Joseph Schumpeter, a renowned conservative economist and social theorist and one of the contributors to *Postwar Economic Problems*, suggested in an essay appearing in that work that the ''most obvious possibility'' was a continuation, consolidation, and extension of the interventionist policies of the New Deal. ''Such a system will no doubt still be called capitalism,'' he wrote. ''But it is capitalism in

---

[19] Richard Hofstadter, *The American Political Tradition: And the Men Who Made It* (New York: Vintage, 1974), p. xxxix.

[20] Ibid., p. xxxiv.

the oxygen tent—kept alive by artificial devices and paralyzed in all those functions that produced the successes of the past. The question why it should be kept alive at all is therefore bound to be put before long."[21]

Schumpeter was not alone. Many observers across the political spectrum doubted that capitalist society could overcome even its economic problems, let alone its social and political ones. Even the rather encouraging economic upsurge of the immediate postwar years did not allay the fears of many economists and intellectuals. It was one thing to have miscalculated the magnitude and duration of an initial postwar boom (most had even allowed for such a possibility); it was another to *keep* the economy at a high level of output. Many liberals themselves were not convinced that Keynesian measures and the restructuring of fiscal and monetary policy could indefinitely forestall an economic collapse or prolonged stagnation, and, America's prosperity at the time notwithstanding, asked themselves how long this new form of capitalism could continue to function.[22]

Thus, at mid-century, the central question posed by the most prestigious and influential members of the American intelligentsia concerning the nation's future involved the viability of a market system that had undergone enormous changes since the turn of the century. Some analysts saw the need for further substantial changes in the system; others predicted the loss of economic efficiency, political freedom, social stability, or possibly a combination of all three if more changes were implemented. Yet all appeared to recognize that the old framework had been shattered beyond repair. It is little wonder that some of them viewed the era in almost apocalyptic terms. No less than the earlier generations of social thinkers who had stood at important turning points in American history, a new cohort braced itself for another period that all sensed would be critical. As they surveyed a society shaken by an economic breakdown, a decade of stagnation and experimental reforms, four years of war socialism, and a postwar expansionary rise that appeared to be nearing its crest, the question they all asked was simple: Could the Broker State work?

[21] Joseph A. Schumpeter, "Capitalism in the Postwar World," in Harris, *Postwar Economic Problems*, pp. 122, 123.

[22] See, for example, Chester Bowles, "Blueprints for a Second New Deal," in Seymour E. Harris, ed., *Saving American Capitalism: A Liberal Economic Program* (New York: Knopf, 1950), pp. 13-39.

THE THINKERS

I The Technological Imperative: John Kenneth Galbraith and the New Industrial State

Joseph Schumpeter

We have seen that the function of entrepreneurs is to reform or revolutionize the pattern of production by exploiting an invention or, more generally, an untried technological possibility for producing a new commodity or producing an old one in a new way, by opening up a new source of supply of materials or a new outlet for products, by reorganizing an industry and so on. . . . This social function is already losing importance and is bound to lose it at an accelerating rate in the future even if the economic process itself of which entrepreneurship was the prime mover went on unabated. For, on the one hand, it is much easier now than it has been in the past to do things that lie outside familiar routine—innovation itself is being reduced to routine. Technological progress is increasingly becoming the business of teams of trained specialists who turn out what is required and make it work in predictable ways. The romance of earlier commercial adventure is rapidly wearing away, because so many more things can be strictly calculated that had of old to be visualized in a flash of genius.

John Kenneth Galbraith

It is not my instinct to be unduly modest, but let me say that I'm not authoring a revolution. Rather, I'm taking advantage of one that is already well along. Circumstances are the enemy of neoclassical economics, not Galbraith.

JOHN KENNETH GALBRAITH

Chapter 2   *The New Capitalism*

In the midst of the postwar quandary over America's economic future, an article entitled "Monopoly and the Concentration of Economic Power" appeared among a collection of essays published on behalf of the American Economic Association under the title *A Survey of Contemporary Economics*. The author, recently arrived at Harvard and employed as a lecturer in economics, had been an editor at *Fortune* magazine the previous year. The article examined the treatment of monopoly and "monopoloid forms" of business enterprise in the scholarly literature of the 1930s and the antitrust action taken during the Roosevelt administration. Discussing the theory that monopoly power and concomitant market imperfections were largely responsible for cyclical fluctuations in the economy, the writer suggested that the discovery by economists that oligopoly was a widespread and probably ineradicable phenomenon was not a sufficient cause for despair. True, oligopoly was a general and dominant element in the economy. True also was the fact that, once this was recognized, "to prescribe the elimination of monopoly became tantamount to demanding a wholesale revision of the economic order." Yet these facts need not, he argued, provoke undue alarm. In fact, he believed that the discomfiture of economists in the face of the apparent demise of the old competitive mechanism was altogether unnecessary, since "Without doubt there are many imperfect markets in which a 'workable' competition yields the same effective solution, or has the same social effect, that the textbooks have associated with pure competition." Surveying the problems of analysis and public policy apparently raised by the revelation that, for the most part, pure competition no longer (if indeed it had ever) existed, the essay concluded that

> The dilemma may be more intellectual than real. We do live in an industrial community where oligopoly—or, more horrid word, private collectivism—is the rule. But, strangely, we do live. Our dissatisfaction with our world is less the result of having known any other than of having constructed a model of another economic society, the *rationale* of which we know and which is more companionable to our sense of elegance and order. We shall never find anything so agreeable in the world we have. But perhaps there will be compensation, once we have ex-

changed elegance for actuality, in a greater rate of progress in understanding what we have.[1]

This thesis, expanded in a book published some four years later, was to make its author a celebrity and add the first of many phrases to the vocabularies of both economists and laymen. The argument would later be greatly revised. Yet it is certainly one of the most extraordinary ironies of modern social thought that a man who was later to be identified as one of the chief critics of American capitalism should have first risen to prominence by proclaiming a harmonious balance of economic forces to exist in the postwar United States.

But this fact is hardly more remarkable than the man himself. By the time *American Capitalism: The Concept of Countervailing Power* appeared in print, its forty-four-year-old author, John Kenneth Galbraith, had already seen an outstanding career in the academic world, in journalism, and in public service. Furthermore, he would continue in future years, as he had in the past, to combine the activities of a scholar, social theorist, administrator, political activist, and social critic, moving back and forth from the university to the arenas of politics, government, and world affairs. Galbraith's craggy countenance was to become an increasingly familiar fixture of the American intellectual and political scenes, where he was to leave an indelible imprint of his presence and ideas during the decades following World War II. With a keen and incisive prose style and a rapier wit in both oral and written forms of expression, he was to create armies of admirers and adversaries, leaving few in the neutral camp. This six-foot-eight-inch former Canadian, however, was relatively unknown to the American public and even to many of his professional colleagues until *American Capitalism* was published in 1952.

The son of Scotch-Canadian farmers, Galbraith was born in Ontario, Canada, in 1908. His father, part of the agrarian reform movement in Ontario, was known locally as something of a firebrand whose inveterate opposition to conservative politics was often dramatically, if somewhat crudely, expressed on a variety of occasions. Once, accompanied by his six-year-old son to a political rally, the elder Galbraith climbed to the top of a manure pile, promptly—though not entirely convincingly—apologized to the assembled crowd of listeners for speaking from the Tory plat-

---

[1] J. K. Galbraith, "Monopoly and the Concentration of Economic Power," in Howard S. Ellis, ed., *A Survey of Contemporary Economics* (Homewood, Illinois: Richard D. Irwin, 1948), vol. 1, pp. 127-128.

form, and then launched into a speech that lambasted the present government and its policies. The child, John Kenneth, was to inherit his father's iconoclastic and reformist temperament, though not his style of argument.

Possessing a formidable intellect, the younger Galbraith was eventually to enter the Ontario Agricultural College at Guelph, where he studied agricultural economics and animal husbandry until his senior year when he obtained a research assistantship in agricultural economics at the University of California at Berkeley. Galbraith supported himself during this period of graduate study by doing research in the problems of honey marketing in California as well as on general agricultural conditions in the state. He later became head of the departments of Economics, of Agricultural Economics, of Accounting, and of Farm Management at the Davis branch of the university. The radical climate prevalent at Berkeley during the early 1930s together with its most obvious immediate cause—the Great Depression—soon led him away from the narrow confines of agricultural economics to more general concerns. Moreover, one of the professors at Berkeley, Leo Rogin, was holding graduate seminars at which Keynes's ideas were being discussed long before the Keynesian Revolution took place. Offered a position at Harvard upon completion of his doctoral program in 1934, Galbraith reluctantly accepted it and headed east.

At Harvard, Galbraith soon became interested in, and indeed part of, the great debate on the structure of modern large business organizations and the nature of market and price behavior under conditions of "imperfect competition," a controversy touched off by the work of Chamberlin, Robinson, and Burns on the one hand and by Berle and Means on the other. It is therefore not surprising that Galbraith's first professional articles as an economist dealt with these matters and drew heavily on the ideas and insights of the aforementioned economists and social theorists.[2] It was the book *Modern Competition and Business Policy*, however, published in 1938 and coauthored by Galbraith and businessman H. S. Dennison, that sought to integrate the findings of these scholars and, in addition, to recommend public policies commensurate with the changed structure of capitalist institutions in America. Examining this new structure, Galbraith and Dennison concluded that a return to the supposedly pure competition of the past was, for all practical purposes, impossible. Convinced that the current predominant form of industrial organization often led to inefficiencies and

[2] See J. K. Galbraith, "Monopoly Power and Price Rigidities," *The Quarterly Journal of Economics*, 50 (May 1936), 456-475, for an example of Galbraith's early work.

low social performance in general, Galbraith and Dennison advocated the mandatory participation of poorly performing corporations in a system of mild indicative planning coordinated by a congressionally appointed commission. They also proposed a reworking of incorporation procedures, the modification of certain internal corporate policies and regulations, and the establishment of minimum standards regarding wages and hours of employment.[3]

But this call for a substantial restructuring of the American economy was to have little impact, since its publication coincided with the ascendancy of Keynesian theory, which did not require such reforms. What the economy needed, Keynes proposed, was not major surgery but only regular medication for an indefinite, though limited, period and a changed external environment. Galbraith himself was no longer moved to investigate the problems of industrial organization and was soon converted to the new Keynesian doctrine.

Galbraith not only accepted the new theory, but, together with economists such as Alvin Hansen, Seymour Harris, and Paul Samuelson, was instrumental in the task of spreading the creed as Harvard became the center of Keynesian theory in the United States. And, as he later recalled, adherents were sought within, but also far beyond, the confines of the university, as Hansen "persuaded his students and younger colleagues that they should not only understand the ideas but win understanding in others and then go on to get action. Without ever seeking to do so or being quite aware of the fact, he became the leader of a crusade. In the late thirties Hansen's seminar in the new Graduate School of Public Administration was regularly visited by the Washington policy-makers. Often the students overflowed into the hall." "The officials," Galbraith relates, "took Hansen's ideas, and perhaps even more his sense of conviction, back to Washington."[4] Indeed, like many who have instructed would-be missionaries, the young Keynesian theorists often succumbed to their own zeal and went to Washington themselves, as did Hansen, Harris, Samuelson, Alan R. Sweezy, Walter Salant, and large numbers of their students and colleagues at Harvard, becoming members of the New Deal intelligentsia.

Galbraith went also, joining the National Resources Planning Board at

[3] See H. S. Dennison and J. K. Galbraith, *Modern Competition and Business Policy* (Oxford: Oxford University Press, 1938), p. 83.

[4] J. K. Galbraith, "How Keynes Came to America," in J. K. Galbraith, *A Contemporary Guide to Economics, Peace and Laughter*, edited by Andrea D. Williams (New York: Signet, 1972), p. 50.

the end of the decade. His work there was followed by a short stay at a teaching post at Princeton, a stint at the National Defense Advisory Commission, and, finally, an appointment as head of the Price Section in the Office of Price Administration (OPA) in 1941. As the United States entered World War II and comprehensive controls were placed on wages and prices (a measure that had been proposed by both Keynes and Galbraith in the spring of 1941), Galbraith's agency expanded from a small number of offices in a single building to a vast bureaucracy employing many thousands of persons. He performed his duties efficiently and energetically—too much so, in the view of many, and his enemies in both business and government multiplied almost as rapidly as his employees. Galbraith reciprocated this animosity, later recalling that "I could not conceal my dislike for the lobbyists, trade association representatives, professional business spokesmen and hireling Establishment lawyers who sought to associate patriotism with the need for even more money than they were already making."[5] Opposition to Galbraith's policies reached a peak by 1943 when Lew Hahn, head of the National Retail Dry Goods Association, held up a copy of *Modern Competition and Business Policy* before a Congressional committee and claimed that Galbraith was attempting to use OPA authority to "change the business structure of the nation under the guise of war necessity."[6]

Even worse for Galbraith was the replacement of the head of the OPA by a former senator whose assistant, the manager of an advertising agency, Galbraith particularly resented. The feeling was mutual, as the latter railed against "the professors and theorists whom Dr. Galbraith represents."[7] The New Deal intelligentsia were being steadily edged out of power, and Galbraith's subsequent resignation was not an isolated incident. After leaving the OPA, he spent several months as an editor for *Fortune* magazine, where he remained until the war ended.

After Germany's defeat, Galbraith was made one of the directors of the United States Strategic Bombing Survey, an investigative effort mounted in order to find out precisely how effective the Allied bombing of cities had been in disrupting German war production and hastening the defeat of the Nazis. Statistical data were amassed and analyzed, German production figures were checked, extensive and intensive interviews were conducted (Galbraith personally helped to interrogate two of Hitler's production

[5] J. K. Galbraith, *A Life in Our Times: Memoirs* (New York: Ballantine, 1982), p. 179.

[6] Leonard Silk, *The Economists* (New York: Basic, 1976), p. 110.

[7] Quoted in ibid., p. 111.

chiefs, Fritz Sauckel, the minister of labor recruitment, and Albert Speer, the arms minister)—a monumental work of analysis that led its managers to an astonishing, yet irrefutable conclusion: Allied strategic bombing had done virtually *nothing* to slow up the production of armaments. It was found that German factories, often located on the outskirts of town, either had escaped destruction or were rapidly put back into operation; the flow of arms had not only continued unabated, but even increased, finally dropping off only in the very last stages of the war. In addition, the capital and productive facilities that were destroyed had nothing to do with basic requirements for food, shelter, and clothing, the losses being confined to nonessential goods and services. The workers from bombed-out shops and factories producing the latter, their productive potential unimpaired but now unemployed, flooded into war industries, ending a labor shortage in that sector that had been caused by irrational government policies and the unwillingness of the population to sacrifice various luxuries and comforts. The study therefore concluded that, if anything, Allied bombing had actually *increased* the efficiency of German war production. Galbraith was long to remember the results of the Strategic Bombing Survey; more importantly, as an economist he was to ponder the implications of its findings for understanding the nature of modern industrial production: the extraordinary productive capacities of modern economies; the trivial nature of much that they produced; and the supreme importance of human resources in industrial civilization.

After briefly serving with the State Department and receiving the Medal of Freedom for his years of government service, Galbraith went back to *Fortune*, and shortly thereafter to Harvard. Having written articles after the war on the problem of inflation, the issue of price control, and their relation to current economic conditions (which later became a book, *A Theory of Price Control*), his main attention was increasingly focused on the larger questions he had first discussed over a decade before: the problems of industrial concentration, oligopolistic power, and imperfect competition. The analysis and solution he was now in the process of formulating, however, were quite different from those that he had offered in *Modern Competition and Business Policy*. No longer was he to stress the flaws and inefficiencies of American business structure and economic organization. His altered view, presently to be set forth in detail, was that the Broker State *could* work, and his book *American Capitalism* was written to show how and why.

American Capitalism: THE BROKER STATE DEFENDED

Not for nothing was Galbraith's book accorded recognition and praise by the vast majority of economists, social theorists, and most of the intellectual community. *American Capitalism* was a comprehensive attempt not only to examine the major changes in the US economy since the Great Depression, but also to totally reformulate the dominant liberal interpretation of the market system in light of those changes and all the others that had occurred since the late nineteenth century. The book foreshadowed Galbraith's later work in its treatment of corporate and market structure, the impact of technology on the US economy, and the role of the state in modern industrial society. It began with the following playful, though highly appropriate lines:

> It is told that such are the aerodynamics and wing-loading of the bumblebee that, in principle, it cannot fly. It does, and the knowledge that it defies the august authority of Isaac Newton and Orville Wright must keep the bee in constant fear of a crack-up. One can assume, in addition, that it is apprehensive of the matriarchy to which it is subject, for this is known to be an oppressive form of government. The bumblebee is a successful but an insecure insect.
>
> If all this be true, and its standing in physics and entomology is perhaps not of the highest, life among the bumblebees must bear a remarkable resemblance to life in the United States in recent years. The present organization and management of the American economy are also in defiance of the rules—rules that derive their ultimate authority from men of such Newtonian stature as Bentham, Ricardo and Adam Smith. Nevertheless it works, and in the years since World War II quite brilliantly.[8]

Americans remained insecure, Galbraith believed, because they had been conditioned to think within the categories of classical, free-market liberalism and could therefore neither rationally explain nor accept a form of economic and social organization that clearly bore only a slight resemblance to the old system. The self-regulating free market of countless small competitors that diffused power throughout society and maximized production was now replaced by a controlled market dominated by several dozen powerful corporations whose ability to affect prices and production

---

[8] J. K. Galbraith, *American Capitalism: The Concept of Countervailing Power* (Boston: Houghton Mifflin, 1952), p. 1. Subsequently cited parenthetically as *AmC*.

levels was, as he acknowledged, known, or at least assumed, by social theorists since Veblen's time. What had bedeviled them and others since before the days of Theodore Roosevelt was the lack of adequate responses to the following questions: How had this state of affairs come about? Was it the result of a conspiracy? A corporate drive for power? Most important, what should be done about it? Should large corporations be broken up, regulated more closely, or even nationalized? These questions were not simply academic. They were real problems of public policy and they required answers.

These issues had come to a head twice before, during both the Progressive Era and the 1930s. Americans had never been in doubt concerning what should be done about monopoly power in its most brazen, open, and pure form. Almost alone among industrial powers, America had attempted to institutionalize its classical liberal ideology, outlawing monopoly and all other consciously constructed barriers to free competition in the Sherman Anti-Trust Act of 1890 (and thus giving the lie to the widespread notion that Americans are inordinately pragmatic). But, as noted previously, economists had found monopoly theory inadequate as an analytical tool since it did not take into account the many intermediate forms of enterprise that typified the real—that is, *oligopolistic*—structure of the economy. In practice, these forms were virtually indistinguishable from actual monopolies with respect to their effects on corporate and market behavior.

Americans had many reasons to oppose and resist the growth of oligopolistic power, but a major one was what many perceived to be its role in bringing on and exacerbating the effects of the Great Depression by keeping prices artificially high even in the face of drastically reduced demand, thus reducing the effectiveness of Keynesian policy—an argument used by the group in FDR's administration that inaugurated the wave of radical antitrust action from 1938 to 1941 which saw more than half of all federal prosecutions undertaken under the Sherman Act until 1941. A third group, oriented toward planning, advised Roosevelt to accept the oligopolistic structure of modern American capitalism, but to bring it under increased state direction and control. (This, of course, had been Galbraith's position when he wrote *Modern Competition and Business Policy*.) Thus, a three-sided battle for influence had been waged throughout the period of the New Deal. The war brought the Keynesians to a dominant position and seemed to validate their ideas, yet even they grew ever more uneasy about the unresolved problem of oligopolistic competition as the postwar period wore on, adding their fear to the general apprehension of the times. Again, a three-way split developed in liberal thought. It was in such a historical and intellectual context that Galbraith offered an explanation and a solution for a dilemma that had perplexed Americans for so long.

As he had in the 1930s, Galbraith insisted that dealing with oligopoly through a great wave of indiscriminate antitrust action would be economically and socially disastrous. Admitting that "a large share of the productive activity of the United States is carried on by a comparatively small number of corporations," he maintained that this was "a normal pattern of capitalist organization" (*AmC*, 6). Any attempt legally to enact the old liberal philosophy of free competition would, he averred, require a radical economic transformation of truly nightmarish dimensions. "To suppose that there are grounds for antitrust prosecution wherever three, four or a half dozen firms dominate a market," Galbraith argued, "is to suppose that the very fabric of American capitalism is illegal" (*AmC*, 58). Moreover, even if such a colossal undertaking could be successfully carried out (and he considered this highly unlikely), it could not possibly, in his view, seriously alter the underlying economic conditions and mechanisms that were responsible for the growth of oligopolies in the first place.

Besides, Galbraith said, the system *worked*. There had been no crash after the war, employment levels remained high, and, in general, Americans had never been so well off. Forget the world of the small entrepreneur, Galbraith urged, for it would not return. Forget the stereotypic image of large corporations as inefficient, greedy monstrosities that stifled economic and technological progress, continually enhanced their own power at the public expense, and collectively unbalanced the natural harmony of the market system, for their image had been greatly distorted. America's main problems were not institutional: they were intellectual and psychological. To prove this, Galbraith methodically blasted away at the logical, empirical, and analytical foundations of beliefs fervently held by the vast majority of Americans.

The end of free competition and the dominance of the small entrepreneur in the industrial sector of the economy was the result, Galbraith wrote, of a natural process of evolution. When an area of industry was first developed, the number of firms tended to reach a maximum within a few years at most. From then on there was generally "a steady decline until a point of stability is reached with a handful of massive survivors and, usually, a fringe of smaller hangers-on" (*AmC*, 36). The causes of this phenomenon were, according to Galbraith, "deeply organic" and had little to do with the conscious machinations of power-hungry corporate leaders. Economies of scale, difficulties in entering an already established field, and the inherently more powerful position of surviving companies both during times of prosperity and depression led inevitably to a mutually reinforcing pattern of consolidation that, he emphasized, was reproduced in an almost identical manner in Western Europe. Any attempt to break up these industrial combinations could never alter these underlying structural tendencies and would therefore be futile.

Even if this interpretation of the origins of existing economic institutions were valid, however, it did not answer those who claimed that, natural or not, these developments were socially and economically harmful. As previously noted, most observers had held monopoly power to be intrinsically inefficient and technologically unprogressive. Firms with substantial market power could, it had always been argued, keep prices artificially high since no adequate competitive pressures existed to force them down to a level where they just covered costs. A corollary of this proposition stated that aggregate industrial output would as a consequence be reduced to a point significantly below the level that would prevail in a freely competitive economy. It was also said that these large companies had little incentive to develop new or improved products and technical processes. Why should they innovate when few, if any, competing firms could threaten to take their markets away from them by developing their own new products and methods? The natural state of such a market would, critics charged, be one of inefficiency and stagnation.

Not so, Galbraith replied. True, in a narrow economic sense, oligopolistic industries were not as efficient as those composed of smaller, more numerous firms. They did expend disproportionate amounts of capital on advertising and other kinds of commercial rivalry—one form of competition that intensified in an oligopolistic system. In addition, their economic power could, if unchecked, lead to a somewhat poor allocation of resources and to a greater maldistribution of income (although Galbraith noted that this need not happen). They also, for technical reasons, tended to produce excessive employment in more competitive industries. But Galbraith maintained that there were important compensatory factors. First, in an economy a large part of whose activity had nothing to do with providing basic necessities, the waste involved in attempts to wean consumers away from one deodorant and lure them toward another, while unnecessary and foolish, could not be deemed a critical economic problem. Second, he argued that large corporations were not backward in the area of research and development. Small firms might have been more technologically progressive than large corporations in an earlier era; but this was already becoming doubtful by the end of the nineteenth century, since the ability to rapidly produce imitations of newly developed products and thereby quickly increase their supply and drive down their prices made the derived advantage of innovation in a freely competitive market only fleeting for small firms that would have little reason to commit the increasingly large sums necessary for many research and development projects. In any case, that era had passed. Modern research and development, now requiring sophisticated, expensive equipment and procedures, large capital outlays, and the talent of highly educated and trained personnel could no longer be carried on extensively by any but the very large industrial firms.[9] Moreover, large enterprises, unlike their smaller counterparts, did have an incentive to invest in innovative projects. Since it possessed substantial market power, the large, innovative firm and, eventually, its imitating rivals would benefit monetarily from a new invention for a reasonable length of time because the innovative firm's increased revenue would not be quickly pared down as the result of cutthroat competition. In fact, Galbraith remarked, technical innovation remained, along with advertising, one of the chief forms of competition in the modern industrial sector.

But even if *this* were true, what would prevent giant firms from intentionally—or even unintentionally—benefitting from their economically advantageous position to the detriment of society as a whole? With the free market largely supplanted by a controlled one, how could one ensure that oligopolies would not use their great power to the disadvantage of workers, farmers, and other businessmen who were under the constraints of a more severe kind of competition? Again, Galbraith seemed to have an ingenious answer. A mechanism to guard against this eventuality already existed, he proposed. People had merely been looking for it in the wrong place!

Under the old system, Galbraith reminded his readers, a balance had resulted from the interplay of economic interests on the same side of the market: sellers competed with other sellers, buyers with other buyers. He conceded that this kind of balance obviously no longer existed. Small businesses as sellers of products and purchasers of goods and human labor certainly could not now compete with huge oligopolies on anything even approaching equal terms. This was also true of individual workers and consumers. But individuals and small producers could use their collective

---

[9] Many of these arguments were, as Galbraith acknowledged, first made by Joseph A. Schumpeter in his book *Capitalism, Socialism and Democracy.*

economic and/or political power on the side of the market *opposite* that of the large corporation. And this, Galbraith pointed out, was precisely what they had been doing for some time. For example, workers selling their labor to a powerful buyer (that is, a large corporation) could negotiate as a group, withholding their labor until they received a reasonable price for it. Similarly, mass retailers could consolidate their firms, set up cooperative buying organizations, and establish chain stores to counter the selling power of large industrial suppliers. Farmers, although too atomized to develop market power independently, could, in conjunction with the state, act collectively to limit production and raise their income to acceptable levels through government price supports, subsidies, or other devices. Similar processes could be seen in action throughout the American economy. Thus, Galbraith maintained, a powerful mechanism was at work that provided the checks and balances that had been lost when the free market disappeared. He called this new mechanism "countervailing power"—a "self-generating force" brought into being by the very existence of concentrated market power.

This new balancing force made extensive regulation and guidance of corporations and the general economy by the state unnecessary and thus invalidated the view which Galbraith himself had held until the late 1930s, since the most sorely afflicted victims of corporate power could now "look after themselves." This did not mean, of course, that the state had no role to play in the economy. Besides ensuring that aggregate demand did not drop enough to precipitate a severe recession, the state would have as a crucial function the redressing of pronounced imbalances in economic power. In this regard, Galbraith wrote: "Without the phenomenon itself being fully recognized, the provision of state assistance to the development of countervailing power has become a major function of government— perhaps *the* major domestic function of government. Much of the domestic legislation of the last twenty years, that of the New Deal episode in particular, only becomes fully comprehensible when it is viewed in this light" (*AmC*, 133).

Galbraith admitted that the development of countervailing power by groups either through their own action or by having it granted to them by the state could not guarantee maximum economic efficiency interpreted within a narrow context, just as this could not be expected when one judged the results of oligopolistic market behavior. But again, as in the latter case, there were important and, in his view, overriding compensations, including a dramatic reduction in the social turmoil that had characterized the earlier twentieth century. Granted, this might not be an ideal arrangement; but Galbraith saw no realistic alternative. It was natural that this development would have involved much legislative and political activity and that it would have been "keenly controversial." After all, he pointed out, those groups that had sought and gained countervailing power for themselves surely did so to use it against those who had had much greater marker power. And, of course, "Those whose power was thereby inhibited could hardly be expected to welcome this development or the intervention of the government to abet it" (AmC, 142).

Not only should Americans not be anxious concerning the countervailing power already given to many groups: they should be willing to see it extended to others, including hired farm workers, unorganized urban workers, and even white-collar employees. Recognizing how state assistance had historically been granted, Galbraith called attention to the fact that government did not bestow countervailing power out of the blue: groups had been forced to seek it. Conservatives, who had been shocked by the results of the New Deal (for example, the Wagner Act, the AAA, and minimum-wage laws), and liberals, who had supported its legislation "without knowing quite why," had actually been witnessing the granting of countervailing power to those with relatively little market power, an act which in fact decreased the overall amount of state regulation that was necessary or that would be requested.

One final—and critical—issue remained: the specter of depression. Nineteen fifty-two was only a dozen years removed from a period that had witnessed an economic collapse so frightening in its dimensions and so unnerving in its effects that many found it difficult to regain confidence in capitalism. Moreover, Keynes's contention that the system was not self-balancing and was therefore in need of guidance and occasional direct intervention by the state had disturbing implications for many Americans, especially businessmen. Keynes was slowly gaining acceptance among politicians, the public, and progressive business groups, but many remained fearful, a condition Galbraith called America's "Depression Psychosis."

Galbraith recognized that while abandoning the free-market model of the economy had created problems that he considered mainly intellectual, the Great Depression was a dire emergency that had demanded immediate action. Summing up Keynes's theory, he observed that its proposals were perfectly compatible with the functioning of a liberal capitalist economy, having essentially left major economic decisions to businessmen and using central control only to affect the "climate" in which they made their decisions in order to ensure economic stability. If this remedy could keep the economy near maximum production and full employment, Americans' most important fear would be a thing of the past. Keynes's ideas had not, it was true, been tested over a long period of time, and they might not be quite as easy to implement as many had at first thought; but Galbraith believed that peace and decreased arms expenditures would make its success likely. And, again, he stressed practical results. Oligopolistic competition was not ideal, but, together with the correcting mechanism of countervailing power, it could operate effectively in a modern economy in a larger system of Keynesian monetary and fiscal policy regulated by the state. Both systems had, at least so far, worked together in an entirely complementary fashion to produce social and economic stability—a synthesis of elements that formed a united front against the threat of economic disaster, social inequities, and political turmoil.

Galbraith's rebuilding of American social theory now appeared to be complete, with a prognosis almost uniformly optimistic. But this was not quite true. His defense of Keynes contained an important caveat—one that appeared also in his discussion of countervailing power. Throughout his book he had warned that one possible condition could not only lessen or even destroy the effectiveness of Keynesian economic policy, but also wreck the mechanism of countervailing power and thus undermine the entire institutional framework established since the New Deal. The Achilles' heel of the Broker State was, he explained, *inflation*.

Keynes had, of course, recognized that a capitalist economy could fall prey to inflation as well as to depression, and, indeed, his remedies for inflation were merely the reverse of those applied to depression. The problem, Galbraith realized, was that while in theory one set of policies was as efficacious and easy to enact as the other, the *practical* differences in applying the two might lead to considerable and even insurmountable difficulties. The reason was simple. No politician would ever be likely to lose votes by advocating cheap money and increased government spending to aid particular groups or to stimulate the economy as a whole; but woe to the politician who called for heavier taxes and fiscal and monetary restraint. Remarking that the implementation of Keynesian measures was "not symmetrical," Galbraith warned of this unseen flaw in the system and predicted that "inflation, not depression, is the greatest present and well may be the most persistent future tendency of the American economy" (*AmC*, 186-187).

Galbraith, who had earlier tried to relieve Americans of their Depression Psychosis, now admitted that this malady had at least one beneficial effect: it acted to promote economic restraint. But by the fall of 1950, few were thinking of depression as the United States prepared to fight the Korean War. More ominously, concomitantly with this lapse of economic apprehension there occurred "the sharpest price increase in modern American history." Changed public expectations and increased business borrowing and buying for inventories were fueling a "continued interaction of prices and wages" (*AmC*, 201).

This was even worse than it seemed, since Galbraith's theory had the same drawback as Keynes's: countervailing power worked under conditions of limited demand precisely because neither sellers nor buyers benefitted disproportionately from depressed prices. On the consequences of strong demand, Galbraith's views were clear: inflation destroyed the entire framework of countervailing power. This was true because high demand and low supply threw dominant market power into the hands of the seller—an adverse state of affairs that would be especially significant and most clearly visible in the labor market. In addition, inflation—unlike depression—did benefit groups whose incomes moved rapidly upward with prices or even faster.

What could be done to ease inflationary pressure? Galbraith denied that heavy taxation alone could work. In peacetime this would either create socially and politically intolerable slack in the economy or, under the pressure of military expenditures during the emerging cold war, place unacceptable constraints on the level of production. He also rejected the position of those in the business community who urged a greater volume of production as a solution, since this would only generate additional income to match the increased production and, even more importantly, reinforce the inflationary cycle through the aforementioned use of unequal market power. As the only acceptable alternative during periods when the level of demand became dangerously high, Galbraith advocated a combination of higher taxation and wage and price controls. He was completely aware that controls would be difficult to implement and were at best an imperfect solution. But he believed even more strongly that, whatever plan was adopted to combat the problem, *something* would have to be done. Controls were preferable to inflation, since to allow high inflation to rage openly had social and political effects that were "vicious": it weakened and discredited governments and social institutions, rewarded productive individuals and scoundrels equally, and, as history demonstrated, threatened democracy itself.

Arguing that "capitalism, as a practical matter rather than as a system of theology, is an arrangement for getting a considerable decentralization in decision," Galbraith consistently defended it as the only means available to a democratic society for managing the production and distribution of economic goods. Seeing socialism and communism as possible only in simple or industrializing societies, he argued that the aim of public control in the economic sphere was to satisfy social needs and wants more adequately. Government therefore could not arrogate to itself economic decision making and ignore public choice and pressures without "abandon[ing] the very job which it set out to perform" (*AmC*, 177). Hence, Galbraith's defense of the system was predicated on his belief that it could now be made to function effectively enough without direct intervention by the state in corporate decisions or even in the general economy on a massive scale for prolonged periods. Yet there existed a "major danger to decentralized decision," Galbraith declared in the final paragraphs of his study, and "It does not come from depression." The threat lay in the opposite direction: war or preparations for war could lead, as they had during the Korean conflict, to inflationary pressures requiring drastic centralization under government control—a control demanded, ironically, by a conservative Congress (*AmC*, 207).

Finally, Galbraith cautioned that no one could be certain regarding the nature or effects of the government intervention that would be necessary should countervailing power disappear. If wise tax policy were adopted and controls kept to the minimum necessary, he guessed that "the effects may not be far-reaching." He again added, however, that inflationary pressure could bring "a major revision in the character and constitution of American capitalism," while world peace would make the outlook "a good deal brighter" (*AmC*, 208).

This concluded a book that marked a turning point in American social theory. As an analysis and intellectual justification of American economic developments in the wake of the New Deal and the Keynesian Revolution, *American Capitalism* was widely acclaimed and perceived as a milestone in economic and social thought. Praising the book as a "brilliant work of synthesis as well as a development of new ideas," C. L. Christenson in *The Journal of Political Economy* saw the theory of countervailing power dispelling the "intellectual tension" in economics that had existed since the 1930s and predicted that it "probably has still greater significance as a

stimulus to further analysis than it acquires in its initial form.''[10] Joan Robinson noted that while she and Edward Chamberlin had ''damag[ed] the
orthodox system,'' their new analysis ''did not replace it with an equally
coherent scheme of ideas and, ever since, the theory of prices has been in
a scrappy and unsatisfactory state,'' leaving many who could therefore still
easily hold onto old beliefs by largely denying the passing of old-style
competition or by minimizing the effects of market imperfections. ''Professor Galbraith,'' Robinson wrote, ''makes a clean sweep of all such arguments.''[11] Paul Homan, writing in *The American Economic Review*,
lauded Galbraith's ''highly untrammeled outlook and incisive analytical
powers'' and added that, although the book was written primarily for non-
professionals, his thinking ''deserve[s] the careful attention of his professional colleagues.''[12]

Reviewers did have some reservations concerning *American Capitalism*. In Homan's judgment, for example, Galbraith had ignored ''the extent and force of the 'real' competitive elements and the necessity of retaining them unless we are to embark upon a radically revised version of
American capitalism.'' Homan also thought Galbraith a trifle too optimistic regarding the ease of preventing a major recession and believed that he
underestimated ''the play of forces now loose in the world which might re-
allocate the whole balance of power, in unpredictable ways.'' Christenson,
taking a different tack, wondered ''whether apparent 'countervailing
power' may be growth of new power under circumstances that limit 'original' private power only slightly if, indeed, at all.'' The reviewers, in
short, felt that Galbraith was rather too sanguine in his view of America's
recent past and immediate future—a kind of criticism that was rarely to be
heard in future evaluations of his writings.

But such reservations were smothered in the surrounding waves of laud-
atory welcome for the first major reevaluation and reinterpretation of
American economic liberalism since the Progressive Era. With one bold
thrust Galbraith had confounded and outflanked both the antitrust and the
planning groups within the liberal coalition, while shoring up the defenses
of the Keynesians. But conservatives fared no better at his hands, since he
had, after all, seriously damaged the credibility of the competitive, neoclassical model of the economy. In addition, his prediction in *American
Capitalism* that no political party would hesitate to use monetary and fiscal

[10] C. L. Christenson, *The Journal of Political Economy* 60 (June 1952), 275-276.

[11] Joan Robinson, *The Economic Journal* 60 (December 1952), 925-926.

[12] Paul T. Homan, *The American Economic Review* 42 (June 1952), 429.

policy to forestall cyclical economic downturns and that conservatives would be forced to bid farewell to classical liberal ideology in practice, if not in theory, was to prove completely accurate. The Eisenhower administration did indeed use Keynesian policy during both the 1953–1954 and the 1957–1958 recessions. Moreover, as Galbraith had foreseen and later noted with some satisfaction, even moderately conservative Republicans found it neither politically possible nor desirable to dismantle the basic institutional apparatus that had been established or expanded during the New Deal, although some judicious trimming was accomplished.

A NEW AFFLUENT SOCIETY: THE THEORY OF SOCIAL BALANCE

The events of the next several years seemed to confirm Galbraith's conclusions virtually without qualification. As the decade of the 1950s wore on, the unextinguished apprehension and anxiety regarding America's economic soundness gradually diminished. As government demonstrated its resolute determination to prevent depression, nearly all sectors of the economy participated in the first phase of the greatest, most sustained, and most universal wave of prosperity in American history. The Gross National Product soared from $318.1 billion (1954 dollars) in 1950 to $428 billion in 1959. Real per capita consumption (1960 prices) jumped from $1,350 in 1945 to $1,824 in 1960. The business sector, the core element of the economy, astonished its critics by producing a higher volume of goods than ever before. In spite of the oligopolistic structure of American business (the 500 largest industrial firms accounted for more than 50 percent of sales and more than 70 percent of profits in manufacturing and mining during these years), production per firm (1954 prices), which had stood at $56,600 in 1929 had, despite ten years of economic stagnation during the Depression, climbed to $72,200 by 1950. By 1960 it had reached $87,000, meaning that output per firm had increased almost as much in the single decade of the 1950s as it had in the previous *two* decades. Also, both the number and size of corporations were increasing rapidly.[13]

The picture was not, of course, unblemished. Nonetheless, its flaws seemed to be effectively counterbalanced by positive signs and tendencies. There was a slight rate of inflation; but income rose far more rapidly. Cer-

---

[13] Harold G. Vatter, *The U.S. Economy in the 1950s: An Economic History* (New York: W. W. Norton, 1963), pp. 53, 3, 152, 150.

tain industries and geographical regions grew slowly; but new industries and new areas of the country more than compensated for this by expanding their production at a phenomenal rate. Poverty remained; but studies seemed to show that its extent was diminishing, with the proportion of the population at a ''low income'' status dropping from 26 percent in 1947 to 19 percent in 1957.[14]

One might expect that a man who had done his best at the beginning of such an apparently prosperous and productive decade to prepare Americans for such developments and had defended the new organizational structure of American capitalism would have been highly pleased by these events and trends. But, significantly, Galbraith did not simply take these developments at face value. Thus it was that, much to the surprise of the general public and to the consternation and active displeasure of many of his colleagues, he produced a work that cast doubt on some of the very achievements of this period. Published in 1958, it was the first book in what was to become a trilogy that would irritate and antagonize most sectors of the business community and the economics profession, find a mass readership both in the United States and abroad, and establish Galbraith as one of the most important and prolific social theorists and critics in modern America.

The first chapters of the book Galbraith called *The Affluent Society* explicated his concept of ''the conventional wisdom,'' that is, an established set of ideas found in every culture to explain the world around it and how it operates, providing stability, cohesion, meaning, and predictability in a highly complex and sometimes rapidly changing environment. The conventional wisdom will by its very nature, he hypothesized, seek to deny that this environment has substantially changed; it will in fact insist that the old ideas are adequate and will try to fit any new phenomena into established conceptual and theoretical molds. The ''inertia and resistance'' of the old ideas could only be overcome when events impinged on them to such a degree that some person or group of persons both discredited them and replaced them with *new* ideas.

Galbraith presented this apparently digressive introduction for a reason: he believed that it applied perfectly to the evolution of economic thought since Adam Smith. The new liberal economics that had replaced the old conventional wisdom of mercantilism had as one of its cardinal assumptions the inherent niggardliness of economic production. Beginning with

[14] Ibid., p. 223.

Smith, economists of the modern era had always emphasized the meager per capita yield of production and the resulting paucity of economic goods for the average person. *Aggregate* wealth might increase through long-term saving and arduous toil, but widespread and enduring abundance was out of the question. Economic theorists as diverse as Ricardo, Malthus, and Marx shared this belief, while often basing it on greatly different theoretical premises. Even economists of the late nineteenth and early twentieth centuries felt it necessary to modify only slightly the gloomy predictions of earlier times. Not for nothing had economics been given the sobriquet "the dismal science."

Reality had greatly changed by the middle of the twentieth century, but the pessimism that underlay so much of economic thought had not. As Galbraith observed, "These—productivity, inequality, and insecurity— were the ancient preoccupations of economics." They were to remain so throughout the 1930s, in the face of what was to be "a mountainous rise in well-being" in the near future. Given this unexpected development, it would be only natural that the conventional wisdom would tend to lag behind objective reality, and it did.[15] The reality, Galbraith explained, was that the last of these "preoccupations" had been largely overcome, the second had been largely forgotten, while the first had maintained its position of supreme importance far beyond the point warranted by its contemporary value in providing the basic needs and even comforts of modern civilization.

Inequality, in Galbraith's view, had lost its power to mobilize resentment and action for several reasons. First, the distribution of wealth and especially income had actually changed in favor of poor families since the Depression. Second, the political and social power traditionally associated with great wealth had appreciably declined since the late nineteenth century as some of the businessman's authority and discretionary power was transferred to an expanding state apparatus, some was lost to unions, and even more was given over to professional managers who had taken over the daily operation of large firms. In addition, the social distinction that wealth had once conferred on its possessors who, as Veblen noted, spent large sums on conspicuous consumption had noticeably declined for two reasons: many had come to believe that it was dangerous to flaunt such wealth before the eyes of the poor, and this new reticence to display one's

---

[15] J. K. Galbraith, *The Affluent Society* (Boston: Houghton Mifflin, 1958), p. 77. Subsequently cited parenthetically as *AS*.

possessions in an egregious manner did in fact reduce the clamor for their redistribution; also, how much prestige and satisfaction could one obtain from purchasing material goods and services that many in the lower classes could now increasingly afford? Finally, inequality could be—and was— made a less volatile issue by the simple means of increasing the volume of production. People were far less worried about how their daily ration of pie was divided if the size of the entire pie and, therefore, the quantity they individually received were steadily growing.

Economic security was another concern that had been greatly affected by the enormous expansion of mass production in modern times. The very meaning of this term had radically altered, Galbraith charged, since when businessmen, workers, and farmers now spoke of "security" they no longer meant adequate food, clothing, and shelter, as had their grandparents. What they *really* meant was the minimization of the risks involved in participating in a market system. Just as large firms now sought to control markets and consumer demand to the greatest possible degree, workers, farmers, and others began to worry about the modified exigencies of life in modern industrial society and to seek government aid to prevent what were now perceived to be intolerable hardships. But this, Galbraith reminded his readers, was a recent phenomenon, since "In the grim world of Ricardo and Malthus the ordinary citizen could have no interest in social security in the modern sense. If a man's wage is barely sufficient for existence, he does not worry much about the greater suffering of unemployment" (AS, 107). It was only with increased income and well-being that people realized that they had now acquired something to protect and actually took steps to do so. For Galbraith, the Depression of the 1930s did not provide evidence that modern life was becoming less secure. On the contrary, one reason for the great pain it had caused was the enormous amounts of income and wealth that then existed.

Galbraith thus brought his argument to what many readers must have considered an extraordinary and even shocking conclusion: the struggle for basic economic insecurity was over; risks still existed, but they were of "much reduced urgency." Regarding the one major source of economic insecurity that remained—the possibility of recession—he elaborated and set forth a major proposition of his book, thereby defining a further critical problem of analysis with crystalline clarity: "In the political life of western countries. . .nothing counts so heavily against a government as allowing unnecessary unemployment. It is not the lost production that is mentioned. It is always the unemployment. The remedy is, of course, more employment and higher production. Thus the effort to enhance economic security becomes the driving force behind production.'' Thus it was that only productivity, not equality or security, remained important in the public mind. Production, Galbraith theorized, had now become the ''solvent of the tensions once associated with inequality, and it has become the indispensable remedy for the discomforts, anxieties, and privations associated with economic insecurity.'' This began to explain a ''modern paradox'': namely, that ''as production has increased in modern times concern for production seems also to have increased'' (AS, 119-120). Such a preoccupation with production, however, had to be given some additional justification, especially in a society that was already saturated with consumer goods, many of which were of highly dubious value. This justification was provided by the accepted theory of consumer demand, which held that (1) consumer wants were insatiable and (2) consumer wants originated within the consumer and were to be accepted as given.

On the presumably infinite wants of consumers, Galbraith asked if it was reasonable to assume that after an upper-middle-class family had satisfied all of its basic needs and owned a large stock of luxury items, the psychological satisfaction they obtained from an additional dollar spent on the latter was as great as that which came from the first dollars spent on their daily food and clothes or on a down payment on a house when they were much poorer and could not afford luxuries. Yet neoclassical theory made no distinction among goods. Each new good, no matter how frivolous, was assumed to possess high marginal utility for the individual or family that was not yet fortunate enough to own it.

Plausibility arguments, Galbraith recognized, did not prove that the accepted theory of consumer demand was fallacious. He pointed out, however, that its second assumption was just as crucial as the first and, he suggested, even more vulnerable. It seemed clear, in fact, that since Americans evaluated people largely by their possessions, as production expanded so did the need for acquisition, so that ''the production of goods creates the wants that the goods are presumed to satisfy'' (AS, 155). Moreover, he believed that what weakened the case for consumer autonomy even further was the frenetic activity of large and numerous institutions devoted to advertising and salesmanship, remarking that ''These cannot be reconciled with the notion of independently determined desires, for their central function is to create desires—to bring into being wants that previously did not exist'' (AS, 155). To him the implications were obvious: ''The fact that wants can be synthesized by advertising, catalyzed by salesmanship, and shaped by the discreet manipulations of the persuaders shows that they are not very urgent. A man who is hungry need never be told of his need for food'' (*AS*, 158). Madison Avenue was ''effective only with those who are so far removed from physical want that they do not already know what they want.'' Galbraith dubbed the phenomenon by which wants were created through the process of production the ''dependence effect.''

What were the consequences of this outmoded concern for production? To begin, Galbraith proposed that the drive for ever greater production had been wed to cold war fears, the result being an irrational equation of high production with national security—the ''myth that military power is a function of economic output.'' As his experience as a director of the postwar Strategic Bombing Survey had taught him, military strength depended not on aggregate output but on ''how much can be diverted to public purposes.'' Thus, real national security could be declining even while GNP rose. Furthermore, he argued that security could be bolstered far more by aiding poor nations than by squandering wealth on an endless consumption spree or on wasteful and expensive military weapons.

And this production mania had further consequences. One was the abandonment of liberal reform as post-Keynesian liberals had concentrated on maximizing aggregate output rather than pushing for basic social and economic change, in effect entering into a tacit alliance with conservatives and businessmen whose own interests were thereby served to an optimum degree. Another was a dangerous accumulation of consumer debt on whose continuous increase the process of production had come to depend. Such debt fueled inflationary tendencies within the economy, and, in the event of even a mild downturn in economic activity, its sudden and rapid liquidation threatened a downward spiral of reduced spending, decreased revenues, and increased unemployment, leading to a further liquidation of debt.

But one of the most serious effects of constantly pushing industrial capacity to a maximum level unquestionably was inflation, a phenomenon he now associated primarily with production at or near full capacity. As he recognized, inflation in a free-market economy could not long be sustained, since an economic expansion accompanied by rising prices would be followed by a later contraction that would cause prices to fall. Also, intense competition among firms had an innate tendency to keep price increases within bounds. But in a bifurcated economy characterized by a mixture of oligopoly and freer competition, the response of the economy to changes in supply, demand, or prices was not uniform for each sector or industry. This problem was exacerbated when large industrial unions received wage increases that fueled a wage-price spiral. The result of all this, Galbraith maintained, must be inflation—a condition that hurt all those with little or no market power (that is, small businessmen, farmers, public employees, pensioners, the poor).

As he had in *American Capitalism*, Galbraith stressed that inflation would not be remedied through tight credit. Such a policy could work if carried out, but such action would be effective only if it were so draconian and prolonged that it had a dampening effect on the pricing behavior of large firms, and this would happen only after large increases in unemployment and severe economic dislocations. Another drawback to monetary policy, however, was its unpredictability, acting as it did on the most volatile component of national income—business investment. Fiscal policy was similarly an ineffective and unacceptable means of combating inflation, since in practice it would be difficult to reduce government expenditures greatly. Tax increases, in theory almost as effective as spending cuts, were also difficult to effect when consumers were struggling to maintain their level of consumption in an inflationary environment. Also, the resulting decreased demand could set in motion a chain of events that would reduce economic growth—not in itself a matter of grave concern, given the nonessential nature of most production, but unacceptable because of the ensuing unemployment. Selective wage and price controls might alleviate this problem, but they were widely considered anathema, save in wartime. All this made inflation endemic to the American economy as it was then structured.

Galbraith perceived, however, that there was something else fundamentally wrong with the American economy—a defect that went to the very heart of America's "affluent society." The national obsession with production did more than swell military expenditures, scuttle liberal reforms, destabilize the economy by raising consumer debt to dizzying heights, and push productive capacity to the point of creating chronic inflation. The final and perhaps the most important issue involved what the economy actually produced. It was not just that much of the GNP was, by any reasonable criteria, sheer waste. In addition, much that was produced was downright harmful or dangerous and, even worse, the single-minded concentration on private consumption entailed an inevitable imbalance between the production of private goods and the provision of public services. Galbraith illustrated his point in memorable passages that have justly become enshrined as classics in modern social criticism. Postwar urban newspapers, he wrote,

> told daily of the shortages and shortcomings in the elementary municipal and metropolitan services. The schools were old and overcrowded. The police force was under strength and underpaid. The parks and playgrounds were insufficient. Streets and empty lots were filthy, and the sanitation staff was underequipped and in need of men. Access to the city by those who work there was uncertain and painful and becoming more so. Internal transportation was overcrowded, unhealthful, and dirty. So was the air. Parking on the streets had to be prohibited, and there was no space elsewhere. . . .

Yet while this went on, there were upbeat but anomalous stories of economic growth, advances in income and productivity, and increasing sales figures, leading Galbraith to remark that

> The contrast was and remains evident not alone to those who read. The family which takes its mauve and cerise, air-conditioned, power-steered, and power-braked automobile out for a tour passes through cities that are badly paved, made hideous by litter, blighted buildings, billboards, and posts for wires that should long since have been put underground. They pass on into a countryside that has been rendered largely invisible by commercial art. . . . They picnic on exquisitely packaged food from a portable icebox by a polluted stream and go on to spend the night at a park which is a menace to public health and morals. Just before dozing off on an air mattress, beneath a nylon tent, amid the stench of decaying refuse, they may reflect vaguely on the curious unevenness of their blessings. Is this, indeed, the American genius? (*AS*, 252-253)

This was more than effective social criticism based on a highly developed or esoteric aesthetic or moral sense: Galbraith stressed that these problems were very real and had an objective basis. He proposed that, just as the efficient production of private goods required a proper "mix" of productive factors, so also the economy *as a whole* required an adequate ratio of public to private goods and services—an idea he called the Theory of Social Balance. Social balance would not only forestall the harmful effects arising from an insufficient supply of public goods: it would also, according to marginal utility theory, enable the public to maximize their satisfactions, something that could not be done if the output of public goods were small.

Yet all the forces of private production and its arm of psychological coercion, the advertising industry, spoke exclusively on behalf of private goods. Beyond this, two factors militated against the extension of public services. One was the problem of funding, an area in which, for obvious reasons, state and local governments experienced more difficulty than did the federal government; the other, inflation, struck especially hard at the public sector, because of its highly formalized pay scales. "Nothing so weakens government," Galbraith remarked, "as persistent inflation." And nothing, in his view, so destabilized a society as did the resulting social imbalance, leading in several countries to an "inability to enforce laws, including significantly those which protect and advance basic social justice, and [a] failure to maintain and improve essential services."

The obvious problem was how to restore balance to the economy, and to Galbraith the solution was clear: the public sector needed to be strengthened. The first essential action was investment in human capital, especially in education and in scientific and technical research. These and other public goods—which by their very nature could be purchased only collectively—would not only increase productivity but also enhance the desire for public goods and depress the desire for wants that were contrived. Another benefit, he believed, would be greater economic stability, since the demand for public goods would not be subject to the wild fluctuations of the market for private goods. On the other side of the equation, he sought to dampen the irrational devotion to production by separating this process from the issue of economic security, largely the raison d'être of production in modern market economies. To accomplish this, he proposed an unemployment compensation plan that would not be a flat, temporary, minimal payment, but instead a subsidy whose amount would be geared to the level of unemployment in a given geographical region and thus eliminate a major source of social and economic insecurity while also automatically reversing economic trends headed either for inflation or depression. Galbraith hoped that this scheme, supplemented perhaps by at least a limited system of wage and price controls, might largely eliminate inflation and depression and with them the danger they posed for social balance.

To fund this program Galbraith urged greater reliance on sales taxes as an alternative to increased income taxes. Although such taxes would be a disproportionate burden on low-income groups, this fact and a possible reduction of economic output would, he thought, be more than offset by the benefits gained from social balance. After all, disadvantaged groups would be precisely those who would be helped most by increased public services, while productivity would be spurred by larger investments in human capital. Emphasizing that poverty was still a major problem, especially among farm families and in the area of the Appalachians, Galbraith argued that "Poverty is self-perpetuating because the poorest communities are poorest in the services which would eliminate it" (*AS*, 330). Thus there would be no conflict between the goal of establishing social balance and that of eradicating the continuing social blight that he called a "disgrace."

A lessened concern for production might also, Galbraith speculated, lead to a change in the scope and nature of work itself. To the extent that hours of labor could be reduced, working conditions improved, and people offered the choice of increased leisure over additional material consumption, many of the tensions and problems of an economy straining to produce at a maximum level might well be relieved. As part of his final summation Galbraith wrote that America's problems would not soon be solved, and that indeed many of them were not even yet discovered. But he believed that "one thing is tolerably certain":

Whether the problem be that of a burgeoning population and of space in which to live with peace and grace, or whether it be the depletion of the materials which nature has stocked in the earth's crust and which have been drawn upon more heavily in this century than in all previous time together, or whether it be that of occupying minds no longer committed to the stockpiling of consumer goods, the basic demand on America will be on its resources of ability, intelligence, and education. The test will be less the effectiveness of our material investment than the effectiveness of our investment in men (*AS*, 355).

The critical reaction to *The Affluent Society* was not nearly as positive as that which had greeted *American Capitalism*, especially within the economics establishment. A pedantic, convoluted, and patronizing review article in *The American Economic Review* concluded that "[Galbraith's] work, unreliable and unsystematic in itself, is nevertheless a call to competent students and analysts to direct their attention to the essential descriptive and analytical tasks."[16] A reviewer in *The Economist* decided that the book was "penetrating, fresh, knowledgeable, humane, and—though it gets off to a slow start—entertainingly written," but that it was "also perverse, muddleheaded, provincial and dangerous."[17] The consensus within

[16] Rutledge Vining, *The American Economic Review* 49 (March 1959), 119.
[17] Hamish Hamilton, *The Economist* 188, no. 6004 (20 September 1958), p. 928.

the profession was that Galbraith had some interesting and important things to say, but that most of his arguments were exaggerated, too unorthodox, or simply invalid.

But events in the world at large were to overshadow the negative reactions of many of the critics. During the summer of 1957 as Galbraith was writing the final chapters of *The Affluent Society* and just a few months before it went to press, the Soviet Union successfully tested an intercontinental ballistic missile. Two months later it launched the world's first artificial satellite, Sputnik I. A month after that, Sputnik II was launched. It carried a live dog. These feats were accomplished by a nation whose economy was centrally planned and whose GNP was far below that of the United States.

The impact of these events was overwhelming. American economic, educational, and scientific institutions seemed to have failed a crucial test and were called into question by educators, economists, politicians, and the general public. How was it that Americans could design, develop, and market myriad consumer goods that were the envy of the modern world but had to watch passively and in awe as the Soviets conquered space? Americans could not understand how such a thing could happen to what was ostensibly the richest, most powerful, and most technologically advanced nation on earth. The Soviets appeared to have not only a functioning and rapidly growing economy, but one that could also support remarkable scientific and technical projects.

In retrospect some of these worries were clearly hysterical, irrational reactions bred of cold war fears and insecurities. The Soviets' string of technological accomplishments was not proof per se of economic superiority, since space efforts cannot be considered a function of normal economic activity, which in the Soviet case was in fact badly hampered by overcentralization. But it did indicate that the American monomaniacal emphasis on constantly expanding the nation's GNP was no guarantee of either national security or technological progressiveness. It also revealed a problem that, as Galbraith had tried to show, was intimately connected with a concern for production itself and the employment it made available: the lack of adequate funding for health, education, social services, and basic civilian research.

The disparity between military and social spending during this era is obvious upon even a cursory examination of the statistical record. The data reveal that expenditures by the federal government had a decidedly lopsided structure during the decade that followed the Korean War. Spending

NATIONAL DEFENSE AND DOMESTIC SERVICES
EXPENDITURES, 1953–1962, AS PERCENTAGES OF
TOTAL FEDERAL EXPENDITURES

	National Defense	Domestic Services
1953	64.2%	20.7%
1954	60.2	23.2
1955	57.8	24.5
1956	57.2	25.4
1957	56.6	27.0
1958	52.6	32.5
1959	51.5	32.5
1960	49.3	34.2
1961	47.9	36.5
1962	47.9	36.5

SOURCE: Roger A. Freeman, *The Growth of American Government: A Morphology of the Welfare State* (Stanford: Hoover Institution Press, 1975), p. 226. The calculations are mine.

for domestic services throughout most of this period amounted to less than one-third of all federal expenditures. Military expenditures, which had in the period 1902–1938 averaged less than 25 percent of federal spending, were now occupying a dominant position. And, although the trend was slowly altering as the decade wore on, those expenditures had not lost that position. Since federal expenditures accounted for approximately one-third of the GNP during these years, military spending was a very significant factor in the US economy, comprising between 10 to 14 percent of total GNP. On the other hand, federal spending for domestic services from 1952 to 1962 comprised only between 3.9 to 8.3 percent of GNP. Since military spending from the turn of the century to World War II had averaged about 1 percent of total GNP during peacetime, this marked quite a radical change.[18] Thus, while the sociologist and social critic C. Wright

[18] Roger A. Freeman, *The Growth of American Government: A Morphology of the Welfare State* (Stanford: Hoover Institution Press, 1975), pp. 108-109, 206. It should be noted that the figures shown in the table from the same source actually understate rather substantially the relative size of defense expenditures. For one thing, the figures for military spending upon which the comparison is based do not include veterans' benefits and services or the sums spent on space research and technology in the period 1958–1962, much of which was military or quasi-military in nature. Moreover, it must be remarked that on a federal funds basis—that is, adding up expenditures from *current* appropriations without including revenue from insurance funds managed by the government (such as the huge reservoir of Social Security assets)—the gap between domestic and defense outlays increases significantly.

Mills may have exaggerated when he wrote of a "permanent war economy" and "military capitalism" in America during the 1950s, it has now become increasingly clear that the US economic system from the late 1940s to the late 1960s was what the political scientist James Q. Wilson and the economic historian Harold G. Vatter have called a "semi-war economy," underwritten by huge direct and indirect military spending and both guided and fueled by the complex of ideas, attitudes, and institutions that Daniel Yergin has aptly termed the "National Security State."

Galbraith's concern for social balance is now quite understandable. As the drop in the sum of federal transfer payments and civilian expenditures from 7.4 percent of GNP in 1939 to 6 percent in 1960 indicates, the trend toward an extension of New Deal reforms was halted in the 1950s. *The Affluent Society* was an eloquent argument for increased attention to the issues that had been largely smothered in the conservative atmosphere of the Eisenhower years, and it unquestionably presaged many of the concerns later brought to the fore in the 1960s and 1970s. Those who were later alarmed by environmental and ecological deterioration, poverty, recession, inflation, and the explosive social conditions generated by urban decay and woefully inadequate social investment would have good reason to recall Galbraith's message in *The Affluent Society*.

Chapter 3   *The Industrial State*

The Affluent Society enhanced Galbraith's growing reputation as an important social theorist and critic, and his writings on current domestic and foreign affairs grew in volume. Even as he pondered these issues, however, his attention was being pulled in another direction. Long an activist in Democratic party politics, Galbraith, who had worked as a speechwriter for Adlai Stevenson in 1952 and 1956, became, along with economist Paul Samuelson, an informal economic adviser to an old acquaintance from his early days at Harvard in the late 1930s—John F. Kennedy. Upon Kennedy's election to the presidency, Galbraith was persuaded to accept the ambassadorship to India (a post in which he served with skill, resourcefulness, and distinction), using return trips to Washington at least partly to advance the views he had expressed in *The Affluent Society*. He opposed Kennedy's tax cut (designed to spur America's somewhat sluggish rate of economic growth) and advised against a mechanical and strict adherence to the goal of a balanced budget. On foreign affairs he was, as might be expected, a liberal internationalist, favoring foreign aid, arms limitation, and peaceful coexistence with the Soviet Union.

It is difficult to gauge Galbraith's influence on economic policy during the Kennedy administration precisely, but it was certainly not great. Although Kennedy personally leaned toward many of Galbraith's views and fought to advance them through legislation (including measures on area redevelopment, manpower training, increased Social Security, disability, and unemployment benefits, housing programs, mental health reform, and Medicare), he doubted the willingness of Americans to pay for a greatly expanded public sector. Moreover, Kennedy's primary concerns were, for reasons of ideology and political pressures, elsewhere. The slower economic growth and concomitant higher level of unemployment inherited from the Eisenhower recession of 1960–1961, the increased national security and space expenditures associated with heightened cold war tensions, and the pressure of business interests for reduced taxes all augured ill for new social spending programs.[1] In a letter written to Kennedy from India in mid-1962, Galbraith urged the president to resist those who fa-

[1] See Seymour E. Harris, *Economics of the Kennedy Years* (New York: Harper & Row, 1964).

vored lower taxes. "I needn't remind you (but nevertheless I always deem it wise)," he wrote, "that the glories of the Kennedy Era will be written not in the rate of economic growth or even in the level of unemployment. Nor, I venture, is this where its political rewards lie. Its glory and reward will be from the way it tackles the infinity of problems that beset a growing population and an increasingly complex society in an increasingly competitive world. To do this well costs the money that tax reducers would deny."[2] For immediate political reasons this advice went unheeded. Perhaps realizing the constraints of the period, Galbraith nonetheless remained undiscouraged; yet he wanted to return to Harvard, from which he had taken an extended leave of absence, for he had much unfinished work to take up, particularly a project he had begun even as *The Affluent Society* was still in the process of completion, and for this reason he resigned his post in India in the summer of 1963.

A NEW INDUSTRIAL STATE: THE TECHNOSTRUCTURE AND THE MODERN CORPORATION

Galbraith's new work addressed issues he had raised throughout his earlier career. However, instead of examining the general problems of economic performance and its results in society as a whole as he had in *The Affluent Society*, his present concern was the world of the large corporation—the producer of more than half the goods whose value was seen as paramount by most Americans—and the economic, social, and political milieu in which it operated. It was a timely topic.

As with theories generally, the theory of the firm had responded to changes in the external world ad hoc, with new features simply added on, but no general reformulation of ideas. Thus, the prevailing theory still maintained that capitalists or their representatives had plenary control over corporate policy and that managers, scientists, and technicians, while increasingly important, were essentially hired personnel with no independent power, and that the goal of business leaders was what it had been in the nineteenth century: profit maximization. Textbooks acknowledged the fact of oligopolistic competition; but authors continued to concentrate on the entrepreneurial firm as the basis for understanding the structure and behavior of *all* firms. The market power of large firms was noted in passing; but the unalterable law of supply and demand was said to be far more influ-

---

[2] J. K. Galbraith, *Ambassador's Journal: A Personal Account of the Kennedy Years* (New York: Signet, 1970), pp. 348-349.

ential. The relationship between the large corporation and the state was assumed to be almost exactly what it had been early in the century: besides maintaining a peaceful environment in which to conduct business and providing a minimal amount of essential regulation, the state left the corporation alone—a service that the latter was only too happy to reciprocate. By the mid-1950s many scholars had come to question and ultimately to reject the classical theory either wholly or in part. Galbraith had by this time rejected it entirely and spent ten years developing his own view of the giant corporation.

The end result of Galbraith's labor, *The New Industrial State*, was finally published in 1967. It had a unifying central thesis that was forcefully expounded throughout its four hundred pages: changes and developments in modern technology had drastically altered the structure and behavior of the large corporation as well as the relationship between it and the larger society. Galbraith began his main argument with six basic propositions:

1. Modern technology greatly increased the amount of time required to acomplish an industrial task. This was a result of the minute specialization involved as a task was broken down into its numerous parts.

2. Modern technology greatly increased the amount of capital needed for production. Increased time costs, expensive machinery, and the high salaries of technical specialists contributed to this increase.

3. Modern capital (physical resources and knowledge) tended to be designed for very specific uses and could not easily be adapted to others. Thus, precise capital requirements for a particular use had to be carefully considered in advance, since if the utimate goal were appreciably changed the specialized capital would become worthless.

4. Specialized manpower was needed not only to use complex technology, but also to "organize and employ information" or to "react intuitively to relevant experience" in order to anticipate obstacles and overcome them (that is, to *plan*).

5. Huge and complex organizational structures grew in direct proportion to the degree of specialization. Such structures were necessary in order to coordinate the work of technical specialists.

6. The enormous commitments of time and capital in addition to the organizational and technological requirements and marketing difficulties inherent in the process of production in the large corporation brought about the need for planning.

This last proposition was for Galbraith the most crucial, since on it depended his view of the major role of large firms and those who managed them. On it also hung the fate of the market, for the price mechanism of the market had "ceased to be reliable" for the large corporation, since "Technology, with its companion commitment of time and capital, means that the needs of the consumer must be anticipated—by months or years." The giant firm could not simply *assume* that consumer demand would be adequate. It had to take active steps to *ensure* that it would. Moreover, while simple labor skills and crude materials were easy enough to obtain upon the presentation of adequate cash or credit, "the specialized skills and arcane materials required by advanced technology cannot similarly be counted upon."

The only solution to this problem was to replace the market with planning. Indeed, Galbraith claimed that "Much of what the firm regards as planning consists in minimizing or getting rid of market influences."[3] This could be done by controlling sources of supply and distribution outlets (a process known as "vertical integration"), exercising market power, and entering into long-term contractual agreements. These techniques could not completely eliminate market uncertainty, but could and did greatly reduce it. Moreover, Galbraith noted that this phenomenon was not peculiar to Western market systems: Soviet planners had to perform the same essential tasks and for the same basic reasons, leading him to predict a convergence of the two industrial civilizations.

Technology had, in Galbraith's view, greatly altered the relative importance of the three factors of production in economics—land, labor, and capital—and had therefore also changed the relationship among social groups whose political power and social influence were based on the particular factor of production each of them had historically provided. Aristocratic landowners had provided the crucial element of production in feudal society, hence their social and political dominance during this era. From the late eighteenth century to the early nineteenth century, capitalists had provided the organizational skill and leadership necessary to mobilize capital—the critical resource during that period—and therefore drew power to themselves and away from landowners. Galbraith did not, however, agree with Marx that the new dominant class would be that which controlled the supply of labor, namely, the industrial workers. Power, he

---

[3] J. K. Galbraith, *The New Industrial State* (New York: Signet, 1968), p. 37. Subsequently cited parenthetically as *NIS*.

argued, was instead passing rapidly and inexorably to another group "embrac[ing] all who bring specialized knowledge, talent or experience to group decision-making." This collection of technical specialists that Galbraith called "the technostructure" had, he claimed, taken the reins of power from the old entrepreneurial class. Most importantly, the technostructure was more than a group that made tactical decisions concerning purely technical matters: it was the supreme locus of power in the large corporation. Since this was the only group that could understand and evaluate the issues faced by the corporation, and since even ultimate, strategic decisions were in large measure technical, there was no higher court to which its rulings could be effectively appealed. Power devolved to it virtually by definition. Thus, Galbraith explained, to understand corporate behavior was to understand the motivation of the technical specialists who controlled large firms.

Beginning his discussion by offering a general theory of motivation within social organizations, Galbraith posited the existence of four general types of motivation. The first, compulsion, he associated with the agricultural society of the feudal era, in which it was an effective and appropriate goad to economic production. As urbanization progressed, however, and with it the establishment of a market and factory system, a reliance on such motivation became inefficient. An industrialized, urbanized society obviously required a free, mobile work force with at least a minimum of education, all of which were precluded by the social constraints of feudalism. Modern laborers could not be physically forced to work; even if they could be, efficiency would suffer, since there would be no incentive to develop industrial skills, increase individual productivity, or undertake more difficult or distasteful kinds of tasks. Pecuniary rewards therefore played a much enhanced role as the effectiveness of compulsion receded.

But this kind of incentive had itself given way in part to two other types that developed as the composition of the work force changed from industrial to white-collar occupations. The two kinds of motivation most strongly associated with work in large, bureaucratic organizations were, Galbraith proposed, identification and adaptation. Identification referred to the subordination of one's own goals to those of the organization. Adaptation, the reverse of identification, was the attempt to mold the goals of the organization more closely to one's own. These motivations could affect an individual either separately or in some combination.

With this general schema established, Galbraith was prepared to construct his theory of the modern large corporation. He began by rejecting

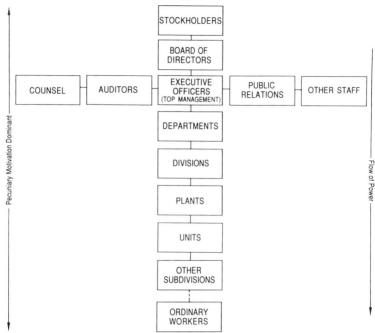

CONVENTIONAL VIEW OF CORPORATE STRUCTURE AND DYNAMICS

STOCKHOLDERS

BOARD OF DIRECTORS

COUNSEL — AUDITORS — EXECUTIVE OFFICERS (TOP MANAGEMENT) — PUBLIC RELATIONS — OTHER STAFF

DEPARTMENTS

DIVISIONS

PLANTS

UNITS

OTHER SUBDIVISIONS

ORDINARY WORKERS

Pecuniary Motivation Dominant

Flow of Power

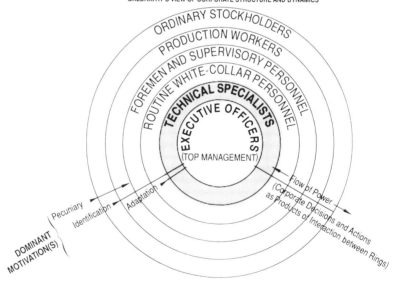

GALBRAITH'S VIEW OF CORPORATE STRUCTURE AND DYNAMICS

ORDINARY STOCKHOLDERS
PRODUCTION WORKERS
FOREMEN AND SUPERVISORY PERSONNEL
ROUTINE WHITE-COLLAR PERSONNEL
TECHNICAL SPECIALISTS
EXECUTIVE OFFICERS
(TOP MANAGEMENT)

Pecuniary
Identification
Adaptation

DOMINANT MOTIVATION(S)

Flow of Power
(Corporate Decisions and Actions as Products of Interaction between Rings)

Shaded Area = The Technostructure (dominant segment of corporate structure–repository of power based on specialized knowledge, talent, or experience).

the model of a "geometric hierarchy" that was so familiar to students of business administration. Authority levels were pictured in conventional textbooks by means of a triangular display of boxes taking the rough form of a tree. A jutting branch on top had boxes representing, in order, the stockholders, the board of directors, and the top management. Descending from this position, branches multiplied, first sideways, with offshoots representing counsel, auditors, public relations, and other staff positions, and then again downward, with boxes for departments, divisions, plants, units, other subdivisions, and finally ordinary workers.

In place of this model Galbraith proposed a radically different one. Imagine, he wrote, a set of concentric circles. Power and influence increased as one moved toward their common center. In the outermost circle lay the ordinary stockholders. Cut off from any real power, their motivation was solely pecuniary: they were paid dividends based on corporate earnings. The next inward circle contained production workers, whose motivation was partly pecuniary (wages) and partly (given the gains of unions and lessened hostility toward corporate goals) based on identification. Moving further inward, one found foremen, supervisors, clerical, sales, and other "routine" white-collar workers who "merge at their inner perimeter with technicians, engineers, sales executives, scientists, designers and other specialists who comprise the technostructure," and for whom the motivations of identification and adaptation became "increasingly important." At the center itself were the "executives or management." Further, Galbraith contended that "The relationship between society at large and an organization must be consistent with the relation of the organization to the individual. There must be consistency in the goals of the society, the organization and the individual. And there must be consistency in the motives which induce organizations and individuals to pursue these goals" (*NIS*, 169). To Galbraith, the broader implications of these propositions were obvious. He deduced that the goals of the "mature" corporation "will be a reflection of the goals of the members of the technostructure," while "the goals of the society will tend to be those of the corporation."

What were the goals of the mature corporation (that is, a corporation in which power had passed from entrepreneurial interests to the technostructure)? Galbraith believed that there were four. First, the technostructure had to ensure that corporate earnings would not fall below a safe level. Low earnings meant less capital available for investment purposes and therefore the need to turn to outside sources of capital (for example, banks), which thus obtained the right to interfere with corporate decisions.

New stock issues were also to be avoided, since they decreased the long-term value of the stock as well as the amount of capital that could be raised through a new issue of securities in the future. Even worse, were the price of corporate stock to decline significantly because of inadequate earnings, outsiders might well be tempted to buy up enough shares to enable them to vote out the firm's managerial elite. The second goal of the technostructure was growth. Growth allowed the technostructure to expand its ranks and ensured its survival by minimizing the risk of reduced output and unemployment in the firm generally and among the technostructure itself. A third goal, technological virtuosity, promoted jobs and business for the corporation, since innovation was an important source of advantage in marketing and was also valued highly in and of itself in modern society. The fourth goal was a rate of corporate earnings that provided for both investment needs and for "a progressive rise in the dividend rate." This rate of return was not, however, to be attained by setting prices at a level that would restrict growth. Social attitudes, Galbraith added, also made adequate earnings "an indication of sound service to the community" (*NIS*, 186).

To some extent, these goals shared much in common with those of the classical entrepreneur, since all firms desired autonomy, growth, innovative skill, and earnings. The crucial difference lay in the order of their relative importance for entrepreneurial and mature corporations. For example, while entrepreneurs personally benefitted from increased earnings and could be expected to pursue them above all else, technical specialists, not owning the company, were not the direct beneficiaries of a policy designed to maximize profits. Profits certainly promoted their welfare, but beyond a certain level were a decidedly secondary consideration. Earnings in mature firms needed to be just high enough to keep stockholders and creditors satisfied.

But Galbraith departed even further from standard theory. Because mature corporations obviously had market power yet had no reason to maximize profits, the question arose as to how prices were set. As he had in *American Capitalism*, he denied that an oligopolistic market led to artificially high prices and an inefficient allocation of resources. Indeed, orthodox theorists themselves agreed on the efficiency of the system, although this contradicted their own theory of oligopoly—a contradiction that they did not resolve.

Nor was this all. If the primary tactical objective of the technostructure was the elimination of market uncertainty, then it had to do more than control prices: it also had to make certain that adequate quantities of the corporation's products were desired by consumers. Returning to a central theme of *The Affluent Society*, Galbraith insisted that large firms did not advertise merely as an acceptable form of competition. They also sought to increase the demand for the products each produced, including those of competitors. Corporations could not rely on consumer demand; they had to *mold* it, both to reduce market risks and to maximize sales. Consumers did not shape production; instead, the converse was true or, as Galbraith put it, the sequence was "revised." He conceded that this process of planning was imperfect and cited the example of the Edsel as one of the system's most notable failures. Nor was consumer sovereignty totally mythical, since outside the industrial system the market still operated more or less according to conventional theory. And, of course, the consumer was not totally passive even in the industrial system. Reality was "plausible but untidy."

Yet mature corporations needed to do still more. They might have market power; they might control prices; and their policies might have a sizable effect on consumer wants and consumer demand. But to what avail if on a macroeconomic scale there were instability, insufficient demand, or other sources of uncertainty? For example, the consequences of mass unemployment in society at large would be equally as disastrous for a corporation as the failure to generate a reliable flow of goods within the firm's own sphere. Modern capitalist economies, no longer self-regulating, required some external, collective entity to ensure a high level of demand and adequate growth in the economy as a whole. That collective entity was, of course, the state.

Galbraith saw the ties between the technostructure of the mature corporation and the state as powerful and mutually reinforcing, and a key section of *The New Industrial State* was devoted to an analysis of this relationship. On its basic nature he wrote of a direct homology between the forces motivating corporate and state bureaucrats and of the overlapping and interconnected interests of the two groups:

> The state is strongly concerned with the stability of the economy. And with its expansion or growth. And with education. And with technical and scientific advance. And, most notably, with the national defense. These are *the* national goals; they are sufficiently trite so that one has a reassuring sense of the obvious in articulating them. All have their counterpart in the needs and goals of the technostructure. It requires stability

in demand for its planning. Growth brings promotion and prestige. It requires trained manpower. It needs government underwriting of research and development. Military and other technical procurement support its most developed form of planning. At each point the government has goals with which the technostructure can identify itself. Or, plausibly, these goals reflect adaptation of public goals to the goals of the technostructure. (*NIS*, 316)

And in case readers did not yet fully grasp the connections between the mature corporation and the state, Galbraith hammered the point home even more forcefully:

No sharp line separates government from the private firm; the line becomes very indistinct and even imaginary. Each organization is important to the other; members are intermingled in daily work; each organization comes to accept the other's goals; each adapts the goals of the other to its own. Each organization, accordingly, is an extension of the other. The large aerospace contractor is related to the Air Force by ties that, however different superficially, are in their substance the same as those that relate the Air Force to the United States government. Shared goals are the decisive link in each case. (*NIS*, 320-321)

Moreover, this relationship did not exist merely with respect to the Department of Defense: it was the *normal* relationship between the mature corporation and executive agencies and "other public bodies" that "underwrite industrial planning with long-term contracts involving large capital outlays and advanced technology."

Until this point the industrial system had been pictured in a generally favorable light. Now, however, came the first hint that all might not be well in the new order. Its central flaw was, in Galbraith's view, well typified by the relationship between the mature corporation and the state. The state, to be sure, provided for economic stability and growth; but because of its adaptation to the needs of large firms, it did so in one particular way: namely, through massive defense expenditures. In addition, the public sector provided routinely and abundantly the capital and services that aided the large corporation, while neglecting social services not useful in subsidizing or extending the power and influence of the latter—a point Galbraith had made at length in *The Affluent Society*. Further, he stressed—as a more general aspect of this problem—that the industrial system ignored or denigrated *all* goals, especially aesthetic ones, not connected to the process of production. This resulted in the suppression of any values that threatened the unrestrained commercialization of life and culture, the despoliation of the environment, and the almost unchallenged supremacy of production and consumption as ends in themselves. Also, because Americans assumed the functioning of a free and responsive market where none in fact existed and where planning had not been developed, there was no public pressure to fill in what Galbraith called the "planning lacunae" of the industrial system that were most conspicuous in the fields of public transportation, housing, and property development. In these and other areas where the market did not work, he advocated its replacement, not by "patchwork planning" that could not be effective, but by strong public authority.

Concerning the possibility of breaking free from the narrow values of the industrial system, Galbraith looked with hope to higher education, since it was, in part, "an apparatus for affecting belief and inducing more critical belief." Freed from the dominance of the industrial system, it could be "the necessary force for skepticism, emancipation and pluralism." This would require that universities no longer allow themselves to be used overwhelmingly as training grounds for the technostructure and that they provide sufficient funding for those fields of study that were not tied to the institutions that the corporate elite served. Leaders drawn from the corps of scientific and technical specialists not bound to the technostructure and from those in "the larger intellectual community" possessed the critical intellect and analytical skills necessary to understand the nature and extent of corporate power and also had the creative intelligence needed to propose alternatives to the goals of the technostructure and its allies. In a final passage strongly reminiscent of Marx's prediction that capitalism would eventually produce its own gravediggers, Galbraith suggested that the modern industrial system had given birth to its own most powerful critics: "The industrial system, in contrast with its economic antecedents, is intellectually demanding. It brings into existence, to serve its intellectual and scientific needs, the community that, hopefully, will reject its monopoly of social purpose" (*NIS*, 406).

The critical response of economists to *The New Industrial State* was unlike that accorded *American Capitalism* or *The Affluent Society*. While the latter two works met with, respectively, acclaim and irritated aloofness, the first excited a storm of controversy. Although it won general public approval and aroused the keen interest of scholars in a number of other disciplines, many economists saw the new theory—an explicit attack on established economic doctrine primarily written for a mass audience— as a direct affront to themselves, their ideas, and their profession. Appearing on best-seller lists for over thirty weeks and later translated into several languages, it was, as one critic in *The Harvard Business Review* somewhat ruefully acknowledged, a "smashing publishing success." *The Quarterly Review of Economics and Business* "sadly recognize[d] the accuracy of Galbraith's charge that 'Scientific truth in economics is not always what exists; often it is what can be handled by seemingly scientific methods.' " Though severely critical of Galbraith's theory (for example, the idea that growth was the primary motivation of the technostructure) and urging its replacement by a better one, the reviewer concluded that "However much the professional economist may have to add, amend, fill in, or construct by way of support, it is a measure of the achievement of Galbraith's work and the importance of its ideas that so much is sure to be attempted."[4]

Most reviews followed in this vein except for one by Robert M. Solow which asserted that, although there were some valuable elements in Galbraith's new work, most of his ideas were either erroneous or borrowed from other theorists and declared that "Professor Galbraith is not the first person to have discovered General Motors."[5] Although not much more critical than several others on substantive issues, Solow, a prominent economist at MIT, also indulged in much tasteless, taunting prose, including ad hominem attacks. His normally unconquerable insouciance shaken, Galbraith unleashed a stinging rebuttal that appeared in the same issue of *The Public Interest*. "The issue," he wrote, "concerns the future of economics in general and of the highly prestigious work with which Professor Solow is associated in particular. That work is within a highly specific frame. Within that frame it is the best of its kind. But it is only good if the frame is reasonably intact. When the frame goes so do the scholars it sustains."[6] Such controversy and bitter exchanges are perhaps not surprising. What *is* surprising is the fact that, five years after the publication of a book that irreverently rent apart established economic doctrine, its author was elected president of the American Economic Association.

[4] Robert Eisner, *The Quarterly Review of Economics and Business* 7 (Autumn 1967), 85, 86-87.

[5] Robert M. Solow, "The New Industrial State or Son of Affluence," in Robert W. Crandall and Richard S. Eckaus, eds., *Contemporary Issues in Economics* (Boston: Little, Brown, 1972), p. 542.

[6] J. K. Galbraith, "A Review of a Review," in ibid., p. 549.

A New Economics: The Broker State Attacked

The rejection of most of Galbraith's ideas in *The New Industrial State* by economic theorists was made at a time when what has been clumsily, though rather accurately, termed the "post-Keynesian neoclassical synthesis" reigned supreme in the economics profession, in governmental and intellectual circles, and in popular consciousness. Much like Freudian theory, from whose main body most of Freud's sober and pessimistic views regarding the irreducible tragedy and suffering of everyday life had been expunged in favor of a simplistic recipe for good living, Keynes's often rather dark and unsettling portrait of advanced market economies with their inherent instability was transformed in the postwar era into an easy prescription for "fine tuning" that could keep the economy in a state of calm equilibrium. Events conspired to make this view seem exceedingly plausible, especially in the United States from the end of World War II until the late 1960s. Rapid economic growth, relatively stable prices, and general social tranquillity had led many to believe that what Keynes had called "the Economic Problem" had at long last been solved. Economists were now almost unanimous in their belief that the continued mathematization of economic relationships and the infinite refinement of econometric techniques were the last frontier of economic knowledge.

But processes were already under way that would dash these hopes and make even Keynes's relatively subdued and more realistic expectations seem too optimistic. Urban turmoil bred by decades of racism, the neglect of social services, and grossly uneven economic development had by the late 1960s produced mass uprisings by blacks in America's largest cities on such a scale that they could be put down only with the aid of state militia or even, on occasion, federal troops. Cold war policy, through its emphasis on containment and global intervention, had led to the Vietnam debacle, a failure that threw open to question not only American foreign policy, but also the massive military expenditures that had both supported that policy and subsidized US industry since World War II. Meanwhile, the confidence of Americans in their economic system was shaken as the prosperity and stability of earlier years suddenly began to erode. Vietnam had, like all wars, spurred inflation; but there now arose, by previous American standards, an especially severe case. As military spending and the money supply were substantially reduced in order to bring inflation under control, economic growth dropped from 4.7 percent in 1968 to 2.3 percent in 1969. This was followed by a precipitous decline in stock market prices and a subsequent mild recession beginning in early 1970. Predictably, unemployment rose to 5 percent in 1970 and to almost 6 percent the next year as the Nixon administration sought to use the standard Keynesian remedies for inflation as had its predecessors. But the increased unemployment was not accompanied by a prompt decrease in prices. Instead, the rate of increase of consumer prices actually *rose* to reach 6.5 percent in early 1970 and then only gradually edged downward to 4 percent by year's end, where it remained until mid-1971. With unemployment hovering at 6 percent (a disturbing figure for those years) the Nixon administration became nervous, and for good reason. Not only was high inflation coupled with high unemployment a politically unhealthful condition: it also defied one of the basic principles of the Keynesian synthesis—the supposedly inverse relationship between price increases and joblessness.[7] It was in such circumstances that President Nixon imposed a total freeze on wages and prices for ninety days. Finally, two years later in 1973 the Arab oil embargo formally and dramatically signaled the end of American self-sufficiency in oil and the beginning of a long-term struggle to obtain the supplies of relatively inexpensive energy needed to fuel an advanced industrial economy.

These phenomena were accompanied by a sizable ferment within the intellectual community, including the economics profession. Neoclassicism, helpless to interpret the economic setbacks of these years, let alone propose effective solutions, was under severe attack from every point on the ideological spectrum—left, right, and center. Articles in respected journals and magazines with titles such as "Economists Are Asking: What Went Wrong?" "What's Wrong with American Economics?" and "Post–Post Keynes: The Shattered Synthesis" told a story of progressive disillusion. A *Business Week* article appearing in mid-1974 went so far as to proclaim in its title: "Theory Deserts the Forecasters: The Thinking of the Past 200 Years Seems Insufficient for Today's Problems." In its pages several of the most prominent economists in America—including two Nobel laureates—admitted that prevailing economic theory was increasingly unable to deal with inflation, shortages of raw materials and energy, and problems in the international economy. The magazine also noted that "If 1973 was a bad show [for economic predictions], 1974 promises to be worse. At the midpoint of any year, economists have usually settled on a consensus forecast for the remaining six months. This year there is not

---

[7] See Robert Lekachman, *Inflation: The Permanent Problem of Boom and Bust* (New York: Vintage, 1973), pp. 19-23; also Leonard Silk, *Nixonomics*, 2d ed. (New York: Praeger, 1973), chapters 1 and 2.

even an agreement as to whether the US is in a recession or a temporarily interrupted boom."[8]

There was no boom. As the months passed it became clear that the US economy was in sharp recession—the worst, in fact, since the 1930s. And yet the rate of inflation remained at almost 8 percent. So exasperating had the situation become that the renowned Harvard economist Wassily Leontief, himself a pioneer in mathematical economics and a recipient of the Nobel Memorial Prize, angrily charged that his profession and especially the Harvard faculty had become overly enamored of mathematical techniques and algebraic formulas, pursuing an abstract scholasticism that bore increasingly less relation to the problems and conditions of the real world. His denunciation was prefigured by his presidential address before a meeting of the American Economic Association (AEA) in 1970, when he told his colleagues that "The uneasiness [in economics] is caused not by the irrelevance of the practical problems to which present-day economists address their efforts, but rather by the palpable *inadequacy* of the scientific means with which they try to solve them. . . . Uncritical enthusiasm for mathematical formulation tends often to conceal the ephemeral substantive content of the argument behind the formidable front of algebraic signs." He concluded further that "In no other field of empirical inquiry has so massive and sophisticated a statistical machinery been used with such indifferent results."[9] Among those who agreed with Leontief was fellow Harvard economist J. K. Galbraith, who had, in fact, made several of these very points in an address before that body one year earlier, when he charged that the neoclassical model was "excluding urgent as well as politically disturbing questions from professional economic vision" and urged listeners not to allow economics to be "comfortable, noncontroversial, increasingly sophisticated in its models and increasingly, and perhaps even dramatically, unrelated to life."[10]

He was to be even more explicit three years later when he stood before the same audience of economists as president of the association. An extraordinary act of recognition and even magnanimity by colleagues for one who had alternately criticized, castigated, and embarrassed his profession for fifteen years, the election of Galbraith to the presidency of the AEA was

[8] "Theory Deserts the Forecasters," *Business Week*, 29 June 1974, p. 50.

[9] Quoted in Gabriel A. Almond and Stephen J. Genco, "Clouds, Clocks, and the Study of Politics," *World Politics*, 29 (July 1977), 515.

[10] J. K. Galbraith, "Economics as a System of Belief," *The American Economic Review* (May 1970), 470, 478.

a remarkable occasion and one that he was determined not to waste. Characteristically, he did not. In a searing blast at established economic theory that must have reddened the faces of many of his listeners, he declared that neoclassical economics was hopelessly out of touch with reality. Yet, the latter fact notwithstanding, the old theory was "not without an instinct for survival. It rightly sees the unmanaged sovereignty of the consumer, the ultimate sovereignty of the citizen and the maximization of profits and resulting subordination of the firm to the market as the three legs of a tripod on which it stands. These are what exclude the role of power in the system. All three propositions tax the capacity for belief." Present theory, Galbraith maintained, played an important role in masking economic realities, especially the fact of power, which was distributed in a vastly unequal manner between the system of large, mature firms and the world of small firms still predominantly under market control. Contrary to the accepted view, there was no "general identity of interest" between the goals of the large business firm and those of small firms and the general public. The imbalance that arose under such circumstances could, he maintained, be remedied only by strong public action.[11] This theme formed the core of a forthcoming book, the third in the trilogy that had begun with *The Affluent Society*.

Economics and the Public Purpose, published in 1973, was an attempt to draw together themes from *The Affluent Society* and *The New Industrial State* and to formulate possible solutions to the current economic dilemmas. In the beginning chapters Galbraith went over much familiar ground, emphasizing the growth of the large corporation, the motivations of its managers, its hierarchy of goals, and its control over prices, sources of supply, and consumer demand. The assemblage of all such corporations was called by Galbraith "the planning system" to distinguish it from "the market system." The market system, composed of about twelve million smaller firms (farms, service establishments, small retail businesses, construction firms, small manufacturers, and others), was, he wrote, a distinct part of the economy that accounted for roughly half of all the business done in the United States. Firms in this part of the economy were generally controlled by entrepreneurs or their families, and their goal was profit maximization. They had little or no control over prices, sources of supply, or consumer demand. This, Galbraith stressed, was the part of the economy that corresponded to the neoclassical theory of economics. The market sys-

---

[11] J. K. Galbraith, "Power and the Useful Economist," ibid. (March, 1973), 5, 6.

tem did operate in a market, albeit an imperfect one; it did tend toward a rough state of equilibrium; and, when this occasionally broke down, Keynesian monetary and fiscal policies could be applied with reasonable effectiveness to bring the system back into balance. By itself, the market system was "broadly stable."

But the other half of the economy—the planning system—was an entirely different matter. This system, characterized by large corporations controlled by their technostructures, was not subordinate to the market. It was, as a result, "inherently unstable." Its upward swings and downward turns were of a highly volatile, cumulative, and self-amplifying nature, and it possessed an intrinsic inflationary tendency. Keynesian policies to counter recession and inflation could not succeed at a tolerable cost in this sector, since mature corporations had escaped from market control.

The instability of the planning system had further important ramifications, since the two systems acted not in isolation, but as interconnected parts of a single economy. Combined, the two systems worked not in unison, but in a lopsided, erratic, and uncoordinated manner. The reason for the constant malfunctioning of the economy was the far greater resources, power, and influence of the planning system relative to the market system. Galbraith contended that this root cause could be found in each of the main problem areas that confronted the American economy.

Calling attention to the "irrational performance" of the economy, Galbraith observed that while certain products in the private sector, such as automobiles, gasoline, alcohol, and "exotically processed foods," were turned out in large quantities, other, more important goods, such as housing, health care, and public transportation—were "endemically in short supply." Neoclassical theory, he reminded his readers, explained the inadequate supply of a product as a consequence of oligopoly and monopoly. Large firms with market power supposedly restricted production in order to obtain higher prices. But then why was the plethora of trivial goods produced overwhelmingly by the *planning* system, not the market system? Neoclassical theorists had no satisfactory answer beyond their belief that, as Galbraith put it, "If things of importance are not produced, it is because consumers understand badly their needs. If the distribution of productive resources seems insane, it is because consumers are insane."[12]

Dismissing the reasoning in the last two sentences as a *reductio ad ab-*

---

[12] J. K. Galbraith, *Economics and the Public Purpose* (New York: Signet, 1975), p. 192. Subsequently cited parenthetically as *EPP*.

surdum, Galbraith found a far more plausible explanation for this phenomenon in the unequal development of the market and planning systems traceable to the organizational superiority and power of the latter, which gave it market influence, economies of scale, an ability to persuade consumers, and government support and subsidies to further aid its activities. This also, he believed, explained the seemingly irrational expenditures of government. He considered it highly significant that "Weapons, aircraft developed to a level of general nonperformance, moon travel, the space shuttle, atomic tests, industrial research and development, [and] highways have ample access to public funds," while "Money for public needs of the highest importance or greatest public convenience—education, police, law courts, street sanitation, urban services of all kinds—is persistently in short supply" (*EPP*, 192-193). This, he wrote, "reflect[ed] the power of the planning system over the state," and was most evident where "public bureaucracies are symbiotically associated with the most highly developed technostructures of the planning system" (*EPP*, 193).

Another failure of the mixed economy was the continued maldistribution of income. Neo-Keynesian theory had predicted a leveling tendency as workers attempted to maximize pecuniary and status rewards by moving from low-paying to high-paying occupations, which should theoretically have been those that by reason of their unpleasant or arduous nature rewarded workers with more money. Yet this was not the case. Wages in the planning system tended to rise rapidly and were relatively immune to inflation, while those in the market system lagged behind. Also, the planning system, with its control over wages, prices, sources of supply, and consumer demand, dominated trade with the market system and used its power to pull resources into its own sphere. Small entrepreneurs could compete with large corporations only by means of "self-exploitation"—that is, by lowering their own wages or lengthening their period of daily work or both. Concerning the idea that high pay for management jobs was simply compensation for their less pleasant nature, Galbraith maintained that this was manifestly untrue. Corporate managers professed to enjoy their work, yet corporate wealth and power made managerial pay (taxed at preferential rates) highly remunerative.

Another of the "anxieties" facing Americans—the impact of the economy on the environment—was also, Galbraith claimed, inadequately explained by existing ideas. Although neoclassical theory recognized the existence of "external diseconomies"—costs of production borne not by individuals or firms, but by society as a whole—they were typically dealt with in a few perfunctory sentences in economics texts. Galbraith, on the other hand, saw them as a direct result of the asymmetrical economic development and growth that produced consumer goods in almost inexhaustible quantities and yet ''accords no similar emphasis and support to the public services which make such increased consumption socially tolerable.''

Finally, Galbraith warned of the cumulative impact of these crises and failures on public morale and social stability. He did not see discontent arising primarily from the industrial labor force, which, because of the acquiescence of corporate managers in granting higher wages and more benefits for these workers (unlike entrepreneurs, managers did not pay for these concessions out of their own pockets and therefore had no reason to resist them unless they appeared to threaten growth or stability), had largely come to accept the goals of the planning system. The outcry would instead come ''from the urban ghettos, from those who work for low wages in agriculture, from the young who have not found employment in the planning system.'' These were the groups that were exploited, he maintained, noting that the violent eruptions in US cities during this period could not be explained by racial tensions alone. Such, Galbraith believed, were the problems of the mixed economy.

Clearly, Galbraith had now moved far beyond his position in *American Capitalism*, having come to a fundamental reappraisal of the Keynesian principles he had for so long espoused and promulgated. First, and most easily, he rejected derived Keynesianism, the synthesis of neoclassical and Keynesian ideas that had dominated the textbooks and economic thought of the postwar era. He now saw in this doctrine an exaggerated and narrow focus on aggregate economic growth and employment levels; a lack of recognition that military spending was not merely a convenient and easily dispensable means of subsidizing investment and growth, but was instead ''functionally integrated'' with the US economy; and an unrealistic split between macroeconomic and microeconomic phenomena that viewed overall economic performance in isolation from the workings of the large corporation.

However, Galbraith had also, though with more difficulty and reluctance, come to repudiate Keynes's original beliefs concerning the viability of a mixed economy the volume and composition of whose output were not monitored or coordinated by any guiding intelligence. Keynes, though accepting the need for governmental regulation of aggregate demand and recognizing the deep and recurrent weaknesses of the economy at this level, had assumed that at the level of the firm there was no need of guidance or restructuring and that the impersonal forces of the market would generally promote socially optimal results in the economy as a whole.[13] In this respect, Galbraith bluntly stated, "Keynes was wrong." He had now come to believe that the entire economy was in need of a drastic overhaul and was prepared to propose reform measures stronger and more overtly radical than any he had previously advocated: the strengthening of the market system; the exertion of increased control over the planning system; and the establishment of national policies to coordinate the activities of both sectors of the private economy.

To begin, Galbraith again called for the "emancipation of belief"—a project to be undertaken by a vanguard of intellectuals in order to weaken the cultural hegemony of the planning system. As part of this preliminary process he urged a new status for women, whose role he had described in earlier chapters (in terms reminiscent of Veblen's *The Theory of the Leisure Class*) as the "crypto-servant functions of consumption administration" in the household. A restructuring of modes of living and of social roles at the household level would mean that "women are no longer available for the administration of consumption." With this task minimized, there would be a "substantial shift in the the economy from goods to services" as well as from the planning system to the market system, which largely provided those services. The state, Galbraith concluded, would also need to take strong and effective action after it first renounced the goals it shared with the planning system. Such action could not be expected to come primarily from the executive branch of government, whose agencies were closely tied to the growth imperatives of the planning system, but instead from the national legislature.

Galbraith's measures for strengthening the market were (1) "General exemption for small businessmen from all prohibitions in the antitrust laws against combination to stabilize prices and output"; (2) "Direct government regulation of prices and production in the market system"; (3) "Strong and effective encouragement to trade union organization in the market system"; (4) "An extension and major increase in the minimum wage"; (5) "A revised view of international commodity organization and a cautiously revised view of tariff protection in the market system"; and (6) "A strong presumption in favor of government support to the educational, capital, and technological needs of the market system" (*EPP*, 245-249). These policies, he stressed, would not be giving the market system

---

[13] See J. M. Keynes, *The General Theory of Employment, Interest, and Money* [1936] (New York: Harbinger, 1964), pp. 378-379.

unfair advantages. They would only be granting it what the planning system already had as a result of its superior organization, market power, and political influence.

Within the planning system itself Galbraith advocated a lessening of income inequality between the highest ranks of the technostructure and the white-collar and blue-collar workers below them. This should be done, he suggested, through aggressive union action, progressive taxation that would not treat executive salaries as "earned" income subject to relatively low tax levies, and legislation that would, in the context of general wage and price controls, specify maximum differentials between various levels of compensation. One final measure to reduce the grossly unequal power of the large firm was a plan "to convert the fully mature corporations—those that have completed the euthanasia of stockholder power—into fully public corporations." The state would buy out shareholders with fixed interest-bearing securities, preventing the inequality resulting from this rentier income from increasing, while "In time, inheritance, inheritance taxes, philanthropy, profligacy, alimony and inflation would act to disperse this wealth" (*EPP*, 261).

Next, Galbraith proclaimed a "socialist imperative," concluding that "other steps toward socialism" would also be necessary. He admitted that old socialist ideas had lost their attractiveness for several reasons, among which was a popular realization that "the larger and more technical of the public bureaucracies—the Air Force, Navy, Atomic Energy Commission—have purposes of their own which can be quite as intransigently pursued as those of General Motors or Exxon" (*EPP*, 265-266). In spite of this, he called for a "new socialism" that was not ideological, but rather "compelled by circumstance." This socialism—consisting, in part, of selective nationalization—would apply to certain "retarded industries" in the market system that were "of peculiar importance not alone for comfort, well-being, tranquillity and happiness but also for continued existence" (*EPP*, 266-267). The failure of these industries to enter the planning system either because of their intrinsic nature or other circumstances brought about a need for state intervention in areas such as housing, medical care, and public transportation. Nationalization would also apply to the type of firm within the planning system whose technostructure "is in peculiarly close relationship with the public bureaucracy," including large weapons firms (for example, General Dynamics, Ling-Temco-Vought, and Lockheed) and any other corporations that did more than half of their business with the government.

In conclusion, Galbraith proposed that fiscal and monetary policy be used together with permanent and comprehensive wage and price controls in an overall system of national planning, since legislative bodies could no longer afford to deal with economic issues solely on a microscopic, particularistic, and piecemeal basis. The planning system did plan, of course, but its individual firms did not coordinate their activities. Neither was there coordination between the planning and market systems; nor, under existing structural arrangements and policies, could any be established. Results of this situation included chronic inflation as well as shortages, bottlenecks, irrationalities, and economic crises and breakdowns of various kinds, such as the "energy crisis" of the 1970s. Society, Galbraith wrote, had to "recognize the logic of planning with its resulting imperative of coordination." He therefore foresaw a necessity for a "public planning authority" to be placed under the "closest legislative supervision." Beyond this he favored the "coordination of planning policies as between the national planning systems" in order to end the constant currency crises between nations, which had at their root uncontrolled domestic inflation. National planning systems, he wrote, required "a measure of international planning" to move the world economy to a less chaotic state.

Thus ended Galbraith's book. Reactions—somewhat predictably—ranged, as one reviewer noted, from "applause to apoplexy." Yet even as the decidedly mixed reviews came in, events in the national economy again cast Galbraith in the role of a prophet. In June of 1973 President Nixon froze most retail prices in an attempt to stop spiraling inflation. During the next year the Ford administration, still determined to fight inflation but equally resolved primarily to use monetary policy to do so, pressed down hard on the money supply. Traditionalists were confounded when this action had little effect on prices, but a substantial impact on employment. As the country slipped into deep recession in 1975, the administration quickly reversed itself and tried to stimulate the economy by loosening monetary controls. The economy responded only sluggishly. In any case it was too late to repair the political damage that had already been done. Jobless rates of more than 10 percent ensured Ford's defeat in 1976. Inflation, meanwhile, continued and even gradually intensified, as did the energy crisis and the problems of urban decay.

ON THE THRESHOLD OF THE EIGHTIES:
THE REFORMER UNBOWED

Economics and the Public Purpose was much more than an intellectual treatise: it was an open call to arms. Since the publication of *The New*

Industrial State Galbraith had become ever more active in the ongoing political debate that spanned the turbulent years of the civil rights movement, the Vietnam War, and the period of urban riots and revolt. An opponent of the war but a supporter of Lyndon Johnson's "Great Society," he began to believe that, at last, the social and political climate was ripe for the kinds of reforms he had advocated as far back as *The Affluent Society*. But as the Vietnam War undermined Johnson's domestic policies as well as his presidency, Galbraith turned elsewhere for political allies. As chair of Americans for Democratic Action (ADA) from 1967 to 1969, he became a member of the "Dump Johnson" movement, swung ADA support behind Senator Eugene McCarthy, and even contemplated running for the Senate in Massachusetts. His personal political involvement peaked with his endorsement of George McGovern in 1972, given as he worked to complete *Economics and the Public Purpose*. McGovern's proposed economic and social reforms, dovetailing at several key points with Galbraith's own, included a redistribution of income and power in American society combined with a fundamental reorientation of priorities both at home and abroad. Somewhat injudiciously, given the manifest ineptness of McGovern's campaign and the public's obvious weariness with political activism and disillusion with social reform, Galbraith predicted victory at the polls.

McGovern's resounding defeat not only shattered Galbraith's hopes for the possible implementation in the near future of the policies he had advocated in *Economics and the Public Purpose*, it also clearly marked the end of the great liberal renaissance that had begun in the mid-1960s and had promised to enact a Second New Deal for the poor, minorities, and the politically powerless who had not participated in America's postwar leap to unprecedented prosperity. Indeed, as in the aftermath of two previous cycles of reform, war, and popular disenchantment, a new conservative movement arose that both challenged liberal views and blamed liberal politicians and activists for the ills of the preceding decade. Undaunted, Galbraith continued to attack the intellectual bankruptcy of established economic theory and the refusal of its adherents to face the realities of a modern industrial economy whose dynamics were no longer adequately described by the doctrine of Adam Smith or even that of John Maynard Keynes and whose problems could not be solved by nostalgia.

Dubbing the new political movement and attitudes the "Conservative Majority Syndrome," Galbraith saw in its drive to cut federal and state taxes while social services deteriorated a self-serving attempt by the technostructure and its allies to improve their lot at the expense of those without the power to resist. Far from abandoning his views, he urged fellow reformers not to succumb to the adverse climate of opinion and to ride out the tide that was pushing against them. Now in his seventies, Galbraith, once a member of the political and intellectual establishments he now so vigorously criticized, was still at the forefront of the assault on the system of belief that, ironically, he had himself helped to erect. In a return to the more radical posture of his youth before the Keynesian Revolution, he now sought to enlist a new generation in the struggle for his vision of a just society. In an address to the Yale graduating class of 1979, he chided the students for their passivity, complacency, and self-absorption. Firing contemptuous barbs at the "great conservative revolt," which, he implied, aimed at restoring many of the principles of laissez-faire for the disadvantaged and powerless while maintaining a system of state socialism for the affluent, he told the students:

> You will see, in this lovely summer, how rich are your public opportunities. You can join the great conservative revolt and serve the fortunate while pretending, even believing, that you are serving the public good. Or you can join Mr. Carter's liberals in Washington and serve the rich by doing nothing at all.
>
> But I do not wish ever to be cynical. Perhaps there are among you those who are without this contemporary instinct for public fraud. If so, another opportunity beckons. One cannot ask you in this age of Jarvis, Gann, and Governor Edward J. King to go out and comfort the afflicted. That would be eccentric. But perhaps you can afflict the comfortable. Perhaps you will wish to join in having honest amusement at the expense of those who, while protecting their income, protest their passion for the public welfare. I promise you, out of some personal experience, that they do not like it.[14]

Thus, appropriately, Galbraith approached the ninth decade of the twentieth century attacking the prevailing economic orthodoxy, calling upon the young intelligentsia to rally to the progressive banner, and reaffirming his own commitment to a just society.

[14] J.K. Galbraith, "How To Get Ahead: From an Address to the Yale Graduating Class," *The New York Review of Books*, 19 July 1979, p. 6. Also see Galbraith's "The Conservative Onslaught" in ibid., 22 January 1981, pp. 30-36.

Chapter 4   *Galbraith and American Capitalism*

Galbraith's impact as a social critic has been widely acknowledged, even by most who disagree with his views. But what of the usefulness of his model and theory as tools for an analysis of modern corporate capitalism? How closely, in other words, do modern capitalist economies resemble the New Industrial State? This issue has enormous significance, since Galbraith's theory implies that "capitalism" as it has been almost universally defined—essentially by private ownership and control of capital in a free market—in a real sense no longer exists in at least half of the American economy. This has, in fact, been the thrust of his argument concerning the basic nature of all advanced industrial economies in the West. To evaluate his position we must, as he did himself, examine the three legs of the "tripod" on which neoclassical theory stands: consumer sovereignty, citizen sovereignty, and the maximization of profits and consequent subordination of the large firm to the market.

Concerning the first question, Galbraith argues that the modern large firm cannot, given the incredibly complex and costly process of modern industrial research, development, and production, leave the problem of consumer demand to chance. Thus, large corporations use the psychological coercion of mass advertising to mold consumer taste and attitudes. So far, one can accept Galbraith's logic. Certainly the large firm—*any* firm, for that matter—would like nothing better than to eliminate the influence of the market and its attendant risks of losses and bankruptcy.

Galbraith, however, goes further than this. He wishes to say not merely that firms want to control consumer behavior, but that they actually do control it. This is, and has always been, the weakest part of his theory, a fact on which his critics have not failed to capitalize. In discussions of corporate sales strategy business leaders continually speak of the constant, costly, and risky process of marketing and the uncertainties and pressures they face daily.[1] Even after discounting for the likelihood of self-serving

---

[1] For a discussion by business executives of this issue and for their views of Galbraith's ideas in general, see Rollie Tillman and Curtis P. McLaughlin, "Six Executives on Galbraith," *The Harvard Business Review* (May–June 1974).

elements in such statements, it is highly doubtful that even huge, "mature" corporations have the kind of power to regulate demand that Galbraith often attributes to them. To say that they *attempt* such regulation is one thing; to say that they succeed is quite another.[2]

Galbraith often cites the phenomenon of vertical integration (the combined control of supply, production, and marketing by the same business organization) in large firms as evidence of the disappearance of the market as an agent for determining demand. But as business historian Alfred Chandler has pointed out, vertical integration does not mean the internal generation of consumer demand; it involves only the internalization of industrial and marketing processes within a single firm in order to ensure a steady and efficient flow of goods through the various stages of production, marketing, and sales once current and long-term market demand have already been estimated.[3] The corporation must therefore still deal with the uncertainty of consumer preferences and with the attempts of competitors to take its customers away. Galbraith thus errs in not admitting the enduring importance of effective, "workable" competition. Mature firms are not subject to all the pressures of companies in a state of pure competition, but they must nevertheless take into account the power and efforts of their rivals, both domestic and foreign. Indeed, Paul Samuelson reminds us that "the large corporation is not an absolute monarch. Ford could not sell Edsels. Lever Brothers could not, with all the wizardry of Madison Avenue, sell Swan Soap. Montgomery Ward was gradually dethroned by Sewell Avery's stubborn stupidity. The great RCA lost hundreds of millions in computers and had to abandon the field ignominiously. General Foods lost heavily in franchise food operations."[4] In short, there still seems to be a good deal of truth in Joseph Schumpeter's remark that even the most beautiful woman in the world cannot sell a poor product.

This criticism does not, of course, vitiate the force or validity of the bulk of Galbraith's critique of modern advertising and the psychological pressure and economic distortion it entails. While corporations cannot, as

[2] Indeed, the very examples of failed attempts to sell products that Galbraith uses to illustrate his point concerning the readiness of the state to insure large corporations against bankruptcy (Lockheed, Penn Central, and, most recently, Chrysler) refute his contention that mature firms have effectively eliminated market uncertainty and can largely control what the consumer buys. Galbraith tries to brush off such failures as imperfections in the planning process; but such "planning" and failures regularly occur in small entrepreneurial firms as well.

[3] Alfred D. Chandler, Jr., *The Visible Hand: The Managerial Revolution in American Business* (Cambridge: Harvard University Press, Belknap, 1977), p. 11.

[4] Paul A. Samuelson, *Economics*, 10 ed. (New York: McGraw-Hill, 1976), p. 512.

Galbraith often implies, create wants *ex nihilo*, they can and do *channel* and *intensify* wants in order to serve their own needs. General Motors did not create the need or the desire for rapid transportation in an urban environment; neither could it ensure that consumers would buy any particular product it wanted to sell. But American automakers could and did manipulate consumers to the extent that they were willing to solve their transportation problems for decades through the purchase of increasingly ornate, inefficient, and often dangerous individual motor vehicles, thereby effectively precluding the development of alternative modes of public transportation. Automobile manufacturers were also able to obtain government subsidies in the form of vast highway systems as well as artificially cheap sources of petroleum products for their customers. Large corporations cannot, as Galbraith claims, control market demand now any more than their predecessors could; but they do have the power to shape demands and markets subject to various constraints.[5]

In short, Galbraith seems to have gone too far in extending the reality of corporate power down to include an ability to control consumer demand. He is on firmer ground in expounding the next cardinal aspect of his theory: the disproportionate power of the planning system and its economic, political, and cultural influence in American life. He convincingly outlines the means by which the planning system uses its enormous power to shift the workings of the market in its favor, rightly seeing this as one of the primary factors behind the unequal development of the two segments of the private sector in the American economy and also as an important cause of the continuing disparity between the resources devoted to the private and public goods.

Yet here again there are flaws and omissions in Galbraith's theory. The first is his failure to note that, unlike Europe, America has espoused a peculiarly harsh brand of economic liberalism that survived long after sev-

---

[5] Here the recent example of Chrysler Corporation is especially instructive. For years Chrysler, like other automobile manufacturers, could use advertising to help sell its products. However, when market demand changed, this firm, plagued by incompetent management and an extraordinary lack of foresight concerning the demand for smaller, fuel-efficient cars, found its "planning" and sales gimmicks totally inadequate and teetered on the brink of bankruptcy, from which it was saved only by timely government intervention. While such disasters are admittedly uncommon in the case of large, established corporations, they could occur only if one assumes the existence of a market mechanism involving at least some autonomous consumer choice. Even nations with centrally planned economies have learned that prices must be geared not solely to production costs, but also to consumer demand, hence their increasing interest in Western marketing techniques.

eral of its salient features had disappeared abroad—a fact that Galbraith, especially in his earlier works, appears to ignore. It is extraordinary testimony to the impact of business dominance and laissez-faire ideology in America that the United States had no system of social security or unemployment benefits until the late 1930s, more than a full generation after such measures had been adopted in most other industrial nations. Similarly, most trade union activities were illegal in America until the New Deal, although they had been accepted in Europe for decades. Furthermore, American backwardness in these areas cannot be blamed on a weakness of corporate development in Europe vis-à-vis the United States, since most European nations not only permitted, but actually encouraged, the formation of cartels. What does seem decisive is the specific structure of social and political power in the United States, since in no other industrial society was the bourgeoisie so openly in control of government. Indeed, a powerful argument can be made that the relative underdevelopment of the public sector in America is traceable in large part to the specific nature of American capitalism.

Also fundamental in promoting the power of the planning system, according to Galbraith's theory, has been the "symbiotic relationship" between the mature corporation and the state. The development of common interests and interlocks between the planning system and government bureaucracies is pictured in his works as one of the most pronounced features of advanced capitalism, and he has been particularly insightful in his description of the economy of weapons firms, an arrangement that Seymour Melman has labeled "Pentagon Capitalism."[6] Military spending has, Galbraith observes, been an important prop for post-Keynesian capitalism in America, filling in investment gaps when insufficient aggregate demand threatened to slow economic growth.[7]

Once more, however, Galbraith betrays a hint of parochialism. For while he implicitly and often explicitly uses America to illustrate the fusion of the state with the planning system, it is in America that the fusion theory least applies. Unlike Germany, France, Japan, and other nations that have

[6] See Melman's books *Pentagon Capitalism: The Political Economy of War* (New York: McGraw-Hill, 1970) and *The Permanent War Economy: American Capitalism in Decline* (New York: Simon and Schuster, 1974).

[7] It should be remarked that the economy of weapons firms—a special case within the planning system—is the one area of the economy whose functioning closely fits Galbraith's theory of planning. Weapons makers have virtually nothing to do with the market, the demand for their products, the prices at which they sell them, and the profits they derive from the sales all being under strict administrative control.

long traditions of strong central governments and are characterized by a great overlapping of political and business elites, America has always been conspicuous for its *de*centralized political structure—the result of its inhabitants' historically and culturally conditioned fear of centralized public authority—and the absence of strong social bonds between bureaucrats and business leaders. The advent of greatly expanded activity on an established and sustained basis by the federal government in America has been very recent, beginning only after World War II. Even now, many European political leaders are amazed at what they consider to be the anachronistic structure of American government: the division of power and responsibility among numerous agencies of the executive branch, two distinct legislative bodies, the judicial system, and a myriad of corresponding state and local governmental units whose jurisdictions often overlap with each other and sometimes with that of the federal government—a complex and unwieldy arrangement of "checks and balances" deliberately designed to frustrate rapid and concerted action and born of a distrust of both state power and direct popular sovereignty. Past and present cooperation between government and business in America is undeniable, but relations have always harbored a strong element of mutual suspicion and even animosity.[8]

That this state of affairs is not universal, but is actually in marked contrast to the experience of many other nations, is evident from Stephen S. Cohen's description of the dealings between corporate managers and government officials in France during negotiations involving the development and acceptance of the National Plan for the French economy.[9] In fact, the very *idea* of centralized planning is anathema to the vast majority of American business executives, who do not trust government bureaucrats attempting direct intervention in economic affairs. The pervasiveness of direct and indirect forms of corruption, bribery, and similar practices in business-government relations throughout American history does not, as some have claimed, prove the fusion theory. On the contrary, as Cohen

[8] For a brief survey of the relations between business and government and their attitudes toward each other in the United States, see Leonard Silk and David Vogel, *Ethics and Profits: The Crisis of Confidence in American Business* (New York: Touchstone, 1976), pp. 198-201.

[9] Stephen S. Cohen, *Modern Capitalist Planning: The French Model*, updated edition (Berkeley: University of California Press, 1977), pp. 65-66. For a view of the relationship between business and the state in yet another country—a study that takes a specifically Galbraithian frame of reference—see Martin Bronfenbrenner, "Japan's Galbraithian Economy," in Daniel Bell and Irving Kristol, eds., *Capitalism Today* (New York: Mentor, 1971), pp. 175-186.

has noted, graft is not needed where a mutuality of interests is genuinely felt; it is required only where close, nonpecuniary ties do not exist.[10]

Galbraith's last major problem involves his view of the reasons for public acceptance of social and economic imbalance. Instead of probing into the psychological and cultural forces behind irrational forms and excessive levels of consumption, he assigns virtually all the responsibility for the overdevelopment of the planning system and the paucity of social services in the economy as a whole to the manipulative workings of the planning system itself. Yet the ease with which Madison Avenue and other private and public agencies of persuasion can alter and mold the opinions of many citizens raises disturbing questions whose implications he does not explore. (How, for example, can one use his model to explain the rampant consumerism in the Communist world, where Madison Avenue does not exist?) Is it possible that in all modern, hierarchically structured societies in which people are denied effective control over their own lives and work they are both permitted and encouraged to seek solace in the obsessive acquisition of material goods and in a vicarious participation in the diplomatic, military, technological, and economic achievements of the nation-state? If so, the solution would lie not merely in redressing economic imbalances, removing old economic elites from power, and supervising the activities of new elites, but rather in the general democratization of society.

SOCIAL THEORY AND THE MODERN CORPORATION: AN INTELLECTUAL HISTORY

Thus far, Galbraith has weakened—but not destroyed—two legs of the tripod; however, neoclassical theory will still stand unless the third prong

[10] Indeed, the historic weakness of the state in America together with the strained relations between it and business gives a more satisfactory explanation for the economic and social imbalance, uneven growth, and lack of coordination to which Galbraith rightly calls attention than does a theory that stresses cooperation between the two. Thomas Cochran notes, for example, that the Great Depression caused more economic damage in America than it did in Europe, because of the lack of sufficient government power to coordinate economic policies and establish adequate relief programs during the early stages of the collapse. (See Cochran, *200 Years of American Business*, [New York: Delta, 1978], p. 175.) Even today, while the governments of Germany, France, and Japan have operated their telegraph, telephone, airline, and railroad systems for decades (with the exception of the airlines, for close to a century), it was only in the 1970s that the United States, under the pressure of an energy crisis, finally moved sluggishly and uncertainly toward more state involvement in energy production and mass transit—a movement reversed under the Reagan administration.

of his attack, his denial of the orthodox theory of corporate motivation, can undermine the most fundamental part of the structure: namely, the assumption of profit maximization. But a discussion of this issue is inseparable from and, indeed, dependent on the central theoretical axis from which all of his major propositions radiate: the alleged evolution of a new form of corporate organization and an elite of technical and administrative specialists who manage it, direct its daily operations, and plan its strategy. This is not a new or a simple question, but it is one that must now be addressed.

The evolution of a managerial class in capitalist societies and the consequent separation of ownership and control initially as a simple division of labor within the large corporation are, as Galbraith acknowledges, well-known facts that were anticipated by Marx and later by social democrats such as Eduard Bernstein in the late nineteenth century. Perhaps one of the first American theorists to call attention to this phenomenon and to ponder its deeper significance for the evolution of capitalism was Walter Lippmann. Lippmann left little doubt concerning who he believed was taking control of the large corporation as it slipped from the hands of entrepreneurs and stockholders. The ''real government'' of the corporation, he announced, was ''passing into a hierarchy of managers and deputies.'' Furthermore, although these new managers had ''no tradition to work with'' and were still surrounded by ''the old commercial morality of the exploiter and profiteer,'' they were, perhaps unknowingly, nonetheless ''revolutionizing the discipline, the incentives, and the vision of the business world.'' ''The real news about business,'' wrote Lippmann, ''is that it is being administered by men who are not profiteers. The managers are on salary, divorced from ownership and from bargaining. They represent the revolution in business incentives at its very heart.'' These were men who ''have to live on their salaries'' and who ''hope for promotion,'' but whose ''day's work is not measured in profit.'' Claiming that ''It is no accident that the universities have begun to create graduate schools of business-administration,'' Lippmann argued that ''it is no longer possible to deal with the present scale of industry if your only equipment is what men used to call 'experience,' that is, a haphazard absorption of knowledge through the pores.'' Management, he saw, was becoming professionalized, and he made it clear that he was not sorry to see this occur.[11]

[11] Walter Lippmann, *Drift and Mastery: An Attempt to Diagnose the Current Unrest* [1914] (Englewood Cliffs, New Jersey: Spectrum, 1961), pp. 48-49; 42-43.

Thorstein Veblen also observed, in a work written just after World War I, that the "Captain of Industry"—the dynamic, powerful, risk-taking entrepreneur whose exploits are legendary in the history of American business—was a figure rapidly disappearing. His preeminence, he wrote, was "not past yet, so far as regards his place in popular superstition and in the make-believe of political strategy, but it is essentially a glory standing over out of the past, essentially a superstition. As regards the material actualities of life, the captain of industry is no longer the central and directive force in that business traffic that governs the material fortunes of mankind; not much more so than the Crown, the Country Gentleman, or the Priesthood."[12] Gradually the entrepreneur lost contact with the operations of large, complex firms whose size and output were constantly increasing. "By insensible degrees," Veblen explained, "as the volume of industry grew larger, employing a larger equipment and larger numbers of workmen, the business concerns necessarily also increased in size and in the volume of transactions, personal supervision of the work by the owners was no longer practicable, and personal contact and personal arrangements between the employer-owner and his workmen tapered off into impersonal wage contracts governed by custom and adjusted to the minimum which the traffic would bear."[13] Veblen succinctly summarized how industry and business "gradually split apart" and how "the tangible performance of so much work as the absentee owners considered to be wise, fell increasingly under the management of that line of technicians out of which there grew in time the engineering profession. . . ."[14] Furthermore, this process had not taken place quickly; it was a long-term and ongoing phenomenon.

Veblen considered the "absentee owners" parasites who served no function other than to drain off resources to their own use, chiefly in the form of "conspicuous consumption." The system of industrial organization was, he believed, wasteful, irrational, and inefficient because of this. Yet he all but dismissed the possibility of a forcible takeover of the industrial machinery by the engineers—those who, in his view, were concerned only with efficiency, technique, and a preoccupation whose existence he posited as a deeply ingrained tendency in humans: the "instinct of workmanship." He looked instead to a "self-made though reluctant abdication of the Vested Interests and their absentee owners," maintaining that it

---

[12] Thorstein Veblen, *The Portable Veblen*, edited by Max Lerner (New York: Penguin, 1976), pp. 377-378.

[13] Ibid., p. 381.

[14] Ibid., pp. 382-383.

should "cause no surprise to find that they will, in a sense, eliminate themselves, by letting go quite involuntarily after the industrial situation gets quite beyond their control. In fact, they have, in the present difficult juncture, already sufficiently shown their unfitness to take care of the country's material welfare—which is after all the only ground on which they can set up a colorable claim to their vested rights." Veblen suggested that "a discontinuance of the existing system of absentee ownership, on one plan or another, is no longer to be considered a purely speculative novelty." For the present, however, he cautioned that "just yet, the production engineers are a scattering lot of fairly contented subalterns, working piecemeal under orders from the deputies of the absentee owners."[15]

The idea that the separation of ownership and control meant not only a new assignment of tasks within the corporation, but also a phenomenon of great social and economic import gradually won acceptance among many economists and social theorists both in the United States and abroad. A few years after Veblen published his thoughts on the subject, J. M. Keynes wrote of "the trend of Joint Stock Institutions, when they have reached a certain age and size, to approximate to the status of public corporations rather than that of individualistic private enterprise," and the "tendency of big enterprise to socialize itself."[16] Keynes did not see this trend as an "unmixed gain," since "The same causes promote conservatism and a waning of enterprise." Believing that this new form of corporate organization contained within it "many of the faults as well as the advantages of State Socialism," he nevertheless interpreted this development as a "natural line of evolution."

Six years later, as interest in the issue continued to build and as the experience of the Great Depression strained the standard description of business structure and corporate behavior, Berle and Means's study emerged, providing empirical data to support a hypothesis that had previously been based largely on indirect evidence and impression. After a careful analysis of the concentration of stock ownership among the largest 200 corporations in America (based on gross assets), Berle and Means concluded that 44 percent of these firms were under the complete control of professional managers. In these corporations, the authors explained, the extreme dispersion of stock ownership in effect allowed shareholders only the options of not voting at all or of turning their votes over to a proxy

[15] Ibid., pp. 445, 464.

[16] J. M. Keynes, "The End of Laissez-Faire," in J. M. Keynes, *Essays in Persuasion* (New York: W. W. Norton, 1963), p. 314.

committee, leading them to write that "Since the proxy committee is appointed by the existing management, the latter can virtually dictate their own successors."[17] Like Keynes, Berle and Means believed that corporate control was being transferred not to a broad technocratic class, but to a narrower professional managerial elite. They were, however, uncertain as to precisely what this meant in terms of managerial and, ultimately, corporate behavior, deciding it was by no means obvious that corporations under managerial control sought maximum profits.[18] What is more, they concluded that if the primary goal of the managers was in fact personal profits, they might well, like Veblen's "absentee owner," adopt the role of plunderer or parasite. Since managers were not the main beneficiaries of increased earnings, "the controlling group even if they own a large block of stock, can serve their own pockets better by profiting at the expense of the company than by making profits for it."[19] What was obvious to Berle and Means was what they did *not* know about modern big business, and their book was not intended to provide a new theory of the corporation.

The next major work to deal with the problem of corporate control, James Burnham's *The Managerial Revolution*, was published in 1941. The thesis of the book was straightforward: capitalism had been in a state of irreversible decomposition for several decades, a condition the primary evidence for which Burnham found in the growing power of managerial specialists. "The completion of this process," he concluded, "means the elimination of the capitalists from control over the economy; that is, their disappearance as a ruling class."[20] Who were the new rulers? Burnham answered that

> Many different names are given them. We may often recognize them as "production managers," operating executives, superintendents, administrative engineers, supervisory technicians; or, in government (for they are to be found in governmental enterprise just as in private enterprise) as administrators, commissioners, bureau heads, and so on. I mean by managers, in short, those who already for the most part in contemporary

[17] Adolf A. Berle, Jr., and Gardiner C. Means, *The Modern Corporation and Private Property* (New York: Macmillan, 1932), p. 87.

[18] Ibid., pp. 121-122.

[19] Ibid., p. 122.

[20] James Burnham, *The Managerial Revolution: What Is Happening in the World* (New York: John Day, 1941), p. 78.

society are actually managing, on its technical side, the actual process of production, no matter what the legal and financial form—individual, corporate, governmental—of the process.[21]

Burnham believed that the supremacy of this new elite was inevitable, since "diverse tasks [in modern industry] must be organized, co-ordinated, so that the different materials, tools, machines, plants, workers are all available at the proper place and moment and in the proper numbers." He noted further that "This task of direction and co-ordination is itself a highly specialized function. Often it, also, requires acquaintance with the physical sciences (or the psychological and social sciences, since human beings are not the least among the instruments of production) and with engineering." He cautioned, however, that he was not speaking of scientists and engineers per se, whom he considered "merely highly skilled workers, no different in kind from the worker whose developed skill enables him to make a precision tool or operate an ingenious lathe," and faulted Veblen's inclusion of this group in the managerial elite.[22] The ideology of this elite was, he claimed, statist, work-oriented, and collectivist, while managers themselves were devoted to the goals of planning, order, discipline, and full employment. In addition, managers, as a rising group, sought power, were willing to make sacrifices and urged others to do so as well, and had an optimistic view of the future. They possessed, in other words, the drives, beliefs, and attitudes that once characterized a rising capitalist class that was now losing its power and was too demoralized and lacking in initiative to meet the world's social and economic needs and thereby regain its old position.

Burnham's dramatic presentation, conditioned by the experience of the Great Depression and the rise of Stalinism in the Soviet Union, fascism in several European nations, and the New Deal in the United States, had even less to say concerning the outlines of corporate structure and behavior or the relationship of the firm to society at large and to the state than did those of most of his predecessors. The reason for this is that Burnham was not primarily interested in these questions. For him, they were incidental to a larger process of political and social evolution—the gradual rise of a managerial elite on a global scale.

Thus, although several writers had speculated generally on the devel-

[21] Ibid., p. 80.
[22] Ibid., pp. 79-80.

opment of managerial control within the corporation, no theorist had by the middle of the twentieth century offered an alternative to the traditional theory of the firm, though many perceived a need for one, the effect of Keynesian theory, World War II, and the economic boom from the late 1940s to the late 1960s having been to divert the attention of most scholars and to shelve an issue that had both interested and troubled social thinkers for more than half a century.[23] Although interest began to revive to some degree by the late 1950s, Adolf Berle could still write in 1959: "Eventually, I suppose, a man will rise . . . who thinks out and writes down a *schema* of the American system in which we live."[24] This prediction proved accurate. During the next several years many schemas were advanced, both in America and abroad.[25] At the same time, the process of building a new theory of the firm was widely undertaken simultaneously by American economists and sociologists, after scattered beginnings in the late 1950s.[26] It was amid such a swirling controversy that another scholar, J. K. Galbraith, wrote *The New Industrial State*, a product of the long debate on the nature of modern corporate capitalism. How, then, shall its main thesis be judged?

[23] Peter F. Drucker's *The New Society: The Anatomy of the Industrial Order* (New York: Harper & Brothers, 1950) and Kenneth E. Boulding's *The Organizational Revolution: A Study in the Ethics of Economic Organization* (Chicago: Quadrangle, 1968), while interesting and important works on the general phenomenon of the rise of large, complex organizations in modern society, were not specifically concerned with the question of corporate structure and behavior.

[24] Adolf A. Berle, Jr., *Power without Property: A New Development in American Political Economy* (New York: Harvest, 1959), pp. 22-23.

[25] In America, some work amounted to little more than general outlines for future inquiry. One of these was Carl Kaysen's article "The Social Significance of the Modern Corporation," *The American Economic Review* 47 (May 1957), 311-319. Two Frenchmen who wrote on the more general problem of modern industrial society were Jacques Ellul, *The Technological Society* (New York: Vintage, 1964) and Raymond Aron, *The Industrial Society: Three Essays on Ideology and Development* (New York: Clarion, 1967). Two Britons, however, did tackle the specific question of modern capitalism and the large firm. One, Robin Marris, wrote *The Economic Theory of "Managerial" Capitalism* (New York: The Free Press of Glencoe, 1964), an influential work that rejected a good deal of the classical theory of the firm. The other, Andrew Shonfield, wrote *Modern Capitalism: The Changing Balance of Public and Private Power* (Oxford: Oxford University Press, 1965). Neither work, however, has the scope of Galbraith's *The New Industrial State*.

[26] See William J. Baumol, *Business Behavior, Value and Growth* (New York: Macmillan, 1959); Richard Caves, *American Industry: Structure, Conduct, Performance* (Englewood Cliffs, New Jersey: Prentice-Hall, 1964); Carl Kaysen, "The Social Significance of the Modern Corporation" and "Another View of Corporate Capitalism," *The Quarterly Journal of Economics* 79 (February 1965), 41-51. The latter article was accompanied in the same issue by two others: "Corporate Control and Capitalism" by Shorey Peterson (pp. 1-24) and "The Impact of the Corporation on Classical Economic Theory" by Adolf Berle (pp. 25-40).

THE CORPORATION IN HISTORICAL PERSPECTIVE:
GALBRAITH AND THE
RISE OF MANAGERIAL CAPITALISM

The crux of Galbraith's theory is that a class of technical specialists—a combination of Veblen's engineers and Burnham's managerial elite—has attained great power within the mature firm. Does such a class exist and does it possess such power? The answer, from all available evidence, must be "Yes, unquestionably." There can be no doubt that a transfer of corporate power to a new elite has gradually taken place in America. Indeed, Galbraith's only major shortcoming in this regard is his apparent conviction that the division of labor between owners and managers began for corporations generally when it did in the auto industry: that is, only well into the twentieth century. Actually, as American business historians have recently shown, the process leading to this arrangement was under way at least sixty years before the new century began.

The world of American business in 1840 was characterized by small, owner-controlled commercial firms and manufacturing enterprises that served local markets whose demand for their output was both quite limited and predictable. This world, whose central figure was the general merchant, was rapidly transformed during the next quarter century by two developments: the harnessing of a new form of energy—steam power—in machinery fueled by coal and the revolution in transportation produced by the building of a transcontinental railroad system. The greatly expanded production resulting from new technologies and the mass markets created by new systems of communication and transportation led inexorably to the evolution of large, specialized firms that strove relentlessly to eliminate the uncertainties and inefficiencies of a chaotic and segmented market system. Large firms in many fields attempted to bring markets under control partly by corporate merger, but more generally and with more comprehensive and permanent results through the integration of supply sources with production, distribution, marketing, and sales operations within a single enterprise. The benefits thus obtained—increased returns to scale, the economies associated with fewer intermediate transactions, reduced transportation, information, and capital costs, and a more reliable flow of goods and money—resulted in cheaper products in huge volumes to satisfy a mass market whose very existence in turn made such production feasible for large manufacturers.

The impact of these developments was not, however, merely economic.

There were more profound and far-reaching consequences. The replacement of the market by the administrative coordination of functions previously performed separately by many individual firms and now carried out by huge, complex, and rationalized business organizations also entailed, by its very nature, the creation of large staffs of professional managers and concomitant hierarchical structures of authority based on technical expertise. Such managerial influence was first seen in the internal organization of the first modern business institutions in America, the railroads, whose rapid development beginning in the middle of the nineteenth century marked the coming of modern corporate structure. But it was only in the third and fourth quarters of the last century that this structure became necessary and dominant in most areas of manufacturing and many areas of retailing.[27]

During the decades when these changes initially took hold, entrepreneurial capitalism barely altered its traditional structure and *modus operandi* at the executive level. At first, professional managers were hired only to carry out middle-echelon functions, while owners themselves continued to act as the top managerial elite. At this stage of development, as the business historian Alfred Chandler has noted,

> Top policy decisions continued to be made by the builders of the firm and their families who remained the major stockholders. They made the long-term plans and allocated the resources to carry them out. Ownership did not become separated from control because the entrepreneurs who built these enterprises had little need to raise capital through the sale of securities. The large volume of cash flow, supplemented by short-term loans from commercial banks, not only paid for inventory but also provided funds needed for plant and equipment.[28]

In such companies "the owner-managers carried out top management functions in a personal and intuitive manner," their firms operating without advanced, analytical cost and capital accounting techniques or long-term planning based on capital budgets and estimates of future market demand. As time passed this arrangement, as might be expected, became progressively inefficient. Although experts were slowly replacing owners in higher managerial positions, owners, their relatives, or their descend-

---

[27] The material in this section is taken largely from Chandler, *The Visible Hand*. Also see George R. Taylor, *The Transportation Revolution, 1815–1860*, vol. 4 of *Economic History of the United States* (New York: Rinehart, 1951), and Cochran, *200 Years of American Business*.

[28] Chandler, *The Visible Hand*, p. 238.

ants still controlled the ultimate decision-making apparatus of most large corporations until well into the twentieth century. As Chandler explains,

> These entrepreneurs and their families continued to look on their enterprises much as the owner-managers of traditional enterprises did. Where family members were no longer the chief executive or in other top management positions, close associates who had been personally selected by the family usually occupied these posts. The owner-managers prided themselves on their knowledge of a business they had done so much to build. They continued to be absorbed in the details of day-to-day operation. They personally reviewed the departmental reports and the statistical data. They had little or no staff to collect information and to provide expert advice. They promoted, hired, and fired their subordinates as often on personal whim as objective analysis.[29]

In a dynamic, complex, and rapidly developing economy, it was not likely that such a system of administration could endure. It did not.

By the time of World War I, the most obvious flaws in corporate organization had been corrected. The rationalization of corporate structure had proceeded *pari passu* with the movement of professional personnel into top managerial slots. Moreover, by this period neither owners nor their families nor their representatives were making or even attempting to make technical decisions at middle levels of authority. And, even more importantly, while the continued predominance of internal financing meant that owners still held a controlling amount of stock in the firm, they almost never became involved in corporate decision making at the level of top management. During the interval between the wars the trend toward bureaucratic organization and greater managerial control continued and was accelerated both by the advancing professionalization of managerial personnel and by the movement toward product diversification and the multidivisional corporate structure typified by General Motors.[30] By the 1950s this process was essentially complete: managerial control over daily operations in large, established firms was all but unchallenged at every level of corporate administration. Managerial capitalism, a form of business organization first seen over one hundred years before, had now achieved ascendancy in America. The attention Galbraith received and his considerable

[29] Ibid., p. 414.

[30] Ibid., chapters 12-14. Also see Peter F. Drucker's *Concept of the Corporation*, rev. ed. (New York: Mentor, 1975), an updated version of his classic 1946 study of General Motors.

success in advocating his model and theory of managerial control were therefore the result not only of his great abilities as a writer and social theorist, but also of the manifest nature of a sizable reality few could any longer deny.

Where, then, lies the controversy? The dispute does not center on the *existence* of managerial capitalism, but rather on what precisely the latter term means and implies. Critics of Galbraith's thesis admit that professional managers fully "control" the "mature" corporation in the sense that they make all tactical policy decisions (that is, all decisions that must be based on technical expertise), but maintain that this control does not extend to broader issues of corporate strategy. Charging that family control has not disappeared as fully as Galbraith and other writers have claimed, they argue that, although the formal organizational structure of entrepreneurial capitalism is no longer viable for the large firm, its ghost lives on and exerts palpable influence on managerial decisions. The old entrepreneurs that once personally ran these enterprises are, quite clearly, gone. Many have proposed, however, that their descendants or family representatives still own controlling shares of company stock that allow them, at a minimum, the negative power of a veto over policies of which they do not approve. And, since the interests of these major stockholders can be assumed to be almost purely pecuniary, critics deny that the primary goal of the corporation is in any way different from that of its entrepreneurial prototype. The main goal of both organizations is, they insist, maximum profits.

Those who have attacked the managerial-control thesis have most often based their challenge on the evidence marshaled by the managerialists. Some, for example, have questioned Berle and Means's assessment of the extent of managerial control among American firms.[31] Other scholars, such as Robert Larner, agree with the managerialists that owners have been effectively eliminated from power; yet they find no significant difference between management-controlled and owner-controlled firms in terms of the profit rates characteristic of each type of corporation. The results of his work suggest, in Larner's words, that "the nature of financial incentives and the structure of pecuniary rewards in management-controlled corporations are such that executive compensation and income have been tied to

---

[31] See, for example, Maurice Zeitlin, "Corporate Ownership and Control: The Large Corporation and the Capitalist Class," *American Journal of Sociology* 79 (March 1974), 1073-1119, and Philip H. Burch, Jr., *The Managerial Revolution Reassessed: Family Control in America's Large Corporations* (Lexington, Massachusetts: Lexington, 1972).

the diligence of managers in pursuing the interest and welfare of stock-holders.'' Indeed, Larner points out that managers are themselves often stockholders, whose income from dividends and rises in stock prices adds substantially to an already considerable salary. ''Although managers may hold only a small fraction of the outstanding common stock in the typical large corporation,'' he explains, ''still the dollar value of their stockhold-ings is large enough to give them an important stockholder interest in the enterprise they manage. Managers are thus a tiny (in numbers) subset within the larger set of all stockholders, and not a completely separate group with distinct interests that conflict with those of stockholders.'' Therefore despite the fact that, as he acknowledges, some studies confirm the managerialist proposition that growth has become the ultimate goal of corporate activity in mature firms, Larner is led to conclude that the effects of the separation of ownership and control regarding corporate goals and stockholder influence have been ''minor.''[32] Such criticism together with the absence of conclusive evidence to support the managerialist thesis have inevitably muddied the waters of the New Industrial State.

Another kind of criticism leveled at managerialist theory emphasizes the stockholdings of large institutional investors—banks, fire and casualty companies, insurance companies, mutual funds, and pension funds—which have, since World War II, been constantly growing as a proportion of total security holdings in large American firms.[33] David Kotz has noted the accumulation of corporate stock held by large institutions and most often controlled by the trust departments of commercial banks, especially on behalf of pension funds. Although giving a figure for the percentage of owner-controlled companies that is even lower than Larner's (Kotz's esti-mate is 13.5 percent), Kotz maintains that Larner mistakenly listed many firms as management-controlled that were really under *financial* control.[34] Meanwhile, Jeremy Rifkin and Randy Barber have reported that, in addi-tion to gaining influence in the corporate power structure, large commer-

[32] Robert J. Larner, *Management Control and the Large Corporation* (New York: Dunellen, 1970), pp. 61, 66.

[33] On the expansion of institutional stockholdings, see Raymond Goldsmith, *Institutional Investors and Corporate Stock: A Background Study* (New York: Columbia University Press, 1973).

[34] David M. Kotz, *Bank Control of Large Corporations in the United States* (Berkeley: Uni-versity of California Press, 1978), pp. 116-118. Kotz's study indicates that 34.8 percent of the 141 largest nonfinancial corporations in the United States in 1967–1969 were under financial control, 5.7 percent were controlled by both financial and owner interests, and 42.6 percent had no identifiable center of control (implying management control).

cial banks have obtained control of the huge capital reserves of union pension funds, using them to enhance their own economic power as well as to
subsidize the workings and coordinate the general interests of a corporate
capitalism that has become increasingly predatory and economically inefficient.[35] This position is in fact taken by almost all the aforementioned
critics of managerialist theory, who either explicitly or implicitly aver that
managerial capitalism has as its main objective the coordination and rationalization of corporate activity and power on behalf of a capitalist
elite.[36] Kotz, for example, declares that "the managerial stratum remains
what it was created to be: servants of the capitalists, although well-paid
and influential servants. The basis of economic power is not expertise but
ownership and control over abstract capital—that is, ultimate power re-
sides with the bankers who are the major stockholders in and the creditors
of the modern large corporation. It is still a plutocracy."[37] In a similar
vein, historian and social critic Christopher Lasch has taken scholars to
task for accepting a good deal of managerialist theory, writing that "They
repeat the mistake made by earlier students of the 'managerial revolution,'
who argued that managers constituted a 'new class.' In reality, both the
growth of management and the proliferation of professions represent new
forms of capitalist control, which enable capital to transcend its personal
form and to pervade every part of society."[38]

But opposition to managerialist theory has not come exclusively from
the left. Neoclassical theorists, quite naturally, have been in the forefront
of the attack. Paul Samuelson, the de facto dean of establishment economics, has succinctly stated the majority view of his profession:

> Experts are increasingly in demand. But Galbraith exaggerates the
> unilateral power that they can exercise. Those who control the plurality
> of stockholders' votes—themselves usually a minority—still call the
> tune. The minute the company hits upon hard times and slow growth,
> the whiz-kid expert is reminded of the layman's definition of the ex-
> pert—"a bastard from out of town." All this applies, as well, to the
> Soviet computer expert who gets too big for his breeches, or the Chinese

[35] Jeremy Rifkin and Randy Barber, *The North Will Rise Again: Pensions, Politics and Power in the 1980s* (Boston: Beacon, 1978). Zeitlin and Kotz also mention this phenomenon.

[36] This is also, of course, the Marxist and Marxist-Leninist position on managerial capitalism.

[37] Kotz, *Bank Control of Large Corporations*, p. 148.

[38] Christopher Lasch, *Haven in a Heartless World: The Family Besieged* (New York: Basic, 1979), p. 191.

physicist who begins to preach about world peace. The technostructure is put in its place by the men of ultimate power.[39]

Concerning the goals of the mature firm, Samuelson admits that "Large corporations do certainly have the elbow room for unilateral action denied to a small farmer or conventional family enterprise. They can give money to slum clearance. They can relax in their pursuit of profit. They can pursue growth even when it is more that of cancerous than of healthy cells." But, having made these concessions, he denies that mature corporations can behave in a manner radically different from that of entrepreneurial firms, noting that "If one minority group of management lets profits languish so that the common-stock holders do not get capital gains, another ring of capitalists will stage a successful 'takeover.' The new crew may not be gentlemen from Princeton, but this is the mixed economy's way of cutting its losses." Arguing that "the large firm is neither absolute monarch nor slave to impersonal market forces," Samuelson explains that "For every case where it pays some management to overstress growth at the expense of profitability, there is a case where losses are cut on activities that didn't work out. Only those who knew the old-fashioned owner-entrepreneur realize how often he failed to maximize profits in the pre-Berle-Means days, and how more commercially rational are modern corporate cost-minimizers and capital budgeters."[40]

Who has won the debate? Do we have, as both radical and orthodox theorists have argued, some version of a neoclassical system or instead, as Galbraith proposes, a "New Industrial State"? Paradoxically, the evidence, taken as a whole, indicates that we have neither—and both. To say that a period is an age of transition has become to some degree a cliché and a truism, and therefore almost meaningless. Yet this phrase is clearly accurate and, in fact, indispensable in any discussion of the present state of modern capitalism. What is becoming ever more obvious is that Galbraith and his critics have grasped and illuminated different parts of a complex reality that is still unfolding.

To begin, it seems clear that Galbraith and others have indeed overstated their case regarding the passing of stockholders' influence, the impotence of outside financial interests, and the power of the managerial and technical specialists who run the large corporation. Stockholders can no longer actively intervene in corporate affairs on a regular basis, and it is also true

[39] Samuelson, *Economics*, p. 512.
[40] Ibid.

that stock ownership has in general become greatly diffused, with majority ownership now almost nonexistent. But these conditions often make it even easier for individual or institutional shareholders with relatively small percentages of corporate stock to have a major impact on the firm. Moreover, aroused stockholders have periodically joined together to fire corporate officers whose performance has greatly displeased them.[41] It would also be premature to suppose that capitalists and their descendants have been mainly excluded from power in Western societies. Evidence that a relatively cohesive capitalist elite still exists, although in a weakened state, has been convincingly assembled by many researchers.[42] There can be little doubt that this elite regularly intervenes in both corporate affairs and politics to further its perceived interests, and that it remains the chief economic beneficiary of managerial capitalism. Professional managers and other technical personnel, though possessing power within the firm, have not gained full independence from stockholder and financial interests, whose influence exerts important constraints on their behavior.[43] Nor is it clear that they have always wished to do so. Far from challenging the present system of economic and political power, the vast majority of managers and technical experts would like nothing better than to enter it themselves. There is, in short, no reason to assume an irreconcilable conflict between capitalists and the technostructure. Just as the emerging bourgeoisie of premodern Europe built up economic power largely for the purpose of entering the upper ranks of feudal society (that is, the aristocracy), so have most managerial and technical specialists in modern capitalist society embraced

[41] As many observers have pointed out, there have been a significant number of corporate takeovers since the publication of *The New Industrial State*, and there is strong evidence that management personnel must be constantly aware of stockholders' desires. Shorey Peterson has pointed out that "At [stockholders'] meetings, stockholders, frequently highly knowledgeable, raise pertinent and sometimes embarrassing questions, occasionally with devastating effect. . . ." He also quotes an experienced executive who has written: "You can get up at the annual meeting and ask anything you want. The press will be there to listen. If your questions are embarrassing enough, and pungent enough, major changes will result. The management can be ousted through the anger that one stockholder can set off. . . . Every day of the year an expression, 'The stockholders would scream if we did that,' is heard echoing through the board rooms and the luncheon clubs of the financial community." (Peterson, "Corporate Control and Capitalism," p. 22.) It is true, however, that the greatest danger to managers is increasingly hostile takeovers by rival firms or by individual "corporate raiders," the most unscrupulous and infamous of whom in the mid-1980s was Ivan Boesky.

[42] See, for example, G. William Domhoff, *The Powers That Be: Processes of Ruling-Class Domination in America* (New York: Vintage, 1979).

[43] See Edward S. Herman, *Corporate Control, Corporate Power* (Cambridge: Cambridge University Press, 1982).

as a goal either status as independent entrepreneurs or, more likely, a line of steady ascent up the corporate hierarchy. In the short run, surely, this state of affairs—a system of shared power between the technostructure and the capitalist class, with the partial co-optation of the former into the latter—will continue.[44]

But in the long run this is likely to change. Just as the bourgeoisie eventually used their growing economic power and social status to gain political power on their own behalf, it may well happen that the technostructure will come fully to dominate both the planning system and society in general. It is also possible that the intelligentsia as a whole will consciously or unconsciously participate in this transformation. As a number of scholars have clearly shown, the "New Class" does exist and has increasingly become a major force in the years after World War II, especially since the explosion of higher education in the 1950s.[45] This development, as Everett Ladd and Charles Hadley have pointed out, has already led to an important and noticeable cleavage:

> [Entrepreneurial business] is no longer a major interest collectivity. Managerial business remains an important stratum. But it experiences peculiar fracturings which could not have been contemplated in earlier periods. Increasingly large segments of the broad new middle class, of the professional and managerial community—primarily those at once the most affluent and secure and most closely associated with advanced technology—cease to function as defenders of business values. More to

[44] Again, such a bipolar system of power finds a direct homology in the history of modern Europe, since even after the aristocracy lost much of its political power and legitimacy in the liberal revolutions of the late eighteenth and early nineteenth centuries, it still shared political and, to a significant extent, economic power with the newly ascendant bourgeoisie until World War I swept away almost all that remained of the old order.

[45] Ladd and Hadley define this new elite in the following manner: "College training . . . defines the outer boundaries of the intelligentsia. We use *intelligentsia* to include those persons whose background and vocation associates them directly in the application of trained intelligence. It includes, that is, not only intellectuals—people involved in the creation of new ideas, new knowledge, new cultural forms—but as well that larger community whose training gives them some facility in handling abstract ideas, or whose work requires them to manipulate ideas rather than things. Thus, school teachers, scientific and technical workers, the burgeoning managerial class which directs the bureaucracies both private and public, people involved in other aspects of the 'knowledge industry' than teaching such as editorial staff of newspapers, magazines, and television networks, college-trained housewives who maintain a keen interest in cultural and political ideas although at least temporarily out of the labor force—all these and others in comparable positions comprise the stratum." Everett Carll Ladd, Jr., and Charles D. Hadley, *Transformations of the American Party System: Political Coalitions from the New Deal to the 1970s* (New York: W. W. Norton, 1975), p. 186 n.8.

the point, they cease to think of themselves as "business" in the historic sense. They become incorporated into a rising new class, the intelligentsia, responding to intellectual values and orientations rather than those traditionally associated with business. At the same time, part of the business community, especially those linked to newer enterprises and the top managers, continue to promote business values and reflect relative conservatism.[46]

What is new about this stratum is not, of course, its existence, but rather its growing size, its access to media and a vast communications network, and its increasing functional importance in managing advanced societies.

Picking up this theme, sociologist Alvin Gouldner has argued that a New Class composed of a technical intelligentsia and critical intellectuals has indeed acquired a great deal of power and is slowly replacing the old business elite. He correctly observes that the crucial issue in analyzing the trajectory of managerial capitalism is not the proportion of management-controlled firms that exists at any given time, but the *secular trend* of such a number, a vector whose direction and magnitude clearly point toward the growing power of the New Class.[47] In contrast to Christopher Lasch, who sees the evolution of the welfare state with its massive social service bureaucracy as a device used by a capitalist ruling elite to ensure its own domination and even extend its influence by eroding all nonpecuniary social and familial ties and values, Gouldner sees the establishment of this new state apparatus as the result of the political strategy and ideology of the New Class. Responding to Lasch's interpretation of this phenomenon, Gouldner remarks: "Lasch clearly shows the growing influence of various 'helping' professions over the family but, without the least justification, assumes that this is all fundamentally in the service of capitalism and its *old* class. If so, one wonders why they dislike footing the resultant tax bill?"[48] Gouldner writes of the "growing split between the old line bu-

---

[46] Ibid., p. 185.

[47] Alvin W. Gouldner, *The Future of Intellectuals and the Rise of the New Class* (New York: Seabury, 1979), p. 13. Philip Burch, for instance, admits that on the basis of past developments the proportion of large American corporations under management control has been increasing at a rate of between 3 to 5 percent per decade. (Burch, *The Managerial Revolution Reassessed*, p. 104.) At this rate the technostructure, by Burch's own calculation, will have attained full power in a majority of these corporations by the end of the century. Gouldner also catches anti-managerialist critics in a peculiar and revealing contradiction. When attacking the theory of managerial control, these critics assert that absentee owners can decisively influence broad lines of corporate policy. Yet when discussing pension funds through which unions own substantial amounts of corporate stock, they often turn abruptly about and deny that this kind of "ownership" means anything. Who, they ask, really *controls* the corporation?

[48] Gouldner, p. 105.

reaucrats and the technical intelligentsia'' and the fact that ''It becomes ever more difficult even for those *managing* the organization simply to understand the skills of the New Class, let alone to exert an ongoing, close control over them.''[49] Calling attention to the tripartite division of responsibility in all modern bureaucratic organizations, he describes the fundamental conflict that arises in such circumstances: ''The technical intelligentsia of the New Class is controlled by those incompetent to judge its performance and whose control, therefore, is experienced as irrational. The New Class intelligentsia, then, feel a certain contempt for their superiors; for they are not competent participants in the careful discourse concerning which technical decisions are made.'' The New Class, he continues, is controlled by two groups: first, the ''bureaucratic officialdom'' directly above them, and second, ''political appointees'' at the top of the organization who ''represent money capital or politically reliable 'commissars,' '' an arrangement that ''systematically generates tensions.''[50]

Indeed, Galbraith is himself open to criticism for neglecting the dimension of tension and disharmony in the process of social change. His theory seems to suggest a quantum leap from one set of stable social structures to another and is, in this sense, a static and functionalist interpretation of organizational and social evolution. There need not be, as Galbraith claims, ''consistency in the goals of the society, the organization and the individual,'' nor need there be ''consistency in the motives which induce organizations and individuals to pursue these goals''—at least not at any particular time, and especially not during a period of rapid social transformation. It follows from this, of course, that the goals of the mature corporation may *not* be a perfect reflection of the goals of the technostructure, even if—and this is doubtful—the latter were an entity with a unified set of goals.

However, the revelation of a dialectical process of accommodation, conflict, and change within large organizations in the works of many scholars points out the weakness of the view that the technostructure is almost to-

[49] Ibid., p. 50.

[50] Ibid., pp. 51-52. Galbraith, it must be said, is not totally oblivious to these divisions. See Myron E. Sharpe, *John Kenneth Galbraith and the Lower Economics*, 2d ed. (New York: International Arts and Sciences, 1974), p. 101. I believe, however, that my criticism is still valid.

It should also be mentioned that the rise of the New Class is not ignored in socialist and communist countries. Marxist-Leninist scholars in the Soviet Union, for example, have written extensively on the historical significance of the rise of the technical intelligentsia. See D. M. Gvishiani, S. R. Mikulinskii, and S. A. Kugel, eds., *The Scientific Intelligentsia in the USSR: Structure and Dynamics of Personnel* (Moscow: Progress, 1976) and V. G. Afanasev, *The Scientific and Technological Revolution—Its Impact on Management and Education* (Moscow: Progress, 1975).

tally subordinate to market, stockholder, and organizational pressures. This, I maintain, is intuitively implausible. It is certainly not self-evident.[51] It is to Galbraith's credit that, if he left the historical unfolding of this process largely unexamined, he nevertheless made it clear that the interests and goals of important new social groups cannot be deemed irrelevant in any useful and believable theory of social change. In any case, the plethora of conflicting studies in this field have raised the distinct possibility that there is as yet no completely satisfactory theory of modern bureaucratic corporations. Galbraith himself has been quite open-minded on this issue, and his detractors might do well to adopt a similar attitude.[52]

What have been Galbraith's other chief accomplishments? One of them has clearly been his insight into the evolution of oligopolistic markets and big business and their relation to other institutional developments and to modern industrial society in general. It is not true, as some have maintained, that Galbraith's theory of oligopolistic market behavior and the mature firm is a mere popularization or rehash of findings already established. One of his intellectual biographers has noted, for example, that "Galbraith's anatomy of the mature corporation goes beyond the theoretical framework of the microeconomics of the Chamberlin-Robinson tradition," and that while other economists have developed new theories of the modern firm, "few have related the larger dynamics of the industrial sys-

---

[51] If Galbraith can be accused of technological determinism, scholars like David F. Noble can be taken to task for neglecting the imperatives of technology and the relative autonomy of professional groups and institutions. In his book *America by Design: Science, Technology, and the Rise of Corporate Capitalism* (New York: Knopf, 1977) Noble concludes that the development of science and technology in early twentieth-century America was profoundly affected and carefully guided by capitalist groups, institutions, and values. But while he clearly shows the exertion of control by the forces of corporate capitalism over technical specialists and their work during this era, neither his evidence nor his argument invalidates a theory of growing technocratic power. Obviously, new technologies and social strata must evolve in *some* kind of economic, social, and cultural milieu, and existing dominant social classes and organizations will attempt to co-opt these new forces and groups and to adapt their roles to their own purposes. To some degree, they are always successful, at least initially. Thus, Noble's almost tautologous demonstration that the new technologies and elites early in this century served the purposes of corporate capitalism is not surprising—indeed, any *other* conclusion would be. The point is that groups and institutions sooner or later press to further their own interests and values, which tend to be asserted ever more strongly as these groups gain in social importance and legitimacy.

[52] Concerning corporate goals, Galbraith has cautioned that "It's a mistake to search for a unique solution to this problem. We are dealing with the order of a thousand corporations, some larger, some smaller, some more powerful, some less powerful, some more technically oriented than others, some extensions of the state, as in the case of General Dynamics or Lockheed. No one should conclude that the goal-structure of all these firms will be the same." Sharpe, *John Kenneth Galbraith*, p. 102.

tem to the rest of American society as vividly and lucidly as he. . . ."[53] Like all innovative thinkers, Galbraith has borrowed much from theorists of the past. But his reformulations of existing ideas and their synthesis with new ones distilled from the realities of the late twentieth century have had a great impact on the present generation of intellectuals and the broader public, and have played a significant part in bringing many of them—albeit often kicking and screaming—into the modern era of advanced corporate capitalism.

Another of Galbraith's major achievements has been his successful effort to demonstrate the crucial role of managerial and technical experts in the evolution of corporate capitalism into its present form. Until relatively recently, histories of American business had focused almost entirely on the trials, tribulations, and miscellaneous exploits of famous (and sometimes infamous) entrepreneurial wizards and buccaneers, meanwhile ignoring the most important development of all: the rise of a class of managerial and technical specialists and a transformation that left in its wake an economic system greatly different from the one described in classical theory. While not searching far enough back in time for the origins of this transformation, Galbraith has nevertheless produced works that have prompted scholars to give these origins and the role of managerial personnel in American capitalism the emphasis they deserve. What is more, his writings on the development of managerial capitalism have provoked a lively and important debate on the similarities and differences among modern American, European, and Japanese forms of corporate enterprise and their roots, as well as on the nature of modern bureaucratic organizations in general.[54]

---

[53] Charles H. Hession, *John Kenneth Galbraith and His Critics* (New York: New American Library, 1972), pp. 210-211. It is precisely the unrealistic nature of the models and theories of establishment economics, increasingly unable to account for phenomena in the actual world of imperfect competition and bureaucratic firms, that has prompted the humorous but nonetheless meaningful witticism, "Among economists, the real world is often a special case."

[54] For instance, it is readily acknowledged by most researchers that in Japan profit maximization is *not* the primary goal of corporate managers. For a variety of economic, social, and cultural reasons, large Japanese firms, many scholars have forcefully argued, prefer steady growth to an all-stops-out push for profit. See, for example, Peter F. Drucker, "Economic Realities and Enterprise Strategy," in Ezra F. Vogel, *Modern Japanese Organization and Decision-Making* (Berkeley: University of California Press, 1975), pp. 228-248. Also see Edwin O. Reischauer, *The Japanese* (Cambridge: Harvard University Press, Belknap, 1977), pp. 179-195.

In view of the countless man-hours spent on model building and empirical reseach directly related to Galbraith's ideas, the allegation of many that his theories have generated few testable hypotheses is indeed strange.

Finally, we have seen that, although Galbraith's theoretical propositions have not all been verified, this is not always because they do not have great merit, but because the sea change that is engulfing modern market societies is incomplete. Seemingly contradictory views may in such circumstances be found to reflect, on closer examination, not totally incompatible evaluations, but differences of emphasis traceable to different theoretical perspectives on a reality that is itself often contradictory. In short, much of the divergence between the views of Galbraith and those of his critics on the nature of modern capitalism is comparable to that which might arise if two biologists, one highly conscious of Darwinian principles, the other not, were to encounter the first amphibians who ventured tentatively upon dry land millions of years ago. While the latter biologist might point out—with much justification—that these creatures share many of the physical and behavioral attributes of fish and cannot move far or for long periods from the water, the former would argue with equal vehemence that these animals represent a new and important form of life and that their anatomical structure and manner of living differ radically from those of their piscine ancestors. Galbraith is, obviously, a Darwinian, although one who often sees hair and lungs where perhaps he ought still to see scales and gill slits.

J. K. Galbraith has rightly earned, but has not always been given, recognition as a major figure in American intellectual history, ranking equally with Veblen as a critic and scholar. Indeed, his work has placed him firmly in the institutionalist tradition begun by Veblen. No less than Veblen, he has refused to ignore the element of power in economic relationships or the irrationalities and wastefulness of an industrial system whose overriding concern is the individual aggrandizement and conspicuous consumption of its members. He has also, like Veblen, exhibited an acute sensitivity to the dynamics of social evolution that has allowed him to perceive and examine changes that others had denied and to adopt the perspective of an alien observer, viewing accepted and conventional beliefs and institutions with an eye for their anthropological peculiarity, historical impermanence, and evolutionary development. Galbraith has, in short, played a truly unique role in postwar social thought. As Paul Samuelson, his sometime critic, has written: "The objective scholar must assert that economics will never quite be the same as in the days before the Galbraith triology."[55] Neither, one should add, will American social theory.

[55] Samuelson, *Economics*, p. 512.

THE THINKERS

II The Ironic Quest: Michael Harrington and the Socialist Dream

Werner Sombart, 1906

If, as I have myself always maintained and often stated, modern Socialism follows as a necessary reaction to capitalism, the country with the most advanced capitalist development, namely the United States, would at the same time be the one providing the classic case of Socialism, and its working class would be supporters of the most radical of Socialist movements. However, one hears just the opposite of this asserted from all sides and in all sorts of tones. . . . In fact, an assertion of this kind cannot fail to awaken our most active interest, for here at last is a country with no Socialism, despite its having the most advanced capitalist development. The doctrine of the inevitable Socialist future is refuted by the facts. For the Socialist theorist as well as for the social legislator nothing can be more important than to get to the root of this phenomenon.

Michael Harrington, 1965

With the exception of the United States, socialism is what the most democratic forces in the West call their dream.

Michael Harrington

Chapter 5   *The New Poverty*

By the late 1950s most American intellectuals had apparently come to terms with the new order to which capitalism had given birth. With the exception of Galbraith, few serious thinkers had broken with the verities of the past, instead remaining wedded to the revitalized liberal doctrine first enunciated by Lippmann and Croly and now seemingly confirmed by America's spectacular postwar economic success. Even Galbraith, while breaking with liberal tradition to an ever greater degree as his ideas evolved, did not adopt a literally radical rethinking of liberal theory (that is, one that proceeded from its philosophical roots) until the early 1970s. Even then, he continued to accept the inevitably disproportionate power of the technostructure; he essentially rejected the notion of the working class as one of the primary agents of social change in the modern world; and he accepted hierarchical, bureaucratic organization as the dominant institutional form of modern industrial society.

Yet there has long been an alternative intellectual framework in the United States that has given pointedly different answers to questions involving social welfare, power, social change, hierarchy, and legitimacy. Unlike the European version of this philosophy, its American counterpart has not exercised significant influence in the last half century. It remains, nonetheless, in spite of its myriad forms and guises, the only relatively coherent and fully articulated institutional alternative to modern capitalism—one whose very existence is felt by many in America as a warning and a threat, but which for others is instead what it once was for relatively large numbers of Americans: a cherished dream and a noble quest for justice and democracy. For them the dream still exists. The quest goes on.

Prologue: Poverty in American History

We have already observed that the rebirth of American capitalism after World War II had left its once confident critics confounded and confused. Yet, although many now believed large-scale economic deprivation to be a thing of the past—especially in view of the undeniable surge in average real income during these years—it was becoming increasingly evident to others that this hopeful view was not well-founded. When President Lyndon Johnson visited Appalachia at the beginning of 1964 to build political and popular support for his proposed War on Poverty, he was genuinely shocked by what he saw, as his predecessor, John F. Kennedy, had been a few years before. ''I saw the poor that day in Appalachia with my own eyes,'' he later recalled. ''And I believe that through my eyes, and through the eyes of reporters and photographers who traveled with me, all America saw them too: the gaunt, defeated men whom the land had abandoned; their tired, despairing wives; their pale, undernourished children—all holding up homemade signs of welcome as we visited their hills. I will not forget them.'' Having spoken to one of these people, a man who was trying to support a family of nine on a yearly income of four hundred dollars, Johnson noted how ''The tragic inevitability of the endless cycle of poverty was summed up in that man's fear: poverty forcing children out of school and destroying their best chance to escape the poverty of their fathers.''[1]

This was not, of course, the first time Americans had discovered—or rediscovered—poverty in their land. Sixty years before, Robert Hunter, whose classic book *Poverty* helped spur on the Progressive movement, had deplored the fact that ''There are probably in fairly prosperous years no less than 10,000,000 persons in poverty; that is to say, underfed, underclothed, and poorly housed.''[2] And, sixty years before *this*, R. C. Waterston had told a church meeting: ''In the crowded metropolis how many a desolate hovel, and damp, dark cellar, gives shelter to human life! Thus, amid congregated thousands, the desolate widow may weep in solitude, and orphan children sigh for a home.''[3]

Clearly, America is no stranger to poverty. The difference in the 1960s was that, while Americans had never quite been able to reconcile themselves to the reality of poverty in their country, its coexistence with an unprecedented and extraordinary general prosperity was a fatal blow to their lingering belief that involuntary poverty was not only rare, but most often the result of character defects—principally sloth. The new con-

[1] Lyndon Baines Johnson, *The Vantage Point: Perspectives of the Presidency, 1963–1969* (New York: Popular Library, 1971), p. 79.

[2] Robert Hunter, *Poverty* (New York: Macmillan, 1904), p. 337. Also see Robert H. Bremner, *From the Depths: The Discovery of Poverty in the United States* (New York: New York University Press, 1956).

[3] R. C. Waterston, ''An Address on Pauperism, Its Extent, Causes, and the Best Means of Prevention; Delivered at the Church in Bowdoin Square, February 4, 1844,'' in David J. Rothman, ed., *Poverty, U.S.A.: The Historical Record—The Jacksonians on the Poor: Collected Pamphlets* (New York: Arno Press and The New York Times, 1971), fifth section, pp. 42-43.

sciousness of poverty in the 1960s and the determination of government leaders to take the previously unheard-of step of consciously and directly using state power and resources to end it was the result of many influences. Among them was the publication of a book in 1962 that exposed and illuminated this condition as had no work of social research and criticism since the days of progressivism, a book that brought forth, by turns, disbelief and shame in the millions who read it or heard of it. Within the next several years its author, a thirty-four-year-old social worker and political activist, would gradually become not only one of America's foremost social critics, but also the chief representative of American socialism.

CHRISTIANITY AND CONSCIENCE: THE MAKING OF A SOCIALIST

Like Norman Thomas, the man whose place he would one day take as America's premier socialist, Edward Michael Harrington was born into a religious, Midwestern, middle-class family in 1928. Although his family was Irish at a time when such a circumstance could have easily meant economic and cultural deprivation, there was little of the strong union of ethnic and class identification common among the Irish of the East Coast. Moreover, Harrington's relatives were well integrated into the community, both economically and socially. His grandfather, he has written, "lived in a big three-story house and grew roses in the back yard." One uncle was a judge, another a corporate lawyer. His father was a patent attorney and his mother had a master's degree in economics from St. Louis University. The son of New Deal Democrats, Harrington grew up in what he has described as a "happy, secure and relatively unresentful world," yet one that retained more than a vestigial intellectual and emotional remnant of the struggle against "British imperialists, Yankee bosses, [and] Protestant princes."[4]

The result of this repressed but still existent in-group feeling was pressure for intellectual accomplishment, a goal that Harrington pursued both at high school in St. Louis and at Holy Cross College at the exacting hands of the Jesuits, an elite Roman Catholic religious order founded as part of the Counter-Reformation and known for its long and arduous intellectual preparation (fifteen years of training, including three years of philosophy

---

[4] Michael Harrington, *Fragments of the Century* (New York: Saturday Review Press/E. P. Dutton, 1973), p. 7. Subsequently cited parenthetically as *FC*.

and four years of theology), its rigorous standards of argument, and its militant commitment to church principles and the dissemination of both theological and secular knowledge. It was the Jesuits who, Harrington wrote, "spearheaded the Catholic movement that emerged as the medieval synthesis was disintegrating and which consciously sought to adapt the old values to the new, capitalist society." They were, he proposed, "the modern critics of the modern world," with a "temptation to heresy . . . [that] was rationalist" (FC, 9). Within a few years of his departure from Holy Cross, Harrington was to reject the theological content of the schooling he had received there, as well as the scholastic, almost catechismal form it had often taken. Nevertheless, his religious education was profoundly to influence his approach to life, to ideas, and to his concept of the relationship between the two, having emphasized, he later recalled, that "knowledge was not free floating; it was always consciously related to ethical and religious values." "The Jesuits," he wrote, "were convinced that ideas have consequences, that philosophy is the record of an ongoing debate over the most important issues before mankind." His subsequent life and social thought were thus indelibly imprinted by the "Jesuit inspiration of [my] adolescence that insisted so strenuously that a man must live his philosophy" (FC, 11,13).

Interestingly, Harrington's philosophy at the time of his graduation was "Taft conservat[ism]." It was, moreover, a conservatism he defended at Yale Law School, which he attended from 1947 to 1948. Gradually, however, his ideas underwent a dramatic change, at least part of whose impetus was paradoxically grounded in the almost rabid anti-socialism of the Jesuits, who had "taught that socialism was immoral because it denied the right of every family to that private property which was necessary to raise children in Christian decency." But the intellectual climate at Yale was to help impart a radically different content to the theological imperative he had internalized at Holy Cross. Yale during these years was staffed by liberal professors and attended mostly by returned veterans, the majority of whom were left-liberals, followers of Henry Wallace, or socialist and communist members of the Old Left of the 1930s. Thus it is not surprising that, on the day he left law school Harrington "switched from Taft Republicanism to democratic socialism without even bothering to tarry a while in the liberal camp in between." He had by now reversed his view of socialism as a system that denied people the right to a decent life. "At Yale," he wrote in his autobiography, "I realized that it was capitalism, not socialism, that denied that right" (FC, 64, 65). Then, at the University of Chicago, where he had transferred to do graduate work in English literature, Harrington found himself in discussions with, among others, Aristotelians and anti-Aristotelians. He "read like a madman to catch up" with his classmates, in the process taking himself yet further from his intellectual roots.

At this point, however, Harrington's conversion to socialism was not based on a deeply felt or thoroughly reasoned belief in socialist philosophy. Indeed, he was later to see his original attraction to socialism as a mixture of "profundities, limitations, inconsistencies—and occasional silliness." His interests having now turned to poetry rather than law, Harrington made a half-reasoned connection among the artistic avant-garde, sexual freedom, and socialist thought, adding a "distinctly aesthetic and elitist dimension" to his leftist leanings reminiscent of what has been called the "Lyrical Left" of the early twentieth century. Like many members of that group, he had come to believe that "Capitalism was not so much cruel and exploitative as crass and vulgar: the bourgeois was hated as a boor rather than as a thief. Thus I thought it only mildly embarrassing to go to a large debutante party at a country club in St. Louis and sit in front of a swimming pool filled with flowers and drink some rich father's whiskey while trying to convince a friend that capitalism was a rotten system" (*FC*, 65).

These feelings and experiences, together with a sympathy for Zionism, had taken Harrington to socialism in the form of a temperamental persuasion divorced from any fully constituted or comprehensive theory or from any practical consequences. But what might have remained only a temporary attraction born of youthful rebellion or, at most, a privately held set of abstract ideas separated from life was soon to become something quite different. After receiving an M.A. degree at the University of Chicago, Harrington had an experience that would dramatically change his life. In the fall of 1949, needing money so that he could travel to New York to write poetry, he obtained a position in the Public Welfare Department of the St. Louis Public Schools through the political influence of a cousin. He was assigned to an old school that had been built in the midst of a "Hooverville" that still stood from the 1930s. As he later explained:

> One rainy day I went into an old, decaying building. The cooking smells and the stench from the broken, stopped-up toilets and the murmurous cranky sound of the people were a revelation. It was my moment on the road to Damascus. Suddenly the abstract and statistical and aesthetic

outrages I had reacted to at Yale and Chicago became real and personal and insistent. A few hours later, riding the Grand Avenue streetcar, I realized that somehow I must spend the rest of my life trying to obliterate that kind of house and to work with the people who lived there.

When I arrived in New York in the fall of 1949 I was still vague about exactly what I was going to do and the drive to write poetry was important to me. As I was running out of money that winter, I took a job as a writer-trainee at *Life* magazine. The personnel director, Jim Crider, was prophetic. He told me that he had been against hiring me but had been overruled by the editors. I asked him why he didn't want me on the staff. "Because," Crider replied, "you are not our kind of person." He was right. Six months later I quit and in less than a year I was at the Catholic Worker. (*FC*, 66)

The Catholic Worker, an organization within the lay apostolate, was founded by Dorothy Day, herself a former member of the Lyrical Left, at the depth of the Great Depression. It was, Harrington noted, "the center for all of the innovative currents within American Catholicism: trade unionism, utopianism, liturgical reform, and interracialism" (*FC*, 21). Beyond this, Harrington knew little of the organization, except that it was "as far left as you could go within the Church." "I did not even know," he later remembered,

> that the Worker was committed to voluntary poverty or that the "staff" shared rooms, clothes, and food with the alcoholics and drifters who were admitted on a first-come-first-served basis. I asked for a job and a young lady told me, "You can work here, but we can't pay you anything." That sounded fine to me and I stayed for almost two years. There were about fifty people living in the house, and breadlines twice a day. Our ideal was "to see Christ in every man," including the pathetic, shambling, shivering creature who would wander in off the streets with his pants caked with urine and his face scabbed with blood. (*FC*, 18)

But members of the Worker's various branches did more than just charity work. They actively and frequently engaged in discussions of innovative Catholic philosophers as well as theorists and writers such as Marx, Dostoevsky, and Freud. After one such discussion at which the social critic Dwight Macdonald was present to do research on Dorothy Day, he told Harrington that "it reminded him of a Trotskyist debate in the thirties, except that the points of reference were Augustine and Aquinas, not Marx and Engels'' (*FC*, 19). Harrington became a staff member of a Bowery settlement house and an associate editor of the *Catholic Worker*, the journalistic organ of the Catholic left. During his stay at the Worker, Harrington participated in an antiwar march (he was a conscientious objector during the Korean War), and through this and other activities was drawn closer to the organizational remnants of the once vibrant American left. Having come to reject Catholic theology, he left settlement work and joined the Young Socialist League.

By the 1950s the socialist movement in America had long been in total disarray, an opposition shattered into countless tiny splinter sects and only the merest shadow of its former self. It was in this milieu that Harrington met its leaders and continued to broaden his understanding of socialist thought. He had meanwhile become a respected and energetic leader within New York radical circles, an informal position whose responsibilities included speaking and organizational work throughout the United States (mainly on college campuses), but which also involved participating in demonstrations in favor of unpopular causes and against American, British, and Soviet foreign policies. ''I was usually assigned to be the picket captain because I was Irish,'' he was to later recall. ''The police would aggressively demand our leader. I would step forward, and they would ask my name. There was usually a stunned silence when I answered and then some remark like, 'Michael, my boy, what are you doing with *these* people?' '' (*FC*, 69).

Living in Greenwich Village during the mid-1950s, Harrington met with radicals of all persuasions. Like all political groups, but especially those not popular in society as a whole, the radicals of the 1950s needed both the mutual support of those who shared their views and the institutional settings in which they could meet and discuss their ideas. For New York leftists, the latter was provided by a nighttime haunt called the White Horse Tavern, frequented by people such as Bernard Cornfeld (then a socialist), Daniel Patrick Moynihan, James Baldwin, Norman Mailer, and Bob Dylan. ''I was in the Horse every night for more than ten years,'' Harrington remembered:

As the people of Konigsberg were said to set their clocks by Immanuel Kant's walks, you would see me, punctually dissolute, appear on week nights at midnight and on weekends at one o'clock. At two in the morning you could usually observe me engaged in an intense conversation of no great importance and at a distance I must have seemed one of Gaddis' squatters. But if I slept until eleven or noon every day, I worked for twelve hours after I got up, reading, writing, or doing socialist organizing. (*FC*, 48)

An observer who had encountered Harrington at a distance during those days has written that "he was intriguing and a little disconcerting—a former Roman Catholic (was he still? nobody was sure) who was a member of the Socialist party, a young Irishman who stood in an oddly filial relationship to the older generation of the New York radical movement. Consciously or not, he had incorporated their style into his own: he liked cafeterias, he talked with his hands, he dentalized his d's and t's. . . . Withal, he looked unmistakably Irish, with the blue-eyed, waif-like pallor and the narrow face of those small boys in blue blazers outside St. Ignatius Loyola at recess time." Indeed, Harrington seemed to some an anachronism, a kind of intellectual time traveler who "evoked an ambiance of the past— of the 1930s. . . . The oddest thing, however, was that he was not at all . . . eccentric."[5]

Members of the socialist group to which Harrington belonged were known as Shachtmanites, that is, followers of Max Shachtman, an American communist who had rejected a nascent Stalinism in the late 1920s and had helped to found American Trotskyism. A close associate of Trotsky, Shachtman traveled with the former Bolshevik leader in Europe after his expulsion from the Soviet Union, wearing sidearms in fear of Stalin's assassins. But by 1939 Shachtman had broken with Trotsky over the issue of the basic nature of the Soviet state and its class structure. Trotsky, in spite of his opposition to Stalinism, continued to defend the Soviet Union as a progressive society. Admitting that the working class had lost its power to a bureaucratic elite, Trotsky argued that this was a temporary phenomenon, and that the regime still objectively functioned on behalf of the workers. Shachtman saw things differently:

Shachtman [Harrington wrote] developed a theory of bureaucratic collectivism in opposition to Trotsky. The state in Russia, Shachtman said, did indeed own the means of production but that did not make it progressive. Where the state owns the means of production, he argued, the crucial question becomes: Who owns the state? There is only one way for the people to own the state—through political democracy and

---

[5] *Current Biography*, 1969, p. 197.

the consequent right to change the policies and personnel of the state. The Soviet bureaucracy, he therefore held, was not a caste temporarily ruling in the name of the workers; it was a new class, the first examplar of a new form of society that was both anti-capitalist and anti-socialist. (*FC*, 73-74)

Harrington found Shachtman's argument—later popularized by Shachtman's associate James Burnham—totally convincing. Moreover, he came to see in Shachtman's theory the possibility of authoritarian and bureaucratic regimes arising not only in the Soviet Union, but—under crisis conditions—in the Third World and, "with the integration of the corporations and the state," in advanced capitalist nations as well, leading him to a "basic proposition: that the future is not going to be a choice between capitalism, Communism, and socialism, but between bureaucratic collectivism, advantageous to both executives and commissars, and democratic collectivism, i.e., socialism" (*FC*, 75-76). This idea was to become a theoretical leitmotiv in Harrington's own thought and writings.

POVERTY AMID PLENTY: *The Other America*

Harrington would one day describe himself in the 1950s as an "itinerant socialist agitator," yet this was only one aspect of his life and work during these years. As a researcher for the Fund for the Republic, he worked on, among other things, a study of blacklisting in the entertainment industry and also wrote extensively on Marxism and communism in journals such as *Dissent* and *Commentary*. "When I could get a plane ticket from the Fund in order to do some work for it," he later wrote, "I would leapfrog from New York to Los Angeles, speaking to socialist groups on the way. More often than not I traveled by bus or hitched rides. . . . But the truly climactic, and most emotional, journey for me took place during the fall of 1958" (*FC*, 88).

Harrington's journey was to take him within a period of three months to every corner of the United States on a whirlwind speaking, fact-finding, and meeting-filled tour that he was later to see as a "personal and political epiphany." But the trip was not special simply as a result of what he was to see and do. As he later recalled, its unusual nature was to no small degree bound up with its historical context. "The sixties," he wrote, "were beginning to stir within the fifties." With the retreat of McCarthyism, the rise of the black and student movements, and the election of the liberal "Class of '58" to Congress, socialists "had the opportunity to become part of a vibrant development and found, *mirabile dictu*, that the theories we had been debating . . . actually referred to reality" (*FC*, 88-89). Thus, after a period of postwar conservatism, America—although few then realized it—was moving into its third major reform cycle of the twentieth century.

Among the few who did sense that change was coming (although they, too, were surprised by its timing) were the members of America's small socialist community, and for good reason. "That Talmudic Marxism I had learned in New York," Harrington recognized years later, "had kept my eyes focused upon poverty and the continuing existence of a working class in America. It was because of my politics that I was able to see the country through which I traveled." It was upon his return from his odyssey across America that an editor from the journal *Commentary* suggested that Harrington write an article about poverty in America. "As I talked to him," Harrington remembered, "and later as I worked on the essay, I realized that I had spent at least seven years doing research. My time at the Catholic Worker and my tours across America had given me a visual, tactile, personal sense of what poverty meant. I was, to be sure, always the middle-class stranger but I had never been, thank God, an objective academician, but always a comrade in the struggle" (*FC*, 89-92).

Harrington's article, entitled "Our Fifty Million Poor: Forgotten Men of the Affluent Society," appeared in the July 1959 issue of *Commentary*. Its central argument was simple and shocking. It was that, out of a population of 180 million Americans, as many as 50 million—that is, roughly one-third—"continue to live below those standards which we have been taught to regard as the decent minimums for food, housing, clothing, and health." These people were a "predominantly urban, white population" who, despite the "striking gains in productivity which have characterized the American economy since World War II," were left far behind in the general economic advance. Even if, Harrington argued, a poverty-line income were set at $3,000 per year (many set the figure between $3,500 and $4,000), "At least 40 million, perhaps closer to 60 million people" still fell below it. Among these were more than a third of the aged, who "live on inadequate pensions in the blighted neighborhoods of the cities—often enough, in the loneliness of rooming houses"; unskilled workers, who, in "an economy growing ever more complex and technical," were "largely doomed from the moment they abandon their studies to seek employment"; marginal and unemployed workers, who were the victims of low wages, plant shutdowns, or moves by industry to other areas; migratory workers displaced by the "revolution in agriculture"; and finally the non-white minorities, who, although comprising a smaller proportion of the poor than whites, suffered from a disproportionate tendency to fall into poverty and, once there, from segregation and especially adverse living and employment conditions.[6]

The poor, Harrington noted, were more prone to both physical and mental illnesses than the general population. They were also forced to live in substandard housing which, paradoxically, constantly cost more to rent because of the chronic housing shortage of the postwar years. In contrast to President Eisenhower's optimistic belief that the voluntary cooperation of "individuals and economic groups at all levels of government" would ensure prosperity, Harrington charged that existing measures such as "urban renewal" often actually made poverty worse and that only a "comprehensive program" could hope to deal with it. But his article ended on a note of pessimism concerning the chances for meaningful change within the immediate future. Until "the rise of some new, deeper impulse in our political life," poverty was likely to remain a major scandal, to "the great damage of our whole society."[7] This article, together with a subsequent essay on urban slums that appeared the next year formed the basis for Harrington's book *The Other America: Poverty in the United States*.

Most people—even those who had read Galbraith's *The Affluent Society*—were totally unprepared to find that poverty of the magnitude Harrington reported still existed in the United States. Galbraith, while calling attention to the persistence of poverty and decrying its existence in an otherwise prosperous nation, had assumed that only two kinds of poverty could still be found in America: insular poverty (scattered pockets of poor in rural or economically depressed areas) and case poverty (people who were poor because of personal, health, mental, or cultural problems). Setting poverty-level income at $1,000, Galbraith had concluded that one family in thirteen—approximately 8 percent of the population—was poor, and could thus write that "in a world of a weekly industrial wage of eighty dollars and a $3,690 median family income, [poverty] can no longer be presented as a universal or massive affliction."[8] Another scholar, Robert Lampman, had decided in a study undertaken on behalf of the U.S. Senate

[6] Michael Harrington, "Our Fifty Million Poor: Forgotten Men of the Affluent Society," *Commentary* 28, no. 1 (July 1959), 19, 20, 21, 22.

[7] Ibid., 19.

[8] Galbraith, *The Affluent Society*, pp. 323, 324.

(using a $2,500 cut-off point) that 19 percent of Americans had a poverty-level income. But Harrington, while not impugning the motivations or scholarship of Galbraith or Lampman and indeed praising their efforts to raise the consciousness of Americans concerning the existence of economic suffering, maintained that their definitions of poverty were seriously flawed. After taking account of postwar inflation, inadequate allowances for family emergencies, and economic fluctuations that periodically raised the population in poverty, Harrington arrived at the conclusion that, *at a minimum*, between 20 and 25 percent of Americans were poor.

Yet if this were true, how could it have gone largely unnoticed for so long? The answer, Harrington explained, was that "The other America, the America of poverty, is hidden today in a way that it never was before. Its millions are socially invisible to the rest of us." Hidden within deceptively attractive Appalachian landscapes and central urban areas that middle-class suburbanites rarely, if ever, entered, the poor were no longer easily seen. And, even when they were, their outward appearance often belied their true condition, for America had "the best-dressed poverty the world has ever known." It was, unfortunately, "much easier in the United States to be decently dressed than it is to be decently housed, fed, or doctored."[9] Others, including the aged and the young, were simply out of sight—the aged because they were immobile, the young because gang violence was largely confined to slum neighborhoods. Finally, those who were not too old, young, sick, or depressed to announce their presence and needs lacked the power to arouse or sustain political attention. Once, as Galbraith pointed out, poverty afflicted the majority; it could not be hidden. "Unlike the poor today," Harrington observed, "the majority poor of a generation ago were an immediate (if cynical) concern of political leaders. The old slums of the immigrants had the votes; they provided the basis for labor organizations; their very numbers could be a powerful force in political conflict. At the same time the new technology required higher skills, more education, and stimulated an upward movement for millions" (*OA*, 7). Thus, as economic conditions improved dramatically after the Great Depression, the majority of these people were pulled up into a new and greatly expanded middle class because they happened to be "at the right point in the economy at the right time in history." Moreover, since the Broker-Welfare State had come into existence in direct response to the

[9] Michael Harrington, *The Other America: Poverty in the United States* (New York: Macmillan, 1963), pp. 3, 5. Subsequently cited parenthetically as *OA*.

pressure of those among the former majority poor with sufficient political power to command its aid and attention, it primarily served their interests, almost by definition. As a consequence, this new institutional arrangement whose "creation had been stimulated by mass impoverishment and misery" ironically and paradoxically "helped the poor least of all." The new poor, Harrington wrote, thus "missed the political and social gains of the thirties. They are, as Galbraith rightly points out, the first minority poor in history, the first poor not to be seen, the first poor whom the politicians could leave alone" (OA, 9).

The central portion of The Other America was, as its author intended, a sociological horror tale of deprivation, waste, abuse, and depression. Purposely minimizing the use of statistical charts and deleting both footnotes and index, Harrington wanted his readers to see and feel vicariously but keenly the scenes and conditions of the "economic underworld" in large urban areas where more than 16 million workers were not covered by the minimum wage and where they performed menial tasks with no job security and no hope for advancement in a "sector of the American economy [that] has proved itself immune to progress." But even skilled blue-collar workers could find themselves unemployed when the economy faltered, or when an industry closed or moved to another part of the country. Indeed, if anything was worse than being poor, it was the process of *becoming* poor, a "horrible sinking experience" that became an ever more likely possibility the older and less skilled a worker was. The result was that millions fell back into varying degrees of poverty (OA, 21, 29).

Another new aspect of poverty in America was that it was "now possible (or rather it is the reality) to have an increase in the number of employed, an expansion of consumption, a boom in production and, at the same time, localized depressions." As a consequence, certain groups were "singled out by the working of the economy to suffer, while all others . . . experience[d] prosperity." Nor did the observed decline in the absolute and relative numbers of blue-collar workers necessarily mean an improvement in wages or status, since although "there are fewer blue shirts and lunch boxes . . . the disabilities of class remain and, in some cases, are intensified" (OA, 30, 31).

But if the lives of the urban poor were grim, those of the rural poor were often worse. Furthermore, Harrington maintained that the problems of both groups were interconnected, pointing out that as a result of lower food prices and the mechanization of agriculture, a "vast exodus" to urban areas had taken place after World War II. He revealed that 1.5 million people left the Appalachians for urban areas during the 1950s, where they became a permanent lower class, illustrating "the workings of a curious dialectic: how a technological revolution in agriculture created the conditions for the persistence of poverty." While a small number of corporate farms and their owners profited greatly from this revolution, the million farms at the bottom of American agriculture were in a position "similar to that of the slum dweller who lacks education: as the big units become more efficient and modern, as invention mounts, the poor fall further behind." (*OA*, 43, 44). Yet rural aid, blocked by conservative groups outside and within government, had allowed only "*ad hoc* and uncoordinated" efforts to alleviate rural poverty while generously subsidizing many wealthy farmers with large holdings.

Worse still was the situation of blacks, who, Harrington noted, were "concentrated in the worst, dirtiest, lowest-paying jobs. A third continue to live in the rural South, most of them merely subsisting within a culture of poverty and a society of open terror. A third live in Southern cities and a third in Northern cities, and these have bettered their lot compared to the sharecroppers. But they are still the last hired and the first fired, and they are particularly vulnerable to recessions" (*OA*, 73). Blocked in their pursuit of occupational advancement through both economic displacement and racism, they were condemned to live in a culture of poverty wherein attitudes and realities reinforced each other. In addition, blacks and other minorities were the victims of at least one circumstance that was historically unprecedented in America. For, not only was there "new poverty," there were also "new slums." Whereas old ethnic slums, although beset by many difficulties, had at least provided their inhabitants with emotional support and values that were of use in breaking into the larger society— something that the majority of older ethnics were eventually able to do— the new slums, as a result of racism, housing shortages, and a despair born of long experience, did not.

And yet there was more. Tragic as these portraits were, they involved groups to which most people in America would presumably never belong—hence an important reason for the perpetuation of such conditions. But there was one group to which *everyone* eventually belonged—the aged. Yet they too were not exempt from the fear and reality of poverty. Almost 60 percent of those over the age of sixty-five were, Harrington revealed, poor even by Galbraith's and Lampman's criteria. This, he believed, was a cruel and mocking reward for those who had worked all their lives, confident that their last years would be spent in at least minimal comfort in one of the world's richest nations.

These, then, were the victims. But what could be done for them and who could do it? To begin, Harrington advocated universal coverage under Social Security, an extension of the minimum wage, national health insurance, civil rights legislation, and a broadening of welfare benefits to include those who actually needed them: the bottom third of society. Private organizations could not begin to deal with the problem, since their resources were comparatively miniscule. Neither, Harrington warned, could state and local governments, dominated by conservative interests opposed to the measures he advocated, be relied upon for solutions. Only the federal government had the power and resources to take these actions and to implement the national planning needed to coordinate them effectively. "The actual implementation of a program to abolish poverty can be carried out through myriad institutions, and the closer they are to the specific local area, the better the results," he added. Administrators, social workers, and planners were already working to do this on a local level, and they could take charge of a national program. "What they lack now," Harrington wrote, "is money and the support of the American people" (*OA*, 171).

Such support could be found, he proposed, among labor groups and the liberal middle class. But there were two main obstacles to major changes in policy. The first was the defection from the New Deal coalition of the South, a region that had previously often opposed financial and business interests. The Democratic party, however, could no longer allow segregation to go unchallenged, and this had cost Southern support for Democratic social policy. Moreover, economic changes in that region had led to a political transformation. "As industrialization came to the South," Harrington explained, "there was a growing political opposition to laws like minimum wage, to unions, and to other aspects of social change. The leaders of this area saw their depressed condition as an advantage. They could lure business with the promise of cheap, unorganized labor. They were interested in exploiting their backwardness." The second obstacle was the political party structure in America. Citing the "irrationalities" of a system in which "each major party contained differences within itself greater than the differences between it and the other party," he deplored what he viewed as the "issueless character" of American politics. "What is needed if poverty is to be abolished," he declared, "is a return of political debate, a restructuring of the party system so that there can be clear choices, a new mood of social idealism'' (*OA*, 173, 174).

But the idealism Harrington hoped for seemed nowhere in sight. The critical reception of *The Other America* was, in his words, ''friendly, if modest,'' but it had not excited nearly the interest one might have expected from a book that had exploded one of America's most popular and long-standing myths. After all, even if its thesis were even *roughly* accurate, the implications were staggering. Harrington had provided almost incontrovertible proof not merely that there was significant poverty in America, but that there was *mass* poverty. If true, this fact was potentially at least as shocking as had been the launch of Sputnik a few years earlier. Yet little response was forthcoming for almost a year, until a review by Dwight Macdonald appeared in a January 1963 edition of *The New Yorker*. Praising Harrington's book as ''excellent'' and ''most important,'' Macdonald surveyed other recent studies dealing with this topic and then proceeded to discuss at almost unprecedented length for a book review (twenty-eight pages) the general issue of American poverty, using many of Harrington's ideas and statistics as a basis for his argument.[10] This review, Harrington later wrote, ''had the effect of a second publication date and made poverty a topic of conversation in the intellectual-political world of the Northeast corridor.'' Even more importantly, the book had caught the attention of the Kennedy administration.

President Kennedy had become interested in newly emerging theories of poverty and had asked his chief economic adviser, Walter Heller, if they had any validity. Heller replied affirmatively and gave Kennedy a copy of *The Other America* and other studies. Unknown to Harrington, who was in Europe with his wife during these events, Kennedy then put in motion an effort to eradicate poverty through a national campaign, assigning Robert Lampman to study the problem for the Council of Economic Advisers.

Back now in New York just before Christmas of 1963, Harrington found himself a national celebrity. ''There were calls,'' he later wrote, ''from London from the British Broadcasting Corporation asking for my advice on a documentary on poverty; a trip to San Diego to speak for the Western Conference of Teamsters; an appearance on ABC network radio to do an instant appraisal of the poverty section of Lyndon Johnson's 1964 State of the Union Message; a call from Walter Reuther's office asking if I would

---

[10] Dwight Macdonald, ''Our Invisible Poor,'' *The New Yorker*, 19 January 1963, pp. 82-132.

be a keynote speaker at the founding meeting of the Citizens' Crusade against Poverty'' (*FC*, 173). It was, to be sure, a time of surprises for Harrington. For, although he did not know it when he arrived back in the United States from Europe, the new Johnson administration was gearing up the federal government for the first national anti-poverty crusade in American history.

Chapter 6   *The Great Society*

In January of 1964, shortly after Harrington's return to the United States, he received a phone call from an old friend, Paul Jacobs, made at the request of Frank Mankiewicz, who, together with Sargent Shriver, had been appointed the day before by President Johnson to work out a program to eradicate poverty. Harrington was asked to come to Washington for lunch. He came, but he was not prepared when "That lunch with Shriver, Mankiewicz, and Jacobs stretched out into two frantic weeks of sixteen- and eighteen-hour work days." Harrington learned of a "bitter struggle within the government" over the best way to attack poverty, some advisers promoting job creation and training, others community action. On these issues Shriver had taken no position, and Harrington and the "small task force" meeting in Shriver's Peace Corps Office conducted a "continuous seminar" to win him over to their views, culminating in the writing of its recommendations—recommendations that "stayed within the rather narrow political limits established by American society." Finally, however, Jacobs, Mankiewicz, and Harrington "decided to state what we really thought without any concern for the constraints of political possibility. We wrote that the abolition of poverty would require a basic change in how resources are allocated. That meant planned and massive social investments and therefore structural changes in the system. To our surprise, Shriver was delighted with our statement and incorporated a good part of it in his first report to Johnson. He returned from the meeting to tell us that the President had said (I paraphrase from memory) that if it took such innovations to complete the work begun by the New Deal, then we'd just have to make them." "It was all very heady and exciting to be arguing with Cabinet officers and indirectly presenting memos to the President," Harrington later admitted (*FC*, 174-175).

It was more than exciting, however, it was also deeply troubling on a political, philosophical, and moral level. The dilemma was obvious and universal among reform-minded radicals: if they worked within a system to reform it, were they merely helping to make exploitative institutions more tolerable? It was a problem that Harrington had been forced to confront even as he wrote *The Other America* and that caused him to rethink his earlier views. "By 1960," he wrote, "I had begun to understand how wrong I had been to accept the simple, revolutionary scenario of the young Marx. The change began when I first made real contact with workers and blacks and realized, among other things, that the Reutherites were the genuine, and utterly sincere and militant, Left-wing of American society. It was furthered by an intellectual process through which I came to realize that Marx himself had abandoned, or revised, some of his earlier polarizations. . . ." Harrington therefore concluded that "Proposing a specifically socialist solution would make it more difficult for the millions of trade unionists, liberals, and men and women of good will to see the reality of poverty. I felt (and feel) that the 'other America' can be abolished prior to a revolutionary reconstruction of American society. I thought (and think) that sophisticated executives might realize they are losing more in the economic underworld than they are gaining from tolerating it" (*FC*, 178-179). This belief led to a book in which Harrington sought to explain how and why the social problems described in *The Other America* had arisen and at the same time to elucidate and justify his concept of modern socialism.

The Accidental Century began by positing a "decadence" in the twentieth century comparable to the "medieval twilight" of the pre-modern era. Harrington proposed that "What is decadent in the contemporary West (always keeping in mind that there is much which is not) derives from an accidental revolution."[1] Defining the "accidental revolution" as "the sweeping and unprecedented technological transformation of the Western environment which has been, and is being, carried out in a casual way," he explained that the present wave of change was historically unique. Whereas the "conscious revolutionists of the past proposed visions which outstripped reality, the unconscious revolutionists of the present create realities which outstrip their vision." "As a result of this development," he wrote, "cracks opened up in every ideology and philosophy. Conservatives unwittingly made a revolution, but it was not the one the revolutionists had predicted, and the antagonists were mutually bewildered" (*AC*, 16, 17). An example of this process was the growth of the "Megalopolis," the sprawling urban complex that had evolved through an anarchic series of mutually reinforcing events and pressures. There was more to this transformation, however, than merely its physical and demographic effects. Harrington pointed out that "it was governmentally encouraged

---

[1] Michael Harrington, *The Accidental Century* (Baltimore: Penguin, 1966), pp. 15-16. Subsequently cited parenthetically as *AC*.

but not democratically planned." It was the US government which in effect created suburbia, while poor people, especially blacks, became "the prime victims of an urban renewal which was supposed to help them" (*AC*, 20). Arguing that a "chasm" had increasingly grown between private and social costs, Harrington cited the examples of the effects of private decisions concerning automobility in changing family structure and sexual behavior and in creating air pollution, and of the machinations of real-estate developers, who had helped create decaying urban centers surrounded by expensive and well-kept suburbs. Admitting that "in a rough way the activity of the entrepreneurs did raise the level of the entire society," he nevertheless maintained that recent developments had "converted the capitalist economy into the near opposite of [Adam] Smith's description"—that is, into one that was becoming increasingly "socialistic" (that is, collectivized by the business class), yet at the same time dysfunctional in terms of its overall effects on society. Reminding his readers of classical liberal theory which stated that private, individual decisions in the free marketplace would lead to the common good, Harrington proclaimed that "Adam Smith has been stood on his head" (*AC*, 37, 36).

Next, in passages hauntingly Galbraithian in tone, Harrington explained that, after World War II, "Capitalism enjoyed an unprecedented internal security from everything but itself." Noting the trend toward oligopoly, administered prices, corporate planning, and the curtailment of market forces, he wrote of the "cold decadence" of a new socioeconomic order in which state capitalism was slowly but steadily and irreversibly supplanting the old system controlled by entrepreneurs and capitalists who supplied the demands of private consumers. Despite the seeming vibrancy of the old liberal ideology in America, the logic of advanced capitalism had led to a system in which "bureaucratized corporations, supported and subsidized by governments, were planning in increasing independence of the laws of supply and demand or the judgments of investors." "Economic life," he wrote, "was more and more dominated by anonymous collectivities, and a relatively few directors were making decisions that affected the existence of almost every citizen. The civilization of capitalism, its ethics, its morality, its philosophy, was being destroyed by the practice of capitalism." All this while businessmen were almost unconsciously molding "new environments and new types of men" (*AC*, 80, 92-93).

But Harrington was forced to confront the fact that the twentieth century had done more than stultify the theory and the practice of economic liberalism: it had also seriously damaged the hopes of socialist reformers. The widespread disillusionment with Soviet-style socialism—a system that was certainly not capitalist, but just as certainly not socialist in either the Marxist or social democratic sense—was obviously a disquieting, and often a personally shattering experience for many on the left. It was, however, to have more general consequences. Along with the mass defection of workers—due to nationalist fervor in World War I, to fascist appeals between the wars, and to the steady rise in living standards after World War II in the "mixed economies" of the West—it had led to the decreased confidence in and appeal of socialism in general and to an "end-of-ideology" school of thought positing the irrelevance of both capitalist and socialist models and theories to the modern world. "So it was," Harrington wrote, "that movements that had once thought of themselves as the cells of a new social order settled on rearranging society rather than revolutionizing it." Rising living standards and the "relative social peace" after World War II might or might not be permanent, but one thing was certain and important: "the West, for the first time in its history, is not fundamentally challenged from within" (*AC*, 124).

Yet the twentieth century, Harrington affirmed, would be indisputably collectivist, the only issue in doubt being the form that this collectivism would take. He sketched a portrait of one possible society that could emerge:

> At the top of the society, there would be a bureaucratic elite; beneath them, technicians and skilled, organized workers; and, at the very bottom, the class of janitors and the jobless, those who perform those functions too menial even to bother mechanizing or automating. And such a group would indeed have an Orwellian helplessness. They would suffer a poverty that had been purged of poverty's one virtue, that of forcing men to fight against their misery. (*AC*, 137)

But there was another possibility: namely, that automation, which had taken a major toll of blue-collar jobs in the 1950s, would begin to displace white-collar workers and middle-level management:

> If this trend were to persist, if a working-class insecurity were to intrude upon middle-class life (and, in the past, one of the most essential differences between the two existences was that the one was cyclic and unstable, the other much less so), a new stratum of society might be energized to seek basic and structural reforms. There would be an obvious danger that such a development would be technocratic and authoritarian, car-

ried on, as in *1984*, at the expense of the "proles." But . . . this need not be the case. (*AC*, 137)

In light of these developments it was no accident that twentieth-century culture raised gloomy, tragic, and even apocalyptic visions of man and society, some of which were not wholly without foundation even under the most optimistic assumptions, since it was possible that "a decent society in which men die from death rather than plagues and famines will have a stark sense of the tragic."

Yet Harrington rejected the fashionable hopelessness concerning reform evinced by those who blamed the destruction of liberal civilization on "the masses." Rightists, he remarked, bewailed the doom of the aristocracy or the bourgeoisie, liberals did the same for educated people, and disillusioned socialists the same for workers. The first two perceptions, he argued, were the results of aristocratic nostalgia and liberal oversimplification, respectively. The third, however, seemed to contain some truth. After all, were not most people beyond the intellectual and cultural attainments hoped for by socialists in the nineteenth and early twentieth centuries?

Harrington did not deny the existence of an intellectually, culturally, and politically stunted group, but he insisted that this deformed species of modern man was to a large extent a social product, maintaining that such a mass "exists by virtue of society's choice. It is not inevitable, for it comes from a repression of natural abilities and talents" shown by America's school dropout rate. Indeed, to the extent that incompetent and debased masses actually existed, he charged that they were a creation of the elite. The West had revolutionized economic and social life, and technology was creating a new civilization. But without revolutionaries or explicit planning, "thought has not kept pace with technology," with the result that "Millions of people are thrust, unprepared, into this unprecedented environment, and then those who systematically did not prepare them excoriate them as 'masses,' as vulgar, as lowly, and deplore the way in which they are pulling the high and noble values down" (*AC*, 239).

The final aspect of the accidental revolution, automation, was seen by Harrington as presenting modern capitalism with one of its most fundamental challenges, since it threatened to deprive Western people of one of their most important activities—work—as well as the psychological and economic benefits derived therefrom. The cybernetic revolution—a technological trend that had begun in the second postwar decade and had promised to end scarcity—could, he warned, pose a fatal dilemma for capitalism since, as business relentlessly strove to replace labor with capital in the form of cybernetic machines, it simultaneously (although unwittingly) curtailed consumer income and market demand, thereby creating unemployment, and also quite possibly severing the traditional connection between labor and wages. Under such conditions the economic system could break down, as Marx had predicted. Yet this need not happen, since Marx never considered another possible result of his theory of automation: namely, the abolition of the working class in the Marxist sense simultaneously with or before the collapse of capitalism. Here Harrington did no more than suggest the "extreme range" of options, that is, the extraordinary and yet indeterminate impact of this development.

In conclusion, Harrington posited the necessity of democratic planning as the only alternative to allowing technological change to proceed in a haphazard way. Such a program would entail the rise of a third party in the United States—one that would not arise suddenly, but "through the conflict within the present party structure." The choice, he repeated, was not between "a resolute march to the rear in the name of anticollectivism and a cautious confrontation with the future in the name of a mixed economy," but between a new social order that would be "fundamentally hostile to the values created over the more than two thousand years of Western man" and one that would allow the West to "once more become the promise of the entire world" (AC, 302, 306).

Harrington's concluding remarks were not merely idealistic rhetoric to at least some of those who read them. The evolution of a "new party" was precisely what many American reformers believed they were witnessing in 1964 and 1965 when, he recalled, "it seemed to us socialists that our dream of a political realignment in America was about to come true." With this idea in mind, Harrington and other socialists moved to establish links with organized labor, with intellectuals like Herbert Gans, Bayard Rustin, Irving Howe, and other civil rights leaders and activists, and with the liberal wing of the Democratic party in anticipation of the momentous opportunity that they felt now lay before them. Indeed, it seemed that at the highest levels of government there was a determination to enact the first major set of social reforms since the New Deal.

The Kennedy administration had in fact moved in this same general direction, but its proposals had been quite modest and had, moreover, been blocked by Congress. After Kennedy's death, however, the new administration moved quickly to establish itself as the most reform-minded government since the days of FDR. Indeed, its chief executive, who had entered public life as an officer in one of the New Deal's alphabet-agencies (the National Youth Administration), had seen Franklin Roosevelt both as a heroic figure and as a role model whom he wished to emulate. An activist by temperament, and a reformer whose own background included a Populist father and a rural upbringing amid economic deprivation in the South, Lyndon Johnson officially launched his term in office with a State of the Union Address that called for an "unconditional war on poverty." In a message to Congress two months later in which he proposed passage of an Economic Opportunity Act, he included passages and language that could well have come from Harrington's own pen.[2] The legislation he was proposing would provide "five basic opportunities": the opportunity for poor youth to "develop skills, continue education, and find useful work"; the opportunity for communities to engage in the fight against poverty at the local level with help from the federal government; the opportunity for Americans to enter voluntary service in this effort; the opportunity for workers and farmers to overcome the "particular barriers" that prevented their ascent from poverty; and the opportunity for the entire nation to join in a "concerted attack" on poverty through the establishment of a new executive department, the Office of Economic Opportunity, which Johnson called the "national headquarters" for the war against poverty.

The Economic Opportunity Act, signed into law in August of 1964—merely a few months after its proposal—was a portent of the activism the Johnson administration was to bring to social policy in the mid-1960s. Still, a number of related measures such as free medical care for the aged, increased Social Security payments, and rural aid were effectively stalled by congressional conservatives. It was not until after Johnson's spectacular trouncing of the arch-conservative Goldwater forces in the 1964 presidential election—a contest in which Johnson campaigned on a platform that emphasized the social issues he had laid out early that year—that the Democratic party could move to enact without obstruction the most sweeping domestic reforms in three decades.

Reform at High Tide: The Great Society

The second Johnson administration—swept into office by the greatest electoral victory until that time—seemed at first to justify Harrington's qualified optimism concerning the prospects for reform in the 1960s.

---

[2] See Lyndon B. Johnson, "Total Victory over Poverty," in Marvin E. Gettleman and David Mermelstein, eds., *The Failure of American Liberalism: After the Great Society* (New York: Vintage, 1971), pp. 181-185.

While during the previous year the administration had already passed, in addition to the Economic Opportunity Act, an Urban Mass Transportation Act and a landmark Civil Rights Act, the legislation enacted from 1965 to 1966 was staggering in quantity and in scope. With the forces of the right weaker than they had been in over a generation and therefore unable to offer organized and effective opposition, Johnson's program, which he called "The Great Society," was approved by Congress in short order. Medicare, a program that provided limited, free medical and hospital services for the elderly—something that had been discussed for decades—was now a reality. Social Security benefits were increased and their recipient population was extended. The Fair Labor Standards Act of 1938 was amended, raising the minimum wage. In the cabinet, a new Department of Housing and Urban Development was created and given authority over all public housing, federal intervention in the field of construction, and the FHA. A Demonstration Cities and Metropolitan Development Act passed in 1966 provided federal aid to local governments in order to build "model" neighborhoods. The act also subsidized the rent payments of those not covered by other poverty programs or living in public housing projects. The Elementary and Secondary Education Act of 1965, close successor to the National Defense Education Act of 1964, expanded federal grants to both public and parochial schools in impoverished areas of the country. The Voting Rights Act of 1965 authorized federal action to register blacks in areas of the country where, on a de facto basis, they had been denied the vote. The federal regulation of consumer goods, including new policies involving automobile safety, was expanded, and the first tentative steps toward a national policy on environmental protection were taken. In the sphere of federal programs directed specifically at poverty, appropriations were almost doubled, with additional funds for the depressed regions of Appalachia.

But in spite of these accomplishments, Harrington was disturbed by the limitations of Johnson's policies—the same limitations that, he felt, had plagued the New Deal. To begin with, he had estimated that an effective program to abolish poverty in the United States might cost over $100 billion. Yet, even with the doubling of expenditures that occurred in 1965, total federal spending specifically aimed at the poor amounted that year to only $1.5 billion. Harrington had already complained about what he considered an inadequate level of funding early in 1964 when he met with Sargent Shriver and other members of Johnson's cabinet and poverty task force. During his first meeting with Shriver, Harrington had remarked that

the billion dollars the administration planned to invest in the poverty program was only "nickels and dimes." ("Oh really, Mr. Harrington,"
Shriver replied. "I don't know about you, but this is the first time I've
spent a billion dollars.") Nor was this the only instance of what Harrington
and others considered insufficient or misplaced funding. For example, despite the creation of HUD and efforts to provide a greater quantity of less
expensive shelter for Americans, the housing shortage became more severe in 1966, as bankers, contractors, and speculators used the program to
tap into federal funds. Most of all, perhaps, Harrington was upset by what
Galbraith had called the "reactionary Keynesianism" of the 1964 tax cut,
which, as one observer pointed out, gave the lion's share of benefits to
those with the highest incomes.[3]

Indeed, by 1966 Harrington had already lost any lingering hope that
poverty could be abolished within the existing political framework of the
Broker State. "The Johnson administration's War on Poverty is basically
inadequate," he lamented in an article entitled "The Politics of Poverty."
Although he explained that he did "not want simply to dismiss the Johnson
administration's War on Poverty (or John F. Kennedy's tremendously important first steps in this direction)," he added that he could not withhold
comment on its shortcomings, since there was "no point in fostering the
illusion that a sort of Federal Community Chest is going to get together the
men of good will . . . and by a little more generous welfare-ism do away
with a national shame."[4] Identifying the present reform effort with the
second, that is, Keynesian, New Deal of the 1930s, Harrington called for
its replacement by a "third New Deal"—a "radical liberalism" that
would involve comprehensive democratic planning and "massive social
investments." To say the least, he was not satisfied.

Certainly it would have been unlikely that socialist or even all liberal
reformers would have been satisfied with the programs and policies of the
Johnson administration. They were, as Harrington correctly judged, not so
much the beginning of a new era, but the end of an old one. Virtually all
of the major reforms and programs of The Great Society were ones that
FDR and his followers would have wanted to enact or extend but could not.
None, in other words, entailed a significant departure from the assump-

[3] Michael Harrington, "The Politics of Poverty," in Jeremy Larner and Irving Howe, eds.,
Poverty: Views from the Left (New York: William Morrow, 1968), p. 28; Leon Keyserling, "Eco-
nomic Progress and the Great Society," in Gettleman and Mermelstein, *The Failure of American
Liberalism*, pp. 85-96.

[4] Harrington, "The Politics of Poverty," pp. 13-14.

tions underlying the Broker State. In addition, The Great Society—like the New Deal that preceded it—was, it now seems clear, largely enacted under the pressure and threat of social conditions and widespread unrest that had exhibited signs of turning political. The mass displacement of agricultural laborers, especially blacks, from rural to urban areas from the early 1940s to the late 1960s resulting from rapidly rising agricultural productivity, the subsidies and cutbacks implemented by the New Deal, and the economic and demographic impact of World War II had created dangerous conditions in many large American cities. This led to an increasing amount of anti-social behavior in the 1950s, finally culminating in the large-scale rioting of the 1960s.

Thus, although poverty in America had not quantitatively worsened, there had been very important *qualitative* (geographic and demographic) changes in its nature. Downtrodden sharecroppers, dispersed over a wide area and living under tight community and family controls in a rural environment, had never presented a political problem. Those same people, suddenly thrown into radically different urban surroundings, were another matter entirely. Hence, the decisive impetus to action was the realization by political leaders that poverty by the late 1950s had become concentrated among increasingly discontented and alienated people—especially racial minorities—in large urban centers. In this new setting it was not only socially troublesome: it was also recognized as dangerous by political elites, who wished mainly to preserve the social order and to integrate a new urban electorate into American society and into the ranks of the Democratic party.[5]

There is evidence that Harrington understood, at least to some degree, the political realities that underlay the reforms of the Johnson administration and was willing to accept their limitations while pressing for more fundamental changes. But by 1967 his cautious optimism had been, like that of many reformers in American history, greatly eroded. His disappointment was, moreover, the result not only of the increasingly obvious shortcomings of the administration's approach to the problem of poverty, but of the stalling and partial reversal of the momentum of The Great Society almost as soon as the effort was launched, a development that initially had nothing directly to do with domestic politics.

[5] See Frances Fox Piven and Richard A. Cloward, *Regulating the Poor: The Functions of Public Welfare* (New York: Vintage, 1972), chapters 7-10. Many of the facts and ideas in this section are taken from their book.

WAR AND DISILLUSION: *Toward a Democratic Left*

Coterminous with the escalation of the War on Poverty was the escalation of the war in Vietnam, a small Asian country that had won its independence from French colonial rule in 1954. At the height of American involvement, it was to consume more than $30 billion per year—20 times the amount spent in 1965 to end poverty—and eventually cost the lives of almost 60,000 Americans and millions of Vietnamese. As the nation's economic resources, psychic energy, and political superstructure became ever more committed to Vietnam, the reform impulse, barely revived after its long dormancy, again rapidly faded. Moderate and conservative forces again came to dominate American politics with the support of a middle class that had come to believe that The Great Society had accomplished little and that, in fact, blamed the programs of the Johnson administration for urban rioting and discontent. At the same time, it was the Vietnam War that, together with the civil rights movement and the social activism spawned by The Great Society, led to a radical questioning of American institutions such as had rarely been seen in the nation's history. Among those who participated in this activity was Michael Harrington.

His hopes for meaningful progress toward social change extinguished and by now thoroughly disenchanted with Johnson's policies, Harrington sought to come to terms with the social and economic irrationalities of what some now called the "Welfare-Warfare State." In *Toward a Democratic Left*, published in 1968, he recalled with disappointment and some bitterness the promises of The Great Society. Yet he did not believe that its promises had been "mere dishonesty," or that the nation's ills could simply be blamed on President Johnson or on a mythical "bloated Wall Street plutocracy." Those responsible, he believed, did not desire to cause or prolong suffering at home or in the Third World; however, they did "just as certainly refuse, out of a sophisticated self-interest, to do what is necessary to end their agony." This suffering could be ended, he proposed, only through "vigorous democratic conflict and a vivid social imagination"—things that flew in the face of what Harrington called America's "utopian pragmatism," that is, its commitment since World War II to middle-of-the-road policies of incrementalism and technocratic problem-solving.[6]

Harrington believed that Americans in the 1950s and 1960s had adopted

---

[6] Michael Harrington, *Toward a Democratic Left: A Radical Program for a New Majority* (Baltimore: Penguin, 1969), pp. 3-4. Subsequently cited parenthetically as *TDL*.

a worm's-eye view which aimed, at best, at avoiding "social explosions," while not taking account of the systemic evils that tended to produce them. Using as an example the mutually reinforcing urban problems of "inadequate transportation, central-city decay, racial segregation and high rates of unemployment," he argued that only broad, coordinated, and determined actions could avert coming catastrophes. The groundwork for such a plan had not been laid by The Great Society, since Johnson's own "obsession with consensus" had led him to keep facts concerning the "conflict-ridden practicalities of the future" from the American people and had therefore caused him "to miss one of the greatest opportunities in recent American history." Proclaiming that the "old liberalism does not offer an adequate response to [the] massive historic trends" that were under way, Harrington expressed his belief that "Franklin Roosevelt's New Deal has become a conservative force in American life." "The positive emotions still evoked by the New Deal are radical and liberal," he wrote, "and are clearly related to [the] class antagonisms which presided over its birth. But, beginning with the Second World War, the corporations gradually came to recognize that the welfare state could be made to serve the interests of those who had most vigorously opposed it."[7] Calling attention to a phenomenon he called the "social-industrial complex," he maintained that a "partnership" between business and government often had antisocial consequences, despite the fact that private businessmen could have motives that were benign or even partly altruistic. The problem was that "the catastrophes of the other America do not yield commercial rates of interest," a fact that the abysmal failure of public housing well exemplified.

But if Harrington saw no possibility of a solution through routine politics, neither did he place as much faith in the evolution of a new technocratic class of corporate managers as he felt Galbraith had done in his recently published book, *The New Industrial State*, remarking that "it is not populist sentimentality to insist on democratic participation in the planning process." A technocratic elite, even a sincere one, would become "servants of the old values refurbished" in a corporate system "meshing with the state" but still remaining "powerfully self-interested and, when necessary, anti-social." Did this mean that a full-blown socialization of the economy was needed? Not necessarily. Even in a private economy government could act as a transmission belt of democratic will if pressured to

[7] Ibid., pp. 8, 9, 11, 17, 29, 30.

"democratically plan 'uneconomic' allocations of significant resources" (*TDL*, 106, 101).

What was needed, then, was a form of indicative planning based roughly on the French model, but more democratic in form. Harrington proposed a periodic "Report on the Future" to be made by the president to the nation, outlining a series of economic plans in terms of their relative costs and benefits with respect to various areas of the economy and to different social and economic groups. The subsequent debate, he predicted, would be both inevitable and beneficial, since concealing conflict behind a facade of "consensus" would not cause it to disappear; such a path "simply drives it underground, which is where the democratic forces are at a disadvantage and money talks so persuasively." Minority voices would therefore have to be heard, and government would have to "subsidize dissent at every level of American life" (*TDL*, 117-118). Dismissing the conservative view that the proliferation of bureaucratic agencies, the growth of federal power, and increased government spending had failed to alleviate, and had even caused or worsened many of the nation's social ills, Harrington countered that "the penny-pinching of the American Right did more to promote the problems of the Sixties than any bureaucrat in Washington or any liberal with illusions about Federal omnipotence." Instead of demonstrating the failure of government action, he contended that the experiments of The Great Society "illustrat[ed] the penny wisdom and pound foolishness of getting everyone excited about an imminent utopia and then investing funds that, by official definition, are not enough for a modest reform" (*TDL*, 140-141).

Regarding foreign policy—an important issue in the midst of the Vietnam War—Harrington referred to America's role in the world as an "almost-imperialism," since the United States had "palpable, material reasons for shoring up the injustices of the international economy and society, but it is not inevitably forced to do so," rejecting the view that capitalism requires exploitative actions abroad. On the other hand, he proposed that "The advanced Communist societies benefit from international injustice every bit as much as the corporations" and that the main conflict in the world was not between the Communist East and the capitalist West, but between the "industrialized North" and the "backward South." He acknowledged that there was a close connection between economic and foreign policy interests in American actions with respect to Europe after World War II, for that continent had always been the center of American economic, political, and cultural interests. But it was only with the beginning of the conflict in Korea that "the ideological hostility which was rooted in the serious conflict of interests in Europe began to take on a life of its own in Asia." Rather than seeing US foreign policy during the cold war as simply a "reflex of economic interest," Harrington traced the pattern of worldwide American commitments to, and alliance with, "conservative and reactionary powers" largely to a domestic conservatism that had held sway in the immediate postwar years, when a "Republican, business-oriented Administration held office for two terms, the Dixiecrat-Republican coalition prevailed in the Congress," and America's leaders were "bewildered" by a rapidly changing world—circumstances that led to internal repression and militarization. Harrington agreed with Galbraith's hypothesis in *The New Industrial State* that the funds being shunted to the military-industrial complex could be easily and much more productively used for space exploration, and that therefore "a massive cutback in the billions for defense plus the normal growth of a full-employment economy would provide sufficient funds for rebuilding America *and* going to the stars" (*TDL*, 206). Beyond this, he believed the United States should join with other nations to contribute a percentage of its GNP to the economic development of the Third World and proposed "international economic planning" and "immediate and basic changes in Western trade policies."

With respect to political change in the United States, Harrington felt that neither Black Power advocates nor the New Leftists of the late 1960s offered realistic alternatives to existing parties and policies, since both movements were composed of and dominated by small elites or segments of American society. Similarly, the poor could not effect change by themselves, because they accounted for only 20 percent of the population and were, in addition, the group least capable (for a variety of economic, cultural, and psychological reasons) of forming a strong and effective counterweight to the groups presently holding power. Only a broad coalition of forces—in combination with American labor unions—could hope to form a new and effective political grouping, most likely within the Democratic party. There was even a chance that a new social stratum—a "new class"—could be persuaded to join such an alliance. This would not be the old middle class of small and large businessmen or the new corporate managers. The new class was instead "composed of scientists, technicians, teachers and professionals in the public sector of the society. By education and work experience it is predisposed toward planning. It could be an ally of the poor and the organized workers—or their sophisticated enemy'' (*TDL*, 270). If labor, minorities, and the poor could be galvanized into an effective political force dedicated to the general welfare, and particularly if the new class could be induced to join them, there was, Harrington affirmed, hope for a viable democratic Left.

But there was another possibility. Instead of joining together in a common cause, these groups could become Balkanized, warring factions, filled with distrust and bent on gaining advantages at each other's expense. In such a case, Harrington warned that ''the American crisis would become literally intolerable. There would be incredible problems of urban life, race and automation but no progressive social force capable of resolving them. In the circumstances, violence would be used to suppress the justified rage at the bottom of the society, and fear and cynicism would permeate every level of national life. The moment would be counter-revolutionary, a sort of American analogue to the German breakdown of 1932 and 1933'' (*TDL*, 261). Even worse was the possibility that the new class would ally itself with the existing power structure or become an exploitative, repressive, and hierarchical entity in its own right. It was entirely possible, Harrington wrote, that ''The professionals and the liberals would become more and more horrified by the jungle world at the bottom of the society, which would imbue them with fear rather than compassion'' (*TDL*, 260). If this happened, ''Plannified capitalism would then come to resemble liberalized totalitarianism.''

Harrington, who had supported and worked for Robert Kennedy and then, after his assassination, Hubert Humphrey in the 1968 election, implied in an afterword added to his book in 1969 that the 1972 election could well decide these issues. ''It is the worst of times,'' he wrote, ''because we have lost brave leaders and the nation has moved to the Right; it is the best of times, if we have the audacity to hope and act, because it is possible to assemble a new majority, because there is a road to 1972 which runs toward the democratic Left'' (*TDL*, 302). So ended Harrington's book and the first phase of his intellectual and political journey. So ended also, although he did not yet know it, the great reform movement of the 1960s and the impulse that had sustained it. The year 1972 *would* see a mobilization of the democratic left, but a left greatly weakened by internal dissension and facing an overwhelming opposition. What lay before it was not victory, but instead what had awaited similar movements in the past: a grim—if gallant—last stand.

The Slow Retreat: The Twilight of an Era

The next several years in America were to witness not a dramatic retrenchment of the domestic reforms and programs enacted during the 1960s, but a gradual lessening of enthusiasm for change. (American foreign policy, its architects chastened by the agonizingly slow and embarrassing US withdrawal from the Vietnam quagmire, had been modified through a policy of detente with the major Communist powers; but its underlying assumptions and goals had not fundamentally changed. Policymakers had simply come to believe that the economic, social, political, and military costs of direct intervention had temporarily become too burdensome.) Harrington had worried in 1969 that "When [the Nixon] Administration completes its term, the United States is likely to have more social problems than now, more racism, more urban deterioration." In the opinion of many, his fears were prophetic.

Richard Nixon rode to power in 1968 on a mild but unmistakable conservative backlash against The Great Society, his campaign speeches centering on the suppression of crime and urban rebellion, and the decreased activity of the federal government in economic and social affairs. Once in office, Nixon's rhetoric was accompanied by very modest cuts in domestic spending, moderate fiscal and monetary policies, a proposal for a negative income tax for the poor, and a moderately conservative program of revenue sharing that involved the distribution of federal tax money to cities and states in proportion to the federal taxes paid to the government by each entity. In the spheres of civil rights, child care, welfare, and labor policy, however, Nixon actively used federal power to delay, stall, or nullify the actions of liberals and their supporters both within and outside government.

But, as disheartening as Nixon's policies were to those on the left, the final blow to reformers and their allies was the 1972 election, on which Harrington had pinned his hopes for a unification of progressive groups and a revitalization of the social activism of the 1960s. For a time it appeared that a renewal of strength within a viable American left was not merely a possibility, but was actually taking place. The McGovern coalition, representing the poor, minorities, antiwar groups, and a corps of idealistic youth and committed to a decrease in military expenditures, an expansion of social services, a genuine redistribution of income and wealth, and the general democratization of American society was, on the basis of its platform, the most progressive political alignment within a major us party since the candidacy of William Jennings Bryan in 1896.

However, Harrington's worst fears became a reality. McGovern's forces were abandoned by the labor movement, by the new class, and by the bulk of the Democratic leadership, their massive defeat at the polls thus being a foregone conclusion. (To Harrington's great chagrin, the American Socialist party *also* defected to Nixon—based on his anticommunist policy in Vietnam and his union support—leading to Harrington's break with Max Shachtman and his resignation from co-chairmanship of the party in October 1972.) The reelection of Nixon left no doubt that the election of 1968 had not been merely a breathing space on an extended ladder of social reform, but instead the sign of a rapidly approaching upper limit to such reform within the existing political context. Its chance to gain political power now gone for an indefinite period, the American left was to be condemned to execute a slow retreat into the following decade, fighting constant rearguard actions in an unsuccessful attempt to hold back an ever stronger conservative resurgence.

Harrington had not been caught unawares by these developments, having speculated on just such events in *Toward a Democratic Left*, and undertook a systematic criticism of the ideas of those whom he called the "neoconservative critics" of the welfare state, analyzed the social and cultural malaise in America in the mid-1970s, called attention to the "new crisis of capitalism" under Nixon and Ford (see above, Chapter 3), and offered his own proposals for resolving the nation's mounting economic problems. This analysis largely comprised the core structure of *The Twilight of Capitalism*, which appeared in 1976.[8] The latter constituted what Harrington had not as yet attempted: a general and theoretical analysis of the American welfare state.

Marxist theory, Harrington began, was not a calcified intellectual fossil of no relevance to the present social and economic turmoil in capitalist society, a notion that had resulted from the sloppy or simply mistaken interpretation of Marx's views by several generations of scholars and the use of a crude and bastardized form of Marxist philosophy by modern tyrants such as Stalin. This "pseudo" or "vulgar" Marxism, in which a material "base" determined a cultural, intellectual, and political "super-

---

[8] See Michael Harrington, "The Welfare State and its Neoconservative Critics," *Dissent* (Fall 1973), 435-454; "A Collective Sadness," *Dissent* (Fall 1974), 486-491; "Our Proposals for the Crisis," *Dissent* (Spring 1975), 101-104; and "A New Crisis of Capitalism," *Dissent* (Winter 1975), 5-10.

structure," was symbolized by Marx's statement that "The hand mill gives you society with a feudal lord; the steam mill, society with the industrial capitalist." This led to a misrepresentation of Marxist theory—on occasion, Harrington asserted, by Marx and Engels themselves!

Marx read in a broader context conceived of capitalism, Harrington wrote, "as a system in which the economic, political and social interact reciprocally upon one another." Productive relationships for Marx were human, not technological or material, nor did they determine every aspect of society, although they did produce a "pervasive lighting" in society. They "bathe the superstructure in that pervasive light, they touch and color the totality, but that leaves room for relative autonomies. Art, science, and politics all have their own rhythms."[9] Most crucial was the central insight of Marx concerning capitalism and the relevance of his perceptions for modern capitalist society: simply that the system was rational and planned (though exploitative and authoritarian) at the level of the firm, but irrational and unplanned within the economy writ large.

Indeed, it was the continuing and intensified malfunctioning of the American economy in the mid-1970s which was the best evidence for Harrington that what Marx and Engels called "bourgeois socialism"—something that he believed corresponded to the Keynesian welfare state—was in deep trouble. The thesis that the welfare state was the ultimate answer to the economic disruptions and social conflicts of laissez-faire capitalism, a position commonly advanced in the 1950s, was, according to Harrington, obviously flawed, although he had little doubt that the present "crisis" of capitalism could be overcome through internal modification. Capitalism had, he acknowledged, an "extraordinary adaptability," and that was precisely the problem. It was, in fact, "compatible with widespread, and even totalitarian, planning." In reply to an argument that a "postindustrial society" now existed in which economic power as the dominant force in society had given way to political and managerial power and decisions, Harrington answered that

When the government intervenes into an economy dominated by private corporations to promote the common good, those corporations will normally be the prime beneficiaries of that intervention. The planners may be liberals, or even socialists, but they will not be able to carry out policies that run counter to the crucial institutions of the society unless

[9] Michael Harrington, *The Twilight of Capitalism* (New York: Simon and Schuster, 1976), pp. 60-61.

they have the support of a determined mass movement willing to fight for structural change. Since this condition usually is fulfilled only in exceptional crisis circumstances, the normal tendency of the welfare state, even with the "new men" admittedly much more in evidence and conscious planning taking on a greater importance, is to follow the old capitalist priorities in a new, sophisticated way.[10]

The remainder of *The Twilight of Capitalism* was devoted to an empirical demonstration of the last proposition.

The US economic system was, Harrington proposed, state capitalist in nature. Massive subsidies were given to huge industrial and agricultural enterprises while the public sector strained to provide a minimal safety net for the poor. Tax laws blatantly discriminated in favor of corporate and unearned income, large property owners, and the affluent generally, leading to highly skewed distributions of income and wealth. Monetary and fiscal policy invariably acted to subsidize and encourage private investment at the expense of public spending. The only exception was *military* spending, an area where there was little fear of the spread of government intervention to other parts of the economy, where the goods produced did not compete with those of other firms, and where the institutional structure and the ideology of those who managed it were "profoundly antisocialist." American state capitalism was also prone to stimulate the general economy through the use of tax cuts, all of which from 1964 to 1973 favored the rich.

To the charges of Daniel Patrick Moynihan and other former liberal activists and intellectuals, whom he called "neoconservatives," that the federal government had done too much in the 1960s, Harrington repeated that government did far too *little*, citing as an example the fact that the Office of Economic Opportunity, the "command post" of the War on Poverty, had received less than $10 billion in nine years. He also noted that, despite their charge of excessive egalitarianism, there had been no redistribution of income or wealth in America during the period of increasing federal action. And, to the extent that government intervention did have unforeseen and negative consequences, he pointed to the timidity of state action in the overall context of capitalist constraints in which the welfare state operated. Finally, he excoriated the "romantic medievalism" of those who posited a kind of mythical *Gemeinschaft* before the coming of modern industrial and bureaucratic society. Government, Harrington retorted, did

[10] Ibid., pp. 222-223.

not cause the breakdown of traditional society: it responded to it. Of the undeniable erosion of traditional values in the wake of cultural change, he observed that "England and Sweden are beset by the same cultural convulsions as the United States. Their churches, family structure, et cetera, are no more secure than ours. Yet their health is. The reason is simple enough: they have better-organized medical care than we have."[11]

Did this mean that the American welfare state only benefited the rich and that it *could* only do so? The answer, Harrington confessed, was "ambiguous." To some degree, those who saw the welfare state as an arrangement for "buying off" mass discontent were right. Elites had often used or even initiated reforms to soften the exploitation of those under capitalism. But these theorists were also neglecting other forces, motivations, and results.

Why, then, if these developments were not part of an overarching plan to serve bourgeois interests, did the welfare state primarily function to further capitalist priorities and values? "The essential [point]," Harrington reiterated, "is that the capitalist state is not itself a capitalist: It therefore depends on capitalists. It is that the most honest and incorruptible of public servants wants and works for the maximum happiness of General Motors and Ford."[12] Intimately connected with this relationship between the state and the economy was the tendency of the system to move almost inexorably toward collectivization—a result certainly not predicted or desired by capitalist ideologists. These insights, he concluded, confirmed the utility of Marxist theory, since the welfare state was "indeed an organic whole of reciprocal causality, with a pervasive capitalist lighting and an atmosphere which bathes, but does not predetermine, every relationship within it . . . a process filled with unintended consequences, surprising its rulers as well as the ruled."[13] Instead of the stable system portrayed by its advocates, he called it "a contradictory, crisis-prone, last stage of capitalism," marked by domestic transformation and confusion, international crisis and the loss of Western hegemony, and an increasing cultural and philosophical demoralization, vacuousness, and decadence.

All in all, Harrington painted a bleak picture of modern capitalism and of prospects for reform. Even though he recognized that the reform process begun during the 1960s had long since ground to a halt and had even been turned back, he nevertheless continued to support the existing welfare state

[11] Ibid., p. 292.
[12] Ibid., p. 307.
[13] Ibid., p. 340.

as a necessary attempt to ameliorate the worst abuses of capitalism and as a beacon whose light might eventually point the way toward a new society. Yet even as he finished *The Twilight of Capitalism*, the political activists and ideologues of the right were preparing an even more intensive assault—one that would challenge not only the new liberalism of The Great Society, but also much of the New Deal itself.

THE CRITICAL DECADE: WHITHER THE BROKER STATE?

The election of Jimmy Carter in 1976 marked the rise to power of the most ideologically atypical Democratic coalition in modern American history. The Carter administration sought both a balanced budget and an actual reduction in current outlays for the social programs begun under the New Deal and extended under The Great Society. This development was accompanied—indeed, partly caused by—the ascent to political influence of an increasingly vocal segment of the radical right, whose views had gained the attention of a wide audience by the end of the decade. In addition, there began to take form by the late 1970s a tax revolt led by elements of this movement that threatened to cut the revenues of state and local governments at the very time when they could expect less financial support from federal sources. Meanwhile, economic conditions had worsened as high unemployment and low productivity coexisted with a rate of inflation that climbed beyond 20 percent at one point in the year 1980.

While these events were transpiring, Harrington, now national chairman of the Democratic Socialist Organizing Committee, assailed the proposed cuts in federal spending and the views of the New Right in speeches, articles, and the mass media. Then also a professor of political science at Queens College in New York, he noted in January 1979 that, although Carter's planned budget reductions were "symbolic" since the actual amounts involved would be "quite small," Carter was "the first President to seriously propose repealing parts of [the] New Deal," something that, he observed, even postwar Republican presidents had been afraid to do. Moreover, he bewailed the administration's apparent willingness to retreat on issues of environmental protection, job safety, and progressive taxation, all of which amounted to "an historical reversal of the New Deal tradition."[14]

[14] "The Carter Budget: Are Cuts Too Deep?" *Los Angeles Times*, 21 January 1979, part 5, pp. 1-2.

However one might evaluate Carter's policies, there can be little doubt that the fortunes of the American left had continued to decline. Yet, interestingly, Harrington's response was not primarily a defense of the welfare state, although he continued to maintain that its features were, by and large, eminently defensible. It was instead an attack on the economic system in which the welfare state operated and a counterattack on the views of the New Right. Harrington's views were to be most fully stated in his next book, *Decade of Decision: The Crisis of the American System*.

Simply stated, the thesis of *Decade of Decision* was that American capitalism had reached a critical stage in its development, one that will result in fundamental institutional changes. Calling attention to the business-cycle theory of Joseph Schumpeter, which emphasized the role of innovation in cyclical movements of the economy and which incorporated the observations of N. D. Kondratiev, a Soviet economist who saw fifty-year ''long cycles'' in capitalist economies, Harrington summarized the Schumpeterian theory of business fluctuations that many economists find compelling. Since cycles of innovation ''regularly disturbed the normal equilibrium'' of the economy, ''Is it possible,'' Harrington asked, ''that the period 1945–67 was a gigantic Kondratiev upswing powered by electronics, petrochemicals and the restoration of war-ravaged economies?'' If this were true, it could, he warned, have important—even drastic—implications for American capitalism in the 1980s.

Schumpeter's theory would explain, Harrington argued, why Keynesian fiscal and monetary policies had worked—or had *seemed* to work—so well for an entire generation, but then failed to avert the stagflation of the 1970s. Keynesianism ''worked'' from 1945 to the late 1960s ''Because there was a fundamentally different—ascendant—economic environment.'' There was therefore the distinct possibility that ''Washington's planners merely nurtured, but did not at all cause,'' American postwar prosperity. If so, this meant, by the same reasoning, that ''the successes of 1945–69 also laid the basis for the difficulties in 1970 and after.''[15]

Beyond his discussion of this changed general environment, Harrington examined the structural conditions and policies that, he theorized, were exacerbating the effects of the current Kondratiev downswing. Citing evidence that neither federal spending nor wage or regulatory costs could account for the burst of inflation in the 1970s, he hypothesized that ''The

---

[15] Michael Harrington, *Decade of Decision: The Crisis of the American System* (New York: Simon and Schuster, 1980), p. 57. Subsequently cited parenthetically as *DD*.

evolution of corporate power, its increasing concentration, and its unresponsiveness to the market are . . . structural determinants of the crisis of stagflation. *So also are the specific conditions in four key sectors—food and fuel, housing and health—three of which are not concentrated"* (*DD*, 71, Harrington's emphasis). Why did prices rise more rapidly in these four areas than in those related to nonnecessities? To Harrington, the answer was clear: these sectors had been operating on the basis of a kind of socialized capitalism that guaranteed huge private profits but even larger social costs. In agriculture, for example, subsidies promoted "nonproduction through payments to farmers—rather than simply guaranteeing farm income and enjoying the benefits of maximum output as is done in some other countries." This meant a direct subsidy that was of most benefit to agribusiness and large growers, while also causing "an artificial and expensive scarcity which bids up consumer prices" (*DD*, 75).

The second aspect of stagflation—unemployment—was similarly made more severe by institutional inadequacy. Even though unemployment "menaces employed workers, women, minorities, people on pensions, as well as the Third World, the cause of peace and the protection of the environment," it had not been overcome, because a policy of full employment would exact its *own* price from the corporate and financial elite: namely, increased wage costs (and therefore a redistribution of income), the disappearance of a surplus labor pool, and the consequent lessened manageability of the labor force. But high unemployment had still other, worse, effects on society as a whole, including lost tax revenue from foregone production and related social expenditures (unemployment compensation, food stamps, and the like), amounting to $67.3 billion in fiscal 1976. A related consequence was what has been called the "fiscal crisis of the state," as government under advanced capitalism was forced to take on an increasing share of the costs of running the economy and was thus increasingly unable to balance its accounts.

But the decade of the 1970s had seen more than economic dysfunction: it had also witnessed the apparent acceptance by broad sections of the American public of the social philosophy of the New Right. Remarking that in the late 1970s "Federal and state tax laws were changed in favor of the rich and against the interest of the people, often with the enthusiastic and militant consent of the people who thus helped discriminate against themselves," Harrington pointed out that the phenomenon of people taking such a willing part in their own exploitation was neither new or unusual. "Every society," he reminded his readers, "must produce an ideology which legitimates its inequities and thereby persuades those at the bottom to accept, and even revere, their own inferiority" (*DD*, 108, 108-109). Nor, as Kennedy-Johnson policy demonstrated, were upper-class tax relief and its economic rationalization historically unknown. Thus the "new" corporate ideology of the 1970s not only prevented egalitarian reforms: it also left standing an already existing structure of inequality that was, Harrington believed, both economically unnecessary and socially unconscionable in a society in which a mere 0.5 percent of the population owned 25 percent of all wealth, the bottom 80 percent owned about 23 percent, and the bottom quarter actually had *negative* wealth because of debt.

To the argument of the New Right that planning and government action of the kind advocated by liberals and leftists had already been discredited in the 1960s and could only lead to economic and social disaster, Harrington replied that American capitalism had itself caused upheavals that in some respects rivaled those of the worst days of Stalinism, but that, because they occurred in a democratic society and as a result of what was claimed to be "the work of the objective and impersonal Market," had not called forth indignant cries of outrage from the same conservative who abhorred the idea of social planning. Catastrophes such as the mass displacement of farm laborers in the postwar years and the migration of minority groups and the poor generally into inner cities had created problems that were not, Harrington argued, mainly the work of liberals, although some government policies *were* harmful and some funds had been misspent. The fiscal crisis of urban America had occurred in a context of shrinking tax bases, demographic upheaval, and increasing unemployment; hence, the decay of urban areas could be arrested and reversed only by means of a national poverty policy that could deal with the root causes of poverty at local, national, and even international levels, a key part of which was the abolition of all taxes except a progressive income tax whose returns could then be redistributed to state and local governments according to a formula weighted for poverty, social problems, and population.

Had poverty itself been ameliorated since Harrington had begun *The Other America*? He conceded that, as a percentage of the total population, poverty had decreased—in large part as the result of increased Social Security benefits and the establishment of Medicare, which had reduced the proportional incidence of poverty among the elderly from one third of their number to only 13 percent. Nevertheless, he pointed out "some disturbing facts" about this apparent progress: poverty in absolute terms decreased from 1962 to 1969 and then moved up and down from 1969 to 1976, showing that it was "a structural problem inextricably tied up with the basic economic rhythms of American society" (*DD*, 229). Harrington concluded that there were therefore still about 55 million poor in the United States in 1980, the same number that had existed in 1959 (although it was probable that there were millions more, since the poor were the ones most often missed in a census). He argued that those who posited a significantly lower figure because of the existence of social welfare programs and the "in-kind" income they provided ignored the severe constraints on such forms of "wealth" and "income," the dependency involved in accepting it, and in the case of things such as health care, its inflated value and even the harm it could cause. (Harrington also pointed out that, interestingly, the theory of "in-kind" income and wealth was never applied to the upper classes, despite the fact that they received much more of these kinds of benefits than the poor and that if it were, the distributions of income and wealth would appear even worse than they did.)

The persistence of poverty and egregious amounts of inequality in America was, according to Harrington, the result of the general inadequacy of liberal theory and practice. This could be clearly apprehended from the results of the emphasis put on education and manpower programs under The Great Society and even during Nixon's term of office. Liberals had believed that these efforts would boost productivity and, since intelligence and talent were randomly and normally distributed, move society toward a more egalitarian structure. For a time, this appeared to be working. But liberal hopes were eventually dashed as, surprisingly, income and wealth differentials between classes and even *within* demographic and age groups did not change and as gains in productivity were sharply reduced by the mid-1970s.

Why had more people not entered the middle class? Partly, Harrington explained, this was a result of inadequate funding. But the main reason was that this problem was deeply rooted in social structure. Harrington thus proposed that "although education may facilitate the rise of individuals, it does not, by itself, change class structure" and could not, therefore, fulfill optimistic liberal expectations (*DD*, 261).

Did not these results support the conservative idea that present inequalities were either ineradicable or at least necessary for increased productivity, which would require, after a severe decline in the 1970s, even *greater* pay differentials as well as tax cuts for businessmen as incentives? Not at all, Harrington replied. Increased productivity in the modern world required more, not less equality, since in late capitalist society virtually all absolute needs had been satisfied, leaving the greatest demand for those goods that by their very nature could not be attained by more than a relatively small proportion of the population (for example prestigious and well-paying jobs, homes with scenic views of the ocean, and so forth). Such a condition led to economically wasteful attempts by most individuals to obtain through educational, political, and even legal means those things that only a few individuals could possess. Reducing the cost of finishing second or third in the race for power, prestige, income, and wealth by leveling their distribution and splitting up the possession of each of these rewards could, Harrington maintained, lessen the income, time, and energy devoted to the effort to acquire them, and would thereby increase both equality and productivity.[16]

But was there a constituency to support such changes, given the apparently increasing conservative drift in politics in the 1970s? Here Harrington believed that it was necessary to distinguish between what scholars have called *ideological* and *operational* political positions. While studies have shown the majority of Americans to be ideological conservatives, that is, in the words of two researchers, ''to accept the traditional ideology which advocates the curbing of Federal power,'' these studies have also consistently shown a majority of Americans to be operational liberals who favor wage and price controls, national health insurance, federal intervention in the field of health care, a policy of full employment, and increased federal spending on environmental and urban problems. About this seeming paradox Harrington wrote:

> These data suggest that America is an exceedingly confused nation and this has social, as well as individual psychological, significance. Because America still believes in a Horatio Alger idyll which it instinctively knows will not work in practice, its operational liberalism is truncated. Thus, the presence of a democratic socialist ideology in Europe is at least one of the reasons why unemployment there was half that of the American average during the post–World War II period—or why the United States is the only Western country without a national health system. (*DD*, 290-291)

This political schizophrenia meant that it was ''important to change America in *both* ideological and operational ways, for the two are not unre-

---

[16] Harrington acknowledges that these ideas were taken from Fred Hirsch's *Social Limits to Growth* (Cambridge: Harvard University Press, 1976).

lated.'' This implied the need for ''practical reforms *and* ideological education,'' since there was ''no single, 'natural' majority'' in America that
could be rallied to support a specific set of political views and programs,
and which majority came to the fore depended on many variables (*DD*,
291).

Neither was it true that the working class was shrinking or even disappearing, since the rapidly growing service sector of the American economy
''includes a huge number of people paid much less than blue-collar workers and employed in menial jobs.'' Granting the proposition that a worker
''is not simply a worker, but a member of a race, an ethnic group, a sex, a
geographic community, a generation, etc.,'' Harrington nonetheless called
attention to the fact that ''at certain periods, the basic economic interest
may assert itself as an overwhelming and integrating factor. That happened
in the thirties. It could happen in the eighties'' (*DD*, 300, 302). As before,
however, he stressed that workers could have significant influence only as
part of a broader coalition that included the new class, a group whose political orientation he still viewed as undetermined. The new class, he
wrote, had ''contradictory political tendencies.'' Being educated and
rather affluent, it could adopt elitist, anti-worker views. But to the extent
that it ''now finds itself facing the problems of a stagflation economy, that
class has a self-interest in making a common cause with the workers in a
campaign for full employment through planned social investments.''
Lastly, its college training led that group to an awareness of ''the structural
inadequacies of American society'' (*DD*, 309). Again Harrington expressed his belief that conservative forces could split up a potential labor-
poor-minority-new class coalition by ''pit[ting] poor blacks against organized workers, women against men, New Class environmentalists against
trade unionists fighting for their jobs, etc.'' But he also believed that the
effort to forestall such an alliance could not be successfully undertaken
within the ideological and programmatic framework of the ''old-fashioned
economic conservatism'' of the New Right, since its promotion of business
values and interests was too blatantly pro-corporate. What conservatives
needed, Harrington proposed, was a ''sophisticated reactionary strategy''
that would ''maintain the living standard of some of the workers and the
middle class, and even provide benefits for them, but which would pay for
their security by attacking the poorly organized and the unorganized''
(*DD*, 310-311).

With the election of Ronald Reagan in 1980, one of the most conservative political ideologues in modern American history came to national

power and proceeded not merely to slow the development of the welfare state, but to drastically curtail its workings and fundamentally reorient American social policy and the political structures that directed it. In a book called *The New American Poverty*, Harrington described the acute suffering of those dependent on America's already minimal welfare programs, programs now slashed to levels that often no longer provided for even basic necessities. Reagan, he wrote, was "an authentic radical," but while he was "a man of principle, even a utopian," Harrington charged that "his utopia is, whether he knows it or not, a cover-up for the *realpolitik* of the rich and corporations" and that "It also didn't work."[17] Yet the position he had adopted in *Decade of Decision* still described his assessment of political choices for Americans. Possible futures included a society under the "total and unchallenged control of private, corporate bureaucracies"; a sophisticated conservatism that, in union with a pro-corporate government apparatus, used planning to achieve social stability and serve corporate interests; a hierarchical society dominated by technocrats of the new class—Max Shachtman's nightmare come true; and national democratic planning—the public control of corporate decisions and investments and their subordination to the common good. A new order was arising. Its nature would be decided, either consciously or by default, by the present generation.

[17] Michael Harrington, *The New American Poverty* (New York: Holt, Rinehart and Winston, 1984), pp. 253-254.

Chapter 7   *Harrington and American Socialism*

A recurrent theme in Harrington's writings has been his search for a viable democratic left in America, a country that, virtually alone of all industrialized democracies, has no significant socialist or labor party. Yet Harrington has admitted that he had refrained from even using the *word* "socialism" in his book *The Other America* for fear that it would alienate his readers and distract them from the main themes and problems he wished to discuss. A crucial question which therefore must be addressed in any examination of Harrington's life and thought is the reason why it has been so difficult for him and other American reformers to build support for the kinds of policies and programs that are usually taken for granted in Western European nations and a number of others. Despite the fact that the United States has one of the smallest tax burdens as a percentage of GNP and the least government intervention in economic affairs, Americans have long shown themselves to be suspicious of, as well as openly hostile to, the enlargement of either the size or the influence of the public sector (with the exception of the military), with the result that this sector is markedly smaller and less powerful than that of practically any other market society. Social democratic influence in America has been, in other words, remarkably weak. Why is this so?

THE MISSING LEFT: WHY IS THERE NO SOCIALISM IN THE UNITED STATES?

In what was probably the first comprehensive attempt to deal with these issues, the German social theorist Werner Sombart sought to explain the absence of a strong social democratic movement in America in his book *Why Is There No Socialism in the United States?* published in 1906. Sombart's book opened with the observation that America was "capitalism's land of promise," rich in natural resources, fertile land, with many good rivers, harbors, and a "vast market area." "One can truly say," Sombart mused, "that if one wanted to construct the ideal country for the development of capitalism on the lines required by this economic system, such a country could take on the dimensions and particular characteristics only of the United States."[1] These characteristics, he emphasized, were not merely physical: immigrants to America "had left all remnants of their European character behind in their former homes, together with all super-fluous romanticism and sentimentality. They had left everything of their feudal artisan existence, as well as all sense of traditionalism, and had taken across with them only what was necessary and of service to the de-velopment of a capitalist economy, namely a powerful, unremitting energy and an ideology that turned activity in the pursuit of capitalist aims into a duty, as if it were a response to a command from God to the faithful."[2]

Sombart realized, of course, that the premise contained in the title of his book was, if taken literally, false. There *was* socialism in the United States, he conceded, in the form of not only one, but *two* socialist parties. His point was that, in terms of its impact on politics and on the conscious-ness of workers, socialism was not an important force in American society. Thus, he proposed that the vast majority of American workers—especially skilled workers—and their most important leaders were not attracted to it. This did not mean that American workers never advocated political meas-ures to curb some of the workings of the market, but simply that "the American worker does not embrace the 'spirit' of Socialism as we now understand it in continental Europe, which is essentially Socialism with a Marxist character." Therefore, although Sombart noted elsewhere in his treatise that "the misery of the slums in the large American cities finds its real equal only in the East End of London," he proposed that the "modal" American worker was "not on the whole dissatisfied with the present con-dition of things," that he possessed a "boundless optimism, which comes out as a belief in the mission and greatness of his country," and that he "is not opposed to the capitalist economic system as such, either intellectually or emotionally."[3]

Beyond these observations, Sombart investigated a number of other fac-tors—political, economic, and demographic—that militated against the development of socialism in America, one of which was the extreme dif-ficulty of breaking the monopoly of the two dominant parties in the Amer-ican political system. Furthermore, he stated his belief that, in contrast to

[1] Werner Sombart, *Why Is There No Socialism in the United States?* [1906] translated by Patri-cia M. Hocking and C. T. Husbands (White Plains, New York: International Arts and Sciences Press, 1976), pp. 3-4.

[2] Ibid., p. 4.

[3] Ibid., pp. 17-19.

European parties, "There is no trace of any fundamental difference of viewpoint between the two American parties on the most important political questions." Political parties in America were not "groups of people united in the representation of common political principles," he wrote, although that may have been true at the time of their origins and again for a period during the Civil War. By the end of that war, however, "The complete lack of political principle in the two major parties became quite blatant for the first time. Today, in fact, they are no more than organizations for the common purpose of hunting offices. . . ."[4]

Other influences and circumstances also contributed to the weakness of American socialism, according to Sombart, including lower prices and dramatically higher average American wages vis-à-vis those of Europe. As wages continued to move up both absolutely and relative to European rates, the average American worker could not help but adopt a pro-capitalist mentality. It was in this context that Sombart made his famous remark that "All socialist utopias came to nothing on roast beef and apple pie," a witty bit of hyperbole that has often caused a misunderstanding of his overall thesis. In addition, he noted that the social and political positions of the American worker were appreciably different from those of his European counterpart. For Americans, he claimed, liberty and equality "are not empty ideas and vague dreams, as they are for the European working class; for the most part they are realities," a fact reflected in their attitudes and behavior:

> Anyone who has ever observed, even only fleetingly, male and female American workers as they carry on their life outside the factory or the workshop, has noticed at first sight that they are a different breed of people from German workers. . . . On the street they are like members of the middle class and they act as working gentlemen and working ladies. In the external appearance of the American worker there is not the stigma of being the class apart that almost all European workers have about them. In his appearance, in his demeanour, and in the manner of his conversation, the American worker also contrasts strongly with the European one. He carries his head high, walks with a lissom stride, and is as open and cheerful in his expression as any member of the middle class. There is nothing oppressed or submissive about him. He mixes with everyone—in reality and not only in theory—as an equal.[5]

[4] Ibid., pp. 45, 47-48.
[5] Ibid., pp. 109-110.

Nonetheless, Sombart saw capitalism even under the best, that is, American, conditions as a repressive and conflict-ridden system. "Even American capitalism," he wrote, "puts tight fetters on the individual, even American capitalism cannot deny that it holds its workers in a condition of slavery, and even American capitalism has had periods of stagnation with all their destructive consequences for the worker (such as unemployment, pressure on wages, and so on)."[6] A "confrontational mentality" would therefore have eventually developed among many of those who saw themselves as victims of this social order. But Sombart believed that America offered "another goal" to most of these "dissatisfied wage laborers": they could become independent farmers in the West. There was, in effect, a safety valve that prevented inevitable frictions and discontent from threatening capitalist institutions. Apparently, then, socialism had little chance of gaining support in America.

This was *not*, however, Sombart's conclusion, as one of the last lines of his essay makes clear. *"All the factors that till now have prevented the development of Socialism in the United States are about to disappear or to be converted into their opposite,"* he predicted, *"with the result that in the next generation Socialism in America will very probably experience the greatest possible expansion of its appeal."*[7] Sombart thus believed that the special conditions that had been adverse to the growth of socialism in the United States had only *temporarily* retarded its development. A strong socialist movement was, in his view, indeed possible and imminent.

In this belief Sombart was not the victim of an idiosyncratic delusion. Nineteen hundred and six was a year in which the fear and anticipation of a socialist movement in America was shared by a large number of sober observers. In a letter to William Howard Taft in that year, Theodore Roosevelt deplored the social conditions that, together with "corruption in business and politics, have tended to produce a very unhealthy condition of excitement and irritation in the popular mind, which shows itself in part in the enormous increase in the socialistic propaganda." Those responsible for this "propaganda" were, Roosevelt warned, "building up a revolutionary feeling which will most probably take the form of a political campaign."[8] And, while some of Roosevelt's fears were undoubtedly exaggerated, the fact remains that there was an established and active socialist movement in America in the early twentieth century; moreover, its size

[6] Ibid., p. 115.
[7] Ibid., p. 119, Sombart's emphasis.
[8] Quoted in Richard Hofstadter, *The Age of Reform*, p. 239.

was increasing at what seemed to many to be an alarming rate. Membership in the Socialist Party of America alone during this period often doubled at two-year intervals, growing from 20,763 members in 1904, to 41,751 in 1908, and to 117,984 in 1912, a year in which its candidate for the presidency, Eugene Debs, received 6 percent of the popular vote. There was a socialist member of Congress in 1910 and an additional one four years later. By 1911, 33 American cities were under socialist administrations.[9] Yet only a dozen years later the socialist movement in America was in complete disarray, its membership evaporated, its philosophy unattractive and in disrepute. What had caused such a turnaround?

The failure of America's nascent socialism to live up to its early promise at the turn of the century is bound up, both before and since, with the entire history of the American nation. In tracing key aspects of this history, it is possible to accept in broad outline much of Sombart's analysis, as does Harrington. Sombart was certainly correct in seeing a fundamental difference in the evolution and nature of American institutions, values, and ideology in comparison with those of Europe. The first generation of settlers in New England in the early seventeenth century—those who bequeathed to future citizens the indelible stamp of their political ideas and social perceptions that was later to give America's governmental structure much of its peculiar nature—were political and religious dissenters from the middle ranks of English society. Mainly villagers and artisans, these people were, as Lawrence Stone has remarked, "sick and tired of the financial, military, and administrative centralization which [King] Charles and [Archbishop] Laud were forcing down their throats."[10] Testimony to their dissatisfaction was the emigration of 17,000 of them during the 1630s to New England where, Stone writes, "The political and religious system the emigrants established was based on the principle of localism, meaning the local autonomy and self-government in church and state which Charles had threatened at home. Without either nobles or the poor, it was, and long remained, relatively egalitarian in its distribution of wealth, although it inherited from its English past a sufficient sense of deference to superiors to hold the society together, at least until the 1690s."[11] The social composition of this cohort together with the historical circumstances surrounding its departure from its homeland thus goes far to explain the roots of the

[9] See David A. Shannon, *The Socialist Party of America: A History* (Chicago: Quadrangle, 1967).

[10] *The New York Review of Books*, 5 February 1981, p. 34.

[11] Ibid.

political institutions and cultural attitudes that exist today—roots whose trace memories live on in the American subconscious to exert a powerful influence on contemporary life in the same way that early personal experiences can predispose, if not determine, the attitudes and actions of individual adults.

The creation of a national myth embodied in a "fragment tradition," it has been proposed, is an essential aspect of the founding of new nations by "fragments" of old ones that can reveal much about the subsequent histories of the former.[12] The basic features of America's myth were outlined three and a half centuries ago. It was the kind of myth that, by assuming the reality of a rough social and economic equality, did not encourage the formation of overt and oppositional political movements to obtain what most people imagined they already had. Moreover, strong and often centralized governmental authority of the type used by modern European social democratic states and used extensively in the past even by conservative parties to effect collective goals, would always retain in the minds of Americans the taint of illegitimate force, unwanted interference, and political repression.

This ideological and institutional structure was both reflected and reinforced during the period of the American Revolution, a conflict itself brought about at least in part by the general belief among colonists that this structure was being threatened by a huge, corrupt, repressive administrative apparatus created by Britain to establish a "tyranny" in America. The rationality of the belief in such an intention or possible result has been seriously questioned by knowledgeable scholars, but there can be little doubt that Americans accepted this notion.[13] Of additional significance is the fact that the Revolution was, as Eric Foner has noted, generally "conducted and controlled by an alliance of the colonial ruling classes—merchants, lawyers and large landowners in the northern colonies, slaveholding planters in the South."[14] Under such leadership the rebellion remained focused on the issue of political independence and did not, except for brief interludes, threaten to develop any sustained movement toward internal

---

[12] See Louis Hartz, *The Founding of New Societies: Studies in the History of the United States, Latin America, South Africa, Canada, and Australia* (New York: Harbinger, 1964), passim and especially chapter 8, part 5 by Richard N. Rosecrance.

[13] See Bernard Bailyn, *The Ideological Origins of the American Revolution* (Cambridge: Harvard University Press, Belknap, 1967) and Gordon S. Wood, *The Creation of the American Republic, 1776–1787* (New York: W. W. Norton, 1972).

[14] Eric Foner, *Tom Paine and Revolutionary America* (Oxford: Oxford University Press, 1977), p. xvii.

social change—a circumstance that would have important implications for the future of reform movements in America. Unlike France, a nation whose revolution included a final, radical phase strongly influenced by artisans, tradesmen, philosophical radicals, and members of the lower classes and peasantry, America experienced no similar phase or influence, and consequently had little use for men like Sam Adams, Patrick Henry, and particularly Thomas Paine (who came closest to egalitarian radicalism in the European sense) once its revolution was well under way, and especially after independence was secured.

One result of this is that American nationalism, unlike the French type, has not, with the exception of Republican ideology before and during the Civil War, included a commitment to, or association with, social reform. Nationalism in America has instead been identified almost exclusively with the concepts of independence and national security, and, of equal importance, has been an issue almost totally monopolized by the American business class, a fact that has continually deprived social critics and reformers of an important—indeed crucial—source of legitimation for their ideas, programs, and political action. So strongly have economic liberalism and American nationalism been conceptually joined in the public mind that they are perceived by most citizens as mutually implicative. (Leftists in Europe, despite whatever other vilifications they have endured, have rarely been labeled ''Un-French,'' ''Un-German,'' or ''Un-Swedish.'')

Sombart's hypothesis concerning the absence of feudalism and other ties to the Old World and its effect on American culture and institutions would seem to find support in the foregoing analysis. But this is true only in part. The transplantation of disgruntled refugees to a virgin environment may largely explain the absence of European-style radicalism. That this does not explain the continued and widespread resistance of Americans to more general and less doctrinaire social democratic ideas can be seen from the case of another mass of people uprooted from Great Britain who settled a new land—the Australians.[15]

Significantly, there is as little socialism (in Sombart's sense of the word) in Australia as there is in America. Australians, like Americans, had neither feudal institutions nor an entrenched and rigid class structure to foster its growth. Richard Rosecrance has explained, however, that what they did have was a vivid collective memory of the economic distress and class

---

[15] See Richard N. Rosecrance, ''The Radical Culture of Australia,'' in Hartz, *The Founding of New Societies*, pp. 275-318. I have drawn heavily on this essay for the present discussion.

prejudice that had been endured by the first wave of settlers in the early nineteenth century—the poor, the political radicals, the criminals, who, thrown off the land into cities by the Enclosure movement, comprised the flotsam cast off Britain's shores during the worst period of the Industrial Revolution. Unlike America's first colonists, the first Australians were almost all members of the urban lower classes, whose resentment and hatred of the social order they had left was directed not at the British government per se, but at the upper classes who dominated its workings and who were the chief architects and beneficiaries of the economic and political order that had condemned them to exile. Although later waves of immigrants were made up primarily of lower-middle-class elements, they too had grown critical of the brutal industrial system that had imposed physical hardships and deprivation on so many. Such people were not likely to be— as was even an American such as Thomas Paine—devotees of laissez-faire capitalism. Thus it was that Australia gave birth to one of the world's strongest labor parties. Furthermore, the attainment of national independence in Australia did not entail a reaction against governmental power or colonial repression, since British administration had not been harsh and was ended peacefully with the granting of Dominion status in 1901. The state in Australia was therefore not associated almost exclusively with the maintenance of order and security, the establishment of independence, and the promotion of economic and territorial expansion as it was in America; it was instead perceived as an instrumental force to achieve needed and popular reforms, since the Australians, in Rosecrance's words, "believed that the major constraints on individual liberty were not public, but private." Consequently, while America's national heroes are almost all either military leaders, successful entrepreneurs, political leaders committed to extending or preserving America's territorial boundaries, or frontiersmen pushing westward, Rosecrance has pointed out that in Australia "The real nationalists are fighters of the social struggle."

Yet, however important the circumstances surrounding the establishment of settlements and national institutions are to an understanding of a nation's receptiveness to socialist ideas, subsequent and specific historical conditions, events, and trends must also be reckoned with. There is, for example, the question of social and economic equality. Tocqueville believed that, although there were rich men in early nineteenth-century America, wealth circulated with "incredible rapidity," with the result that men there were "nearer equality in wealth and mental endowments, or, in other words, more nearly equally powerful, than in any other country of the world or in any other age of recorded history.''

To what extent has America lived up to its national myth? Several studies have shown that, despite the relatively egalitarian conditions that obtained during the first generation of settlement, an inexorable trend toward increased social stratification had, by the early eighteenth century, produced a society of significant economic inequality and marked class distinctions.[16] Disparities in income, wealth, and political power had become so pronounced after the rapid industrialization of the late nineteenth century that many feared a mass uprising of the discontented and downtrodden—the very fear expressed above by Theodore Roosevelt. It has long been recognized by students of society, however, that what is crucial in determining the ability of a particular social order to maintain popular allegiance in the face of such inequality is neither the degree of stratification nor the absolute, ''objective'' level of economic well-being, but rather the direction of movement in income, wealth, and status over time, the reference groups to which people compare themselves when deciding if their achieved position is ''fair,'' and the real but also the *perceived* opportunities to become upwardly mobile. For example, research by historian Stephen Thernstrom on occupational mobility in late nineteenth-century America suggests that, at least in large urban areas such as Boston, there was a good deal of movement from one generation to the next.[17]

[16] Some of the most important studies of this transition are: Kenneth A. Lockridge, *A New England Town: The First Hundred Years* (New York: W. W. Norton, 1970); Richard L. Bushman, *From Puritan to Yankee: Character and the Social Order in Connecticut, 1690–1765* (New York: W. W. Norton, 1970); and Michael Zuckerman, *Peaceable Kingdoms: New England Towns in the Eighteenth Century* (New York: Vintage, 1972). On the degree of social stratification in Jacksonian America, see Edward Pessen, ''Inequality in American Life,'' in John H. Cary and Julius Weinberg, eds., *The Social Fabric: American Life from 1607 to the Civil War* (Boston: Little, Brown and Company, 1975), pp. 169-181.

[17] See Stephen Thernstrom, ''Socialism and Social Mobility,'' in John H. M. Laslett and Seymour Martin Lipset, eds., *Failure of a Dream? Essays in the History of American Socialism* (Garden City, New York: Anchor/Doubleday, 1974), pp. 509-527. Herbert Gutman also notes in his study of Paterson, New Jersey, from 1830 to 1880 that ''So many successful manufacturers who had begun as workers walked the streets of that city then that it is not hard to believe that others less successful or just starting out on the lower rungs of the occupational mobility ladder could be convinced by personal knowledge that 'hard work' resulted in spectacular material and social improvement.'' Herbert G. Gutman, ''The Reality of the Rags-to-Riches 'Myth': The Case of the Paterson, New Jersey, Locomotive, Iron, and Machinery Manufacturers, 1830–1880,'' in Stephen Thernstrom and Richard Sennett, eds., *Nineteenth-Century Cities: Essays in the New Urban History* (New Haven: Yale University Press, 1969), pp. 98-124 (p. 122). Stuart Blumin also makes the important point in his study of nineteenth-century Philadelphia that, although the opportunity for economic advancement in that city probably declined markedly by mid-century as

Nevertheless, Harrington and others have emphasized that no theory of the general *embourgeoisement* of the working class can be based on a simple increase in average economic rewards. One could, in fact, expect that a generally prosperous working class would be all the more inclined to support social reforms, especially during or after periods of economic slumps. "In point of fact," as Harrington has written, "to the degree that America was better fed and freer than Europe before World War I . . . it was a provocation to insurgency." Also, average wage levels may hide great inequalities among workers, some of whom could form a permanent underclass.

But Thernstrom's research indicates that if such an underclass existed in late nineteenth-century urban America, it did not settle for long periods of time in any single place. Indeed, demographic studies have shown that America, geographically enormous to begin with, was a nation characterized by an extraordinarily rapid turnover in population in its urban areas, with large numbers of itinerant poor and laborers wandering over the huge land in an atomized state. Such a dispersed proletariat was difficult if not impossible to organize for any kind of political action. The sheer size of the nation also meant, as Daniel Bell has explained, that the great amount of labor violence that did occur from 1870 to 1940 was spread over such a wide area that it could not have the same social or political impact as would an identical per capita amount of unrest in a smaller European country such as France. Therefore, whether or not there actually existed a safety valve for the discontented on the homesteads of the Western frontier (an idea that has been disputed), there was at least one kind of outlet for those on the margin of American society—space.[18] Nor were discontent and violence enhanced through a joining of economic unrest with specifically and independently political discontent and violence, since America, like Australia but unlike European nations, achieved political democracy *before* industrialization with its attendant stresses and strains. Thus it was that not

the result of the dominance of large-merchant capitalism by 1840 (which helped to produce an incredibly skewed distribution of wealth), "a decline in the extensiveness of opportunity does not necessarily make the success ideology less potent. The American Dream is fed, not by such mundane matters as mobility matrices, but by isolated cases of spectacular success." Stuart Blumin, "Mobility and Change in Ante-Bellum Philadelphia," ibid., pp. 165-208 (p. 203).

[18] See Stephen Thernstrom and Peter R. Knights, "Men in Motion: Some Data and Speculations about Urban Population Mobility in Nineteenth-Century America," *The Journal of Interdisciplinary History* 1 (Autumn 1970), 7-35. Concerning Bell's idea of "insulating space," see Daniel Bell, *The Coming of Post-Industrial Society: A Venture in Social Forecasting* (New York: Basic, 1973), pp. 314-316.

only leftists but even classical liberals, who in Europe had been moved to direct and radical action to achieve basic parliamentary rights and liberties, were partially defanged virtually from the outset.

But there is still another American peculiarity that is increasingly believed by scholars to have placed severe constraints on the growth of an effective socialist or social democratic opposition in the United States. This was, of course, the massive waves of immigration between 1870 and 1920. So large were the numbers of foreign arrivals that census data reveal they comprised between 30 to 50 percent (depending on the decade) of the increases in American population during this half century of rapid population growth. This fact was to have enormous significance for Sombart's theory of *embourgeoisement*. For not only is there evidence that American wage and occupational mobility rates were substantially higher than those of Europe, but Thernstrom's work also shows that rates of mobility for second-generation Americans in late nineteenth-century Boston were as high as those of the offspring of native-born stock and almost *three times* as high as those of their immigrant fathers. And, although the chances for the second generation to retain their positions in white-collar occupations were no greater than those of the first-generation immigrants (who remained overwhelmingly blue-collar), both groups evidently found that America offered far more opportunity to rise economically and socially than the lands they had left. As Harrington has proposed, it is this set of unusual circumstances that made Sombart's theory right for the wrong reasons. The "crucial factor" here, as Harrington notes, was not abundance, but foreign birth, since "many of the immigrants, even though living under objectively degrading conditions, saw their lot as improved compared to the old country. They thus had an impression of relative betterment, not relative deprivation." This phenomenon, he points out, also operated in nineteenth-century Europe, as rural dwellers were attracted to cities, having heard of better pay and other advantages to be had there. Increased contentment, though often only temporary, was often the result, as it was for those who came to America between 1880 and 1920 from "the countryside of the world."[19]

The high concentration of ethnics in urban centers also helps to account for the defeat of Populist-reformist forces in the pivotal election of 1896.

[19] Michael Harrington, *Socialism* (New York: Bantam, 1973), p. 159. On the social mobility of American immigrants, see Stephen Thernstrom, "Immigrants and WASPS: Ethnic Differences in Occupational Mobility in Boston, 1890–1940," in Thernstrom and Sennett, *Nineteenth-Century Cities*, pp. 125-164.

While it would seem at first that urban ethnics and Populists had similar grievances arising out of the social and economic displacements associated with America's rapid industrialization and the depression of the early 1890s, ethnic, religious, and urban-rural antagonisms divided the two groups and would continue to do so for more than a generation. Such conditions did not exist in Europe, though they *might* have arisen in Australia as a consequence of the attempts of businessmen and plantation owners to import Asians as indentured laborers. But liberal and especially labor groups succeeded in abolishing the "Kanaka" trade and establishing the exclusionary laws that underlay what became the "White Australia" policy. While rooted partly in racism, the main motivation for this policy was the fear of downward pressure on wages and a weakening of labor power and solidarity.

Racism, however, *was* to play a major role in the American labor movement, although the results, given the context of American society, were to be far different. The American Civil War, while technically freeing black slaves as part of a liberal revolution directed against the essentially authoritarian society of the South, had only partially transformed that social order through war and the period of Reconstruction. The national dominance of the planter elite was ended, but because their regional and local power was not diminished, the South remained basically a rural society tied to single-crop plantation agriculture and planter ideology and thus a reservoir of political reaction and militarism, containing a labor pool of black sharecroppers and agrarian workers who were eventually to move into the industrial cities of the North. What therefore emerged from the post–Civil War era was to a large degree not really a liberal democracy, but rather a *Herrenvolk* nation divided on the basis of race into two interconnected and yet separate societies—a situation from which Northern financial interests benefitted as much as the planter class and industrialists of the South. This political alliance had an enormous stake in dividing American workers against each other and used its influence to end the political cooperation of Southern black and white tenants and to thwart a possible alliance of the latter groups with Midwestern farmers in the 1890s, leading to the formal segregation of blacks for the first time.[20] Thus it was that racism, born in colonial America in the early eighteenth century, received powerful reinforcements from Southern and Northern elites for generations in modern

---

[20] See Jonathan M. Wiener, *Social Origins of the New South: Alabama, 1860–1885* (Baton Rouge: Louisiana State University Press, 1978).

America. This was seriously to weaken the bargaining position of American labor as a whole, while providing economic benefits to a minority, and psychological benefits to a majority, of workers. Blacks, condemned to permanent debt peonage and denied even formal political rights, could scarcely bolster the union movement or alter their position as a formally stigmatized reserve army of labor, remaining unable even by the 1980s to form effective coalitions with whites and other groups who in principle share many of their grievances and beliefs.

The case of Australia was, again, different. Aborigines, although in many ways as oppressed as the freed American slaves, lacked both the numerical strength and the long cultural association with the dominant majority even to *attempt* to enter Australian life on its own terms. Victims of almost total exclusion from any aspect of Australian civilization, their numbers and impact dwindled through cultural shock and the encroachment of settlers, their lands having been gradually closed off to them, causing them to become marginal laborers. Military intervention ended their eventual revolt, contributing to a reduction in their numbers from about 350,000 in 1788 to only about 50,000 by the end of World War II. The treatment and the eventual fate of Australians of color was therefore more comparable to that of American Indians than to that of American blacks. Brutality and racism thus need not reinforce the power of economic elites; that they did so in America again reflects different circumstances.

The alliance among downtrodden Southern blacks, Midwestern farmers, and urban ethnics having been prevented during the Populist era, improved economic conditions and the reforms of the Progressive Era took most of the steam out of America's first modern radical movement. Yet a strong undercurrent of discontent remained, and, although the political strength of the Socialist party peaked in 1912, it continued to be a force whose potential influence was feared by conservatives and moderates. In these respects, its position was similar to that of the British Labour party. Committed to relatively moderate social democratic ideals and programs, they were effectively prevented from building broader bases as a result of the political monopolies established by strong two-party systems that, as Sombart had understood, were able to co-opt progressive leaders and incorporate elements of reform proposals in their own platforms in order to deny the third parties greater influence. Yet Labour emerged as a permanent major party in Britain at the end of World War I, while the American Socialist party went into a steep decline. Why did this happen?

It might well be pointed out that the Labour party in Britain was intrinsically stronger than the American Socialist party, since it functioned in a fundamentally different cultural and social environment. Nevertheless, it is indisputable that World War I, an event that proved an unexpected boon to the Labour party by permanently crippling the Liberals and shaking the nation's faith in some of its most cherished ideas and institutions, had precisely the opposite effect in America (mainly because of America's brief participation, minimal casualties, and insulation from physical destruction). It is true, no doubt, that many of the reasons for this outcome were historically conditioned and almost predetermined, such as the consistent opposition of American socialists to the war—an opposition that could only have been maintained because of the strong pacifist-isolationist streak among American leftists and because of the party's weak ties with America's chauvinistic trade unions (in contradistinction to the Labour party) and that itself caused the party to be subjected to severe repression after the war. And the trouble that plagued American socialists in the 1920s was not only externally caused. Internal party strife also arose in the wake of the Bolshevik Revolution. Foreign-born party members, who had swelled the ranks of the organization in those years, sought to move the party to an extreme revolutionary position—a ludicrous strategy in a postwar America basking in the prosperity the war had brought and ideologically unreceptive to both Marxism and bolshevism—and the party tore itself to pieces in a bitter internecine quarrel.

Nonetheless, the disaster that engulfed American socialism after World War I was at least partly fortuitous. If the United States had endured the social and economic disruptions and human suffering of four years of total warfare and had known the subsequent disillusionment of Europeans with the liberal principles the war had forced their leaders to discard, the resolutely antiwar stance of American socialists would have redounded to their benefit.[21] Such a circumstance would almost certainly have given the party a least a temporary lease on life until its next great opportunity at the time of the Great Depression. As it was, the party in 1932 was a mere shadow of its former self, but even in its weakened state managed a significant revival under the leadership of Norman Thomas. But here the dominance of a two-party system worked against the left, as FDR was pressured into adopting strong social democratic rhetoric coupled with minimal social democratic policies in his second bid for the presidency, having been aban-

---

[21] See C. T. Husbands' introductory essay in Sombart, pp. xxxvi-xxxvii, and Shannon, *The Socialist Party of America*, chapters 5-9. Also see J. A. Thompson, ed., *The Collapse of the British Liberal Party* (Lexington, Massachusetts: D. C. Heath, 1969).

doned and denounced by American business. This left socialists out in the cold as the Democratic party functioned briefly as a European labor party—something it was to do again in the 1960s.

Nor did this end the string of blows fate held in readiness to batter American progressives. America's geopolitical insularity was further to weaken American leftists vis-à-vis their European cousins in the period during and after World War II. While, as we have seen, the war delivered a *coup de grâce* to what remained of reformist momentum in the New Deal and ushered businessmen into direct positions of power, influence, and renewed prestige in Washington, its effect in Continental Europe was dramatically different. European businessmen during the Nazi occupation—whether entirely willingly or not—were put into a position of collaboration with the invaders in order to continue the operation of these industrial societies and therefore faced public opprobrium and delegitimation at the war's end. At the same time, of course, leftists in both Eastern and Western Europe were able to garner nationalist laurels as the vanguard of resistance to Nazi oppression and to enter postwar governments that they often came to dominate. Moreover, the physical devastation wrought by the war led these regimes to use strong measures of state intervention and planning in order both to rebuild their economies and regain their positions in world markets as well as to institute the welfare policies and partial industrial democratization that social democrats had long waited to implement.[22]

Needless to say, what awaited the American left in the two decades after 1945 was not power and prestige, but McCarthyism and the cold war—an outcome perversely appropriate for a movement that could never break out of a downward spiral of disillusion and disaster. Nevertheless, it should be kept in mind that the dramatic eclipse of social democracy in America after 1920 was not written in the stars. It simply happened.

THE IRONIC QUEST: MICHAEL HARRINGTON AND AMERICAN CAPITALISM

Michael Harrington, the leader of the largest splinter group to emerge from the wreckage of a party that once seemed to be a serious contender for political power in America, has obviously inherited a legacy of reformist hopes dashed by the constraints, the vagaries, the accidents, and, most

---

[22] See Albert S. Lindemann, *A History of European Socialism* (New Haven: Yale University Press, 1983), chapter 9.

clearly, by the ironies of American history. But there is also much irony to be found in his own ideas and proposals. There is, first of all, his attempt to use Marxist theory to provide an analytical and ideological framework for moving the United States toward democratic socialism. Marx, he asserts, was not a rigid thinker who dealt in mechanistic schemes and teleologies, but one who instead understood the complexities and ambiguities of economic and social change, and could thus provide insight and hope for the progress of an evolutionary socialism within the institutional structure of the welfare state.

But there is little in Marx's writings to offer encouragement to a reform movement based on such a perspective. The fact is that the mature Marx was basically a hard determinist who assumed that the productive forces of society (land, labor power, machinery, and technology) determined the economic structure (power relations within society), which in turn produced the political superstructure (ideas, law, religion, and so on). He also assumed the inevitability of social revolution as the productive forces evolved and eventually could no longer be controlled by the two tiers of social entities above them.[23] Viewed from this standpoint, Harrington's philosophy is not Marxism at all, but a variant of a more general social democratic ideology. Indeed, none of Harrington's criticisms of American capitalism depend in any way upon Marxist theory or assumptions.

A second, and greater irony is that Harrington's major criticisms of capitalism *as a system* could, with few exceptions, only have been made in the United States. America is, of all the Western democracies, the nation that has generally permitted the highest rates of unemployment, the least amount of social and economic planning, the highest concentrations of poverty, and the lowest levels of social spending. It is also, by no mere coincidence, the nation whose political power structure is most subordinate to the forces of capital and big business. As Harrington himself has come perilously close to admitting in recent years, the fact that almost no other Western industrialized nation allows a large proportion of its citizens to remain unemployed, ill-housed, and without adequate incomes is testimony not to the intrinsic defects or peculiarities of capitalism in general, but to the extraordinary power and the reactionary ideology of the American business class and its political allies. In nations where that class takes

[23] For a scathing review of *The Twilight of Capitalism* that takes Harrington to task for his systems-theory approach to Marxism, see Sidney Hook's article in *The New Republic*, 7 and 14 August 1976, pp. 34-37. For a short, but illuminating and convincing interpretation of Marx as a nineteenth-century determinist, see Peter Singer, *Marx* (New York: Hill and Wang, 1980).

a broader and more humane view (for example, Japan and Canada) or where it has far less power (for example, Australia and Sweden), such conditions are either far less severe or unheard of. (It should be noted, however, that the most socially progressive nations appear to be those that have special characteristics: they have tended to be small and racially and ethnically homogeneous. It should also be pointed out that in social democratic Western Europe, social programs have rarely been aimed at specific ethnic or economic minority groups, but instead at general low-income populations as well as the broad middle classes, or have been provided for the population as a whole. This, as Charles Andrain has observed, is what accounts for their popularity and consequent high levels of funding, which themselves appear to result in a redistribution of income.)[24] Harrington in fact recognizes that the unwillingness to eliminate them is correctly viewed by most other business and government elites as economically counterproductive and wasteful, socially atavistic, and morally intolerable.

And it *has* been the practical struggle for social welfare and social justice that has occupied most of Harrington's time, energy, and thought. Although he has not abandoned other, traditional goals of socialism (for example, the democratization of economic decision making) that, depending on the depth and extensiveness of their implementation if carried out, would in fact require the radical alteration or abolition of some or most elements of capitalist institutions, until recently he has not given them much emphasis or attention, and only a vague programmatic content. The reason for this is that Harrington, unlike American socialists of the early twentieth century, has chosen to work within the Democratic party. This might or might not have been advisable from an immediate tactical standpoint; it certainly would have shocked Eugene Debs, who ran on the Socialist ticket for the presidency in 1920 while in prison for opposing US participation in World War I and received almost a million votes. Debs believed that the object of running for office as a socialist was not to win elections, but to present points of view never expressed by other candidates and to build a political base for the future.

Debs, on the other hand, would no doubt have approved of Harrington's statement of socialism's ideal "vision." Classical socialism, Harrington understands, was not primarily concerned with social reforms, laudable

---

[24] Charles F. Andrain, *Politics and Economic Policy in Western Democracies* (North Scituate, Massachusetts: Duxbury, 1980), p. 200; also chapters 7 and 8 generally.

though the abolition of poverty and the redistribution of income and wealth might be. What it aimed at was social transformation—specifically the elimination of class structures and the power relations they make inevitable—and through this the transformation of the human psyche, freeing it from the self- and interpersonal alienations intrinsic to commodity relations under capitalism. The goal of classical socialism thus was not economic reform, but *economic democracy*.

Yet by identifying socialism with the ameliorative measures of new liberalism, Harrington has been gambling its future on policies which, if successful, entailed no necessary change in power relations in society, and, if unsuccessful, risked the discrediting not only of new liberalism, but also of the democratic left, thus eliminating the latter as an alternative to conservative forces. Such a political strategy could thus lead either to a relatively humane form of the very system he believes to be the ultimate root of the problem, or to a far less tolerable form of that system—the reactionary outcome he fears most of all. Nor, as he implies, can he seek Marxist insight in resolving these dilemmas, for they did not exist for Marx, who believed—as did Sombart—that the political power and socialist consciousness of the proletariat would proceed apace with the development of the productive forces of society. The simple model of human and social behavior accepted by most nineteenth-century Marxists (objective reality → response) has long since been replaced by another view (objective reality → perceptions → response) associated with theorists such as Antonio Gramsci. Indeed, George Lichtheim and others have shown that in capitalist societies the "natural" outcome of workers' organizations and political activities in the absence of other influences has historically been either unfocused and self-defeating violence or ordinary trade unionism, not socialism. Unlike Sombart, Lichtheim knew that what specifically needed to be explained was not why socialism did not evolve spontaneously on a mass basis in America, but rather why a socialist party was not able to organize and *educate* workers effectively. American workers have not received, nor are they likely to receive, such an education within the Democratic party.[25]

[25] See George Lichtheim, *A Short History of Socialism* (New York: Praeger, 1970), chapters 1-4. For a critical review of Harrington's *Toward a Democratic Left* that questions his affiliation with the Democratic party, see Tom Christoffel's article in *The Nation*, 3 June 1968, pp. 736-737. Christoffel writes, in part: "[Harrington] might have argued, in the manner of the traditional left, that the government apparatus can become a positive force after the political system itself is changed. Or, with the New Left, he could have argued that no fundamental change is immediately in sight, so we must look for ways of getting around the federal roadblock as we fight it (using

What are Harrington's prospects for keeping the social-welfare mission and the political-democratic mission of socialism united? If, as he has contemplated, reforms that could sufficiently reduce the social and economic blights of American capitalism to socially tolerable levels are enacted by a conservative government, such a movement might be indefinitely forestalled. Indeed, judging from history alone, the resiliency of American capitalism does not bode well for the left.

On the other hand, if such reforms could be easily undertaken by a political coalition on the right, it is difficult to understand why they have not as yet been attempted or even proposed. If it becomes clear that conservatives cannot—or will not—deal with mounting chaos in the economy and discontent in the broader society, it is by no means impossible that a social democratic coalition will emerge in some form and be given a mandate to do so. Such an event, Harrington has reminded us, occurred in the past during the Great Depression and again during the 1960s. He is certainly correct that key elements in this kind of assemblage—an "invisible mass movement"—exist today within the Democratic party. Emphasizing that these elements, centered around the trade union movement, do not, for historical and cultural reasons, call themselves "socialists," he maintains that their sentiments and policy proposals are in some important respects indistinguishable from those of other social democratic movements. This paradox, he argues, has resulted from the fact that, although American workers have historically ostensibly been militant antisocialists, they have at the same time been "utopian capitalists," believing that, because there was equal opportunity for all under American capitalism, there was no need to join a separate political movement to oppose structural inequality. American capitalism has therefore been, in the words of Leon Samson, a "socialist concept of capitalism," a fact that brings out the greatest irony of Harrington's quest. By de-emphasizing the original socialist goal of participatory democracy, he had ignored what is both socialism's potentially most attractive feature to Americans—with their justifiable fear of concentrated power—and its most devastating critique of corporate capitalism.

But his quest has not ended. In his most recent work, *The Next Left: The History of a Future*, Harrington has moved markedly closer to the original goals and promises of socialist thought. Arguing that the left should not shrink from advocating a "bottom-up democratization of the economy,"

---

what power the Left does have on a grass-roots level). But by trying to use the existing system against itself, Harrington becomes tangled in the political marshmallow of the system he opposes" (p. 737).

he has suggested that pushing the welfare state toward the left is a ''radical project that has become a practical necessity'' and has acknowledged that ''trying to make basic revisions of societal priorities within the framework of corporate-dominated structures does not work.'' Thus, while cautioning that ''neither is there any serious possibility, politically or economically, to transform those structures overnight,'' Harrington proposes that ''each specific reform must . . . make achievable gains that alter the rules of the game. To democratize economic decisions and tax policies is not simply to adopt two discrete and desirable goals; it is to move toward a shift in basic power relations.''[26]

The next decade is indeed a critical period not only for the future of American capitalism, but also for the American equivalent of social democracy, neither of which has faced such great challenges, opportunities, and dangers for fifty years. Thus far, social democratic forces, while capturing control of the Democratic party for short intervals, have not been able to seize the initiative for a prolonged period and become a sustained and powerful political presence in America in their own right and under their own banner. The belief that they can and will do so is the essence of Harrington's socialist dream.

[26] Michael Harrington, *The Next Left: The History of a Future* (New York: Henry Holt, 1987), pp. 16, 178.

THE THINKERS

III Capitalism in Transition: Robert Heilbroner and the Crisis of Business Civilization

Robert Heilbroner,
1959

History, as it comes into our daily lives, is charged with surprise and shock. When we think back over the past few years, what strikes us is the suddenness of its blows, the unannounced descent of its thunderbolts. Wars, revolutions, uprisings, have burst upon us with terrible rapidity. Advances in science and technology have rewritten the very terms and conditions of the human contract with no more warning than the morning's headlines. Encompassing social and economic changes have not only unalterably rearranged our lives, but seem to have done so behind our backs, while we were not looking.

These recurring surprises and shocks of contemporary history throw a pall of chronic apprehensiveness over our times. . . . The bewildering turnabouts of fortune, the abrupt shifts of expectations, the awareness of the innumerable microscopic factors by which our destiny may be affected, all conspire to make of our encounter with history a frightening and disorienting ordeal.

Johan Huizinga,
The Waning of the
Middle Ages

Is it surprising that the people could see their fate and that of the world only as an endless succession of evils? Bad government, exactions, the cupidity and violence of the great, wars and brigandage, scarcity, misery and pestilence—to this is contemporary history nearly reduced in the eyes of the people. The feeling of general insecurity which was caused by the chronic form wars were apt to take, by the constant menace of the dangerous classes, by the mistrust of justice, was further aggravated by the obsession of the coming end of the world, and by the fear of hell, of sorcerers and of devils. The background of all life in the world seems black. Everywhere the flames of hatred arise and injustice reigns. Satan covers a gloomy earth with his sombre wings. In vain the militant Church battles, preachers deliver their sermons; the world remains unconverted. According to a popular belief, current towards the end of the fourteenth century, no one, since the beginning of the great Western schism, had entered Paradise.

ROBERT HEILBRONER

Chapter 8   *The New Pessimism*

During January of 1966 the Dow Jones industrial average reached an interday high of slightly more than 1,000, marking the climax of the most spectacular and longest-lived bull market in American history. The stock market, which had closed the year 1949 at the 200 level, had by the early 1950s exploded in a burst of belated optimism at what seemed to be mounting evidence that this might, after all, be the "American Century" some had predicted at the end of World War II. Taking advantage of the investment opportunities that presented themselves in such abundance during the next decade, many would become rich by gambling on the future of American capitalism.

Investments in the late 1940s were generally sound, most investors being relatively cautious, professional traders—the typical pattern since the crash of 1929. But by the late 1950s this pattern had changed. By 1959, 12.5 million Americans owned common stocks, up 6 million from 1952. In addition, a new kind of investor was appearing: one who did not remember the great disasters of the past and therefore did not fear them. As Robert Sobel has noted, veteran traders believed that these newcomers "bore more than a surface resemblance to the amateur speculators of the 1920s."[1]

Indeed, skepticism and good judgment were abandoned to an ever greater degree as a speculative mania founded on little more than an irrational belief that there was no limit to the rise in stock prices gradually swept across the nation. And, although the final phase of the market surge in the 1960s was marked by the vast expansion of stockholdings and the dominance of trading by huge financial institutions, the stock market continued to attract investors from an increasingly broad cross section of American society and in ever greater numbers—a total of 25 million shareholders by mid-1968, representing a 15 percent increase in just two years. This meant that in 1968 roughly 12 percent of the entire US population were in the market as direct traders. (The corresponding figure for the late 1920s is probably a maximum of 6 percent.)

But even this understates the magnitude of public participation, since by

---

[1] Robert Sobel, *The Last Bull Market: Wall Street in the 1960s* (New York: W. W. Norton, 1980), pp. 47-48.

the late 1950s, as Sobel explains, "Union pension funds, reserve funds of insurance companies, and other large financial aggregates depended upon the fortunes of leading stock issues for income with which to pay out benefits. The so-called little guy was in the market whether or not he wanted to be there."[2] New York Stock Exchange President Keith Funston called this phenomenon "People's Capitalism" (despite the central role of large institutional traders), and it seemed to be bringing the benefits of "free enterprise" to everyone.

By the end of 1968 there were unmistakable signs and warnings—as there had been in 1929—that the bubble might burst, but, as in 1929, they were generally disregarded. The pattern of 1929 was repeated yet again when, as the end finally came, most analysts were slow to recognize the truth. "In fact," Sobel writes, "the great bull market that had originated in the midst of economic and social despair in 1949 finally had come to its conclusion—in a period of new malaise."[3] Indeed, more than twenty years after breaking through the daunting millennial barrier, and despite the dramatic surge in stock prices in the mid-1980s, the Dow average—adjusted for inflation—had not yet again reached the level it had attained in 1966.

And yet, for all the apparently striking similarities to the debacle of 1929, many observers noticed that there were some distinctly odd things about the great decline that would within a decade drive stock prices down to half of their previous real value. First of all, the actual date of the market's peak was to retain no special significance, unlike the day that heralded the previous collapse, which would always be associated with "images of brokers and clients jumping from windows, banks closing, and panic rampant on Wall Street." These symbols were, in fact, missing entirely. "The young lions of the late 1960s didn't jump from windows or put bullets through their temples," Sobel reports. "Instead they got jobs for other organizations or left the district to work elsewhere." The end was to come "not with a bang or a whimper or the long anticipated 'another 1929.' The market caved in amid feeling of numbness, uncertainty, and despair."[4] In short, there was to be no dramatic "crash." What emerged instead was a "saw-toothed pattern," a kind of "kangaroo market," characterized by wild bounces and swings. The result was that "Clients were whipsawed, and millions of them left the arena, most never to return."[5]

[2] Ibid., p. 22.
[3] Ibid., p. 222.
[4] Ibid., p. 223.
[5] Ibid., p. 225.

The apparent causes of the downturn also bore quite noticeable resemblances to those of the previous catastrophic decline. Again, however, there was an important difference. "At first," Sobel explains, "it seemed the declines were caused by the usual factors—excess speculation, weak brokerages, shaky businesses, tight money, recession, political leaders who had lost public trust, and several other developments. All these were familiar to old-timers and students of the market."[6] But, although there were recessions in 1970–1971 and 1975–1976 (the latter quite severe), a new phenomenon had arisen to haunt American and world capitalism, one that was the opposite of that which investors had feared in the late 1940s— an unexplained and continuous rise in the general level of prices. This development was particularly puzzling in view of the fact that the recessions had themselves been at least partly engineered to bring prices down. The disappointing result had not been less inflation, but inflation plus economic stagnation—stagflation—accounting for the seesawing downward spiral of stock prices as investors intermittently believed that successive government policies and actions would end inflationary pressures. (There had been rallies in 1970–1971, 1971–1972, and 1975–1976.) It was this string of repeated failures that, more than anything else, undermined and then swept away the optimism that had sustained the stock market advance of the 1950s and 1960s.

The Great Bull Market of the postwar years was coterminous with and symbolized the renewed faith of Americans in the reformed Keynesian capitalism that had emerged from the economic disaster of the 1930s. Its collapse signaled the beginning of an era of doubt, confusion, and unease which in many respects rivaled that of a similar period of strain four decades before. The new time of troubles for American capitalism would be of longer duration than the last such period, yet simultaneously characterized by less intense pain and a less tangible kind of fear. There would be no general business collapse or the severe shock and bewilderment that had always accompanied such an event. What replaced them was a feeling of disorientation and a diffuse sense of discomfort and discontent, the latter perhaps best expressed by the French *malaise* or the German *Unbehagen*.

Nor was this a reaction to economic dilemmas and disappointments alone. An entire concatenation of events and circumstances—some apparently interconnected, some not—combined to cast doubt on the effectiveness or even the survival of many American institutions, including

---

[6] Ibid.

schools, marriage, the family, and established religions. What seemed increasingly clear to many was that there was a malfunctioning not only of the economic infrastructure of American society, but also of the social and political structures to which it was joined—a possibility that, by and large, had not been raised in the 1930s and that could only make the present conditions worse in their psychological effects. What is more, as the years wore on, the radiating circles of distress seemed to expand ever outward to encompass not just America, but all of Western civilization.

Of the American economic and social theorists on the democratic left who have dealt with postwar American capitalism, one has consistently sought to place it within its widest historical perspective. To him, the preceding events and the ensuing turmoil were neither totally unexpected nor inexplicable, but rather part of the unfolding of a new and disturbing chapter of history. His somber view of that process, more than that of virtually any other American thinker, would place in question the philosophical premises and the institutional structure of American capitalism and, further, of industrial society itself.

HISTORY AND THE FUTURE: SCIENCE, TECHNOLOGY, AND ECONOMIC CHANGE

Robert Louis Heilbroner was born in New York City in 1919. His father, who had worked his way from a life of poverty in North Carolina to the cofounding of a chain of men's clothing stores, died when Robert was five. Soon after this, the family sold its interest in the clothing business, by now a successful enterprise the proceeds from whose sale left its surviving members in very comfortable circumstances, allowing Robert and his two older sisters to be educated in private schools. "I grew up like anyone else in the privileged class," he later recalled. "I was reared during the Great Depression and never knew there was one."[7] As Heilbroner later reflected, an early life in such an economic environment and class position would ordinarily be expected to lead to predictable social and political views. But this was not to be, for, as he subsequently told an interviewer, "for about 10 years [after my father's death], I found myself with another father, so to speak":

He was the family's chauffeur, and he was a fine, warm-hearted man. I loved him very much. But at the same time he was an employee. And

---

[7] Quoted in *Current Biography*, 1975, p. 188.

although my mother was a good person, this man I loved so much was essentially a servant to her. Moreover, he didn't like being a servant. He hated his uniform, called it his monkey suit. I was acutely conscious of the fact that he had been thrust into a position of inferiority by economic circumstances, and I deeply felt his humiliation. I've thought about this story for quite a while now, and I think it explains something about my life and personality and hence about my work. I've found myself pulled between conservative standards on the one hand, and a strong feeling for the underdog on the other.[8]

Entering Harvard University in 1936 with the intention of majoring in writing, Heilbroner happened to take an economics course taught by a radical professor. "It was an awakening," he remembered. "I took to the subject like a duck to water." He graduated *summa cum laude* and Phi Beta Kappa in 1940, majoring in history, government, and economics. After working for a short time at the Office of Price Administration, he became a clerk at Weber & Heilbroner, an experience he did not enjoy. Drafted (thankfully) into the army during World War II, Heilbroner served as an intelligence officer in the South Pacific, where he interrogated Japanese prisoners of war. Discharged in 1946 with the award of a Bronze Star, he became a business consultant with a large commodity trading house.

Still he was unhappy. "I was always expected to be in the business world," he later said, "but I was always uncomfortable with it. I'm afraid I was always an intellectual." As a result of his dissatisfaction, Heilbroner turned to writing articles on economic issues in his spare time. "I always had the urge to write," he later explained, and by the late 1940s he had sold a number of articles to *Harper's* magazine. By now devoting an increasing amount of time to this pursuit, he recalled: "I decided I liked writing more than office work, and I got a year's leave."[9] He would never return.

While working as a free-lance writer, Heilbroner began to take graduate courses at the New School for Social Research. One day an editor at Simon and Schuster who had noticed one of his articles in *Harper's* suggested that he write a book. He also received encouragement in this endeavor from Professor Adolph Lowe, in whose seminar on the economist David Ricardo he was enrolled. An essay by Heilbroner on Ricardo would be expanded and eventually become *The Worldly Philosophers*, a study of

[8] *Psychology Today*, February 1975, p. 98.
[9] *Business Week*, 30 September 1972, pp. 58-59.

economic thought from the Middle Ages to the present. Widely praised by economists, the book was recognized as a highly readable yet thoughtful account of major figures and schools in the history of economic ideas. Over the years, it would go into several editions, be translated into more than twenty languages, and be sold in the millions. Heilbroner's second book, *The Quest for Wealth: A Study of Acquisitive Man*, was also well-received, but it was his third that, when published in 1960, would make him known as an important figure in American social thought.

The Future as History: The Historic Currents of Our Time and the Direction in Which They Are Taking America was written at a time when, although Americans generally continued to be what Heilbroner called "stubborn optimists," there had arisen, especially in Europe, but even to some degree in the United States, a kind of "pervasive anxiety" concerning the course of current events, among which were prominently included the unsettling scientific and technological successes of the Soviet Union in space and the phenomenal and pervasive rise of nonliberal nationalism in the Third World. Slightly more than a generation before, Americans were certain that their values and institutions were in permanent ascendancy; yet now the United States found itself in a position of "defensive insecurity." "The core of our inquietude," Heilbroner proposed, "stems from a more fundamental condition than the feeling of unpreparedness which is only its most acutely felt symptom. At bottom our troubled state of mind reflects an inability to see the future in an *historic* context."[10] If this were so, he reasoned, the task before Americans was obvious: they needed, at long last, to develop a sense of history and their place within it so that their movement within it would not be experienced as a "blind plunge into the unknown." There was a "grand dynamic of history," a "grandiose design" that had to be discovered "if we are to comprehend the meaning of the struggles of our time" (*FH*, 15-16).

Heilbroner began by pointing out that the concept of optimism was itself "*an historic attitude toward the future*" that assumed "plasticity and promise," rejected the idea of an unyielding fate, and was "grounded in the faith that the historic environment, as it comes into being, will prove to be benign and congenial—or at least neutral to our private efforts." But such an attitude, he informed his readers, was historically and culturally specific. "Indeed," Heilbroner observed, "as an enduring trait of national

[10] Robert L. Heilbroner, *The Future as History: The Historic Currents of Our Time and the Direction in Which They Are Taking America* (New York: Harper & Row, 1960), p. 15. Subsequently cited parenthetically as *FH*.

character it could almost be called exclusively American," explaining that "until a few centuries ago in the West, and until relatively recent times in the East, it was the past and not the future which was the dominant orientation to historic time" (*FH*, 16, 17, 18). The idea of progress, he noted, was born during the Enlightenment of the eighteenth century and apparently confirmed during the nineteenth century as the Western world witnessed a vast, rapid, dramatic, and seemingly beneficial technological and economic transformation. Still, this optimistic view soon became "curiously defensive," since the consequences of this transformation were not those expected by previous generations.

What were these consequences? There was, to begin, the seamy underside of economic growth: the new factory system, which, while making more rational and efficient the process of production, at the same time exacted a fearsome price in the form of regimented, exhausting labor—often performed by mere children—under physically and psychologically unhealthful conditions, and the larger industrial system itself, which, by concentrating workers in crowded, dirty, disease-ridden cities and by requiring the application of monotonous and mind-numbing techniques of work, had created a degrading and alienating form of life for millions. There was also the disenchantment of many—including some liberals—with the results of the political awakening and growing influence of a mass public and the dangers this was thought to pose to intellectual and cultural achievements.

But "the crux of the gathering disillusion" was to be found mainly in a third unexpected development: the failure of capitalism to provide what could be judged even a subsistence level of existence for the average worker—something that would not occur in England until a full century after the publication of Adam Smith's *The Wealth of Nations*—coupled with a mounting belief among social thinkers such as Malthus and Ricardo that history was not moving in the direction of unending material and spiritual betterment, and the views of socialist reformers that laissez-faire capitalism would not lead to a "naturally improving" future. Marx did believe in the progressive movement of history, but only because it would, he contended, destroy the very system that Smith had advocated.

By the end of the nineteenth century, there were unmistakable signs of "a weakening European confidence in the forces of technology, democracy, and capitalist evolution," although in an age of expansion, he continued, "well into the twentieth century something of the assured faith of the late eighteenth century remained" (*FH*, 44). But if Europeans entered the twentieth century with a central core of optimism still intact, they would not retain this notion in the face of the brutal and disheartening events and realities that would confront them in the next half-century, since

> From 1914 through 1945 Europe experienced a compression of horror without parallel in history: the carnage of the First World War, the exhaustion of the Depression, the agonizing descent of Germany into its fascist nightmare, the suicide of Spain, the humiliation of Italy, the French decay, the English decline—and finally the culminating fury of World War II. Before the cumulative tragedy of these years all optimistic views failed. Indeed the obvious question was no longer whether the forces of technology, democracy, and capitalism were the agents of a promising future, but the degree to which they should be held responsible for the unspeakably malevolent outcome of the past. (*FH*, 46)

The European belief in progress, born in Europe itself, had been mortally wounded there within the three decades after 1914; it died on that continent by 1945.

Yet if European thought, tempered by history, had long possessed "a characteristic bias—an awareness of profound secret problems of the human condition which neither technology nor democracy nor wealth could alleviate," for historical and geopolitical reasons the American belief in progress remained almost untarnished even after 1945. Only once, during the Great Depression, had Americans' confidence in their course been shaken. Indeed, Heilbroner wrote, "the dazed perplexity which that experience aroused in us, the sense of incredulity that the Depression would not 'cure itself,' the extreme reluctance to believe that its cause might be rooted deep in the historic force of capitalist expansion—all this was testimony to the degree with which our experience with a benign past resulted in a fixity of expectations concerning the future" (*FH*, 54). Yet he cautioned that the American view of history, still very much alive as the 1950s came to a close, was a "parochial and sheltered one. The idea that there may be challenges in history which are irresistible, pitiless, unyielding; the thought that a people may often be not the masters but the prisoners of their time with no alternative but to bow before its demands; the intimation that there may sometimes be very little that a nation can do to bring about a state of world affairs or of domestic society which would approximate its desires—these are all conceptions about history which our optimism makes it extremely difficult for us to consider, much less accept" (*FH*, 57-

58). Still, Heilbroner predicted that Americans were *now* faced—and would be in the future to an ever greater degree—with precisely such unsettling possibilities and challenges.

Heilbroner had little doubt concerning the nature and origin of the first and most obvious challenge. "This," he averred, "is the towering threat of the new technology of war." Not only did the existence of nuclear weapons threaten America with "national extinction": it had two further implications as well. First, it meant that the traditional use and rationale of military force had lost much of its meaning, and that consequently the "contest of ideologies and world influence" would be determined by "the gradual erosion of ideas, the slow pressures of economics, or the virtuosity of political leadership." In addition, usable military power in the atomic age meant the almost certain outbreak of small, conventional wars, leading to a huge US military budget—then a tenth of GNP—and thus to the institutionalization of huge military bureaucracies, a new development in a nation that had traditionally feared and distrusted such entities.

A related challenge was "the general impact of science and technology," a broad phenomenon of which the new military technology was only a part. Without denying the benefits of modern technology, Heilbroner pointed out that in many ways man's own technical devices had created an environment that was "as demanding, incomprehensible, even arbitrary as the environment of nature." Man, he wrote, "makes his peace with technology through social organization," since "technology itself demands organization in order to function. . . ." This implied hierarchical organizations and psychological coercion, both of which led to man's "steadily enforced conception of himself as part of a huge and impersonal social machine" (*FH*, 74).

The second of the "great historic currents" of the mid-twentieth century was "the revolutionary extension of popular political aspiration to the underdeveloped world." Evidence of this new historic force was abundant and seen in the wars, government instability, riots, revolutions, and, perhaps most disturbingly, in the movement toward authoritarian, and usually left-wing, political structures. Further, Heilbroner remarked that, although it might not be immediately obvious to Americans, the seemingly shocking behavior of Third World peoples had, when placed in the perspective of history, a direct connection to the evolution of the liberal political thought of the Enlightenment, itself involving a "revolution of expectations." "What is now happening," he proposed, "is an extension of that essentially restricted revolution on a world-wide scale." Cut off from Western economic development for three centuries, Asian and African nations were suddenly subjected to the disorienting impact of Western contact and economic penetration, whose worst effect was not naked and brutal exploitation—things that already existed—but rather the introduction of "the raw economic drive of capitalism without the social and political underpinnings and protections which blunted that drive at home" (*FH*, 77-78). The Age of Colonialism, however, was over. What had replaced it was "a new sense of impatience, desire, hope."

Heilbroner warned, however, that the struggle for economic development in these lands—a process he called "the terrible ascent"—was "of Herculean proportions and Sisyphean discouragement." Lacking the resources, values, and institutions of industrialized nations and confronted with rapidly growing populations, the former colonial regimes could not permit, as had the West, the glacial slowness of an economic development that proceeded from the bottom upward, allowing a gradual transition from feudal oligarchy to liberal democracy. Parliamentary procedures and structures retarded social change in order to grant freedoms and rights to dissident minorities, a luxury that these societies could not afford. A much more likely development was the rise of the "soldier-ruler," a personage already common in many such nations, together with an authoritarian orientation that could be rightist, but was more likely to lean toward the extreme left.

Such a development was inevitably unsettling to Americans, since, along with the aforementioned impact of scientific and technological change, it had formed one of the powerful currents of change in the twentieth century: the gradual loss of the worldwide institutional and ideological hegemony of capitalism—a hegemony that had not been seriously challenged up to the time of World War I. The First World War, the Bolshevik Revolution, the rise of socialist-inspired nationalism in colonial nations, and the coming to power of the first Western labor governments would halt the massive and indiscriminate export of its values and organizational forms abroad. Yet behind both capitalism and communism lay "the impulsion for material growth and the leverage of a newly unleashed industrial technique," and thus communism, regardless of its professed goals, could fruitfully be viewed largely as an alternative historical manifestation of the same brutal process of industrialization, whose ultimate goal was the extraction of a surplus from human labor in order to provide investment capital for economic growth. Nevertheless, Heilbroner doubted that the functional similarity of this process to capitalist development would make the ideas and institutions it spawned any more congenial to the peoples of the West.

In addition, profound changes were also taking place within Western capitalism itself. There was, for instance, an impetus for state planning in capitalist nations, which could be traced to a number of sources, including the centralizing influence of war and the need to deal with the economic collapse of the 1930s. Citing the amazing statistic that 60 percent of Americans had fallen below the poverty line in 1929, he noted that there had been both a substantial redistribution of income by 1958 as well as an enormous increase in the productive capacity of the US economy that had permitted the growth of the new middle class and had raised the real income of this class far above subsistence levels. Such an economic performance was expected to continue. Heilbroner noticed, however, that an important aspect of America's great postwar economic boom had received little comment: namely, that it had been underwritten by massive military expenditures, which were nonproductive and inflationary and which, in all probability, could not expand further. Given the historical fact of cyclical downturns produced by the instability that Heilbroner called the "endemic weakness of capitalist growth," he posed the question—as had Keynes— of whether an economy not buoyed up by huge amounts of military spending could take up the slack with other expenditures of the magnitude that might be required to maintain economic activity at a sufficient (that is, politically acceptable) level. The only alternative—the adoption of policies that discouraged saving—would curtail investment and therefore economic growth. Defense spending, Heilbroner wrote, "enables us to gain the full benefits of a powerful government planning operation without actually confronting the problems of a true 'mixed' economy." He pointed out that the public sector expanded at the expense of the private, and thus "the movement into overt planning would unquestionably confirm the fact which our movement into covert planning conceals—that we are gradually shifting ever further away from traditional *laissez-faire* capitalism into a new structure of economic responsibilities" (*FH*, 144-145). Yet an unalterable opposition to planning carried with it serious risks for internal social stability and international prestige. The main issue was therefore "what *kind* of planning, what *direction* of growth will best promote our chances for survival while preserving the values of an open society" (*FH*, 149).

A further problem for Americans involved the consequences not of trying to achieve, but of maintaining high levels of economic growth.

Downtrodden ethnic and racial minorities were now performing much of the menial labor in American society, but as the new middle class expanded it would be progressively more difficult to persuade its members to take the routine white-collar jobs that needed to be filled. Moreover, the business sector itself was now less than ever before under the direct compulsion and guidance of market forces, a trend that raised the possibility that Americans might "acquire economic abundance only at the cost of crushing social restrictions." To be sure, this might not come to pass. But Heilbroner maintained that, at the least, "the road to abundance leads subtly but surely into the society of control."

Beyond this troublesome aspect of economic success, there were, however, even more severe problems that involved the relationship between growth and the three "historic currents" discussed previously. An unquestioned devotion to growth that only considered its economic facets threatened to place mankind at the mercy of economic forces and technological imperatives (whose nature he had already investigated) that were beyond its control. Nor would the growth of the American economy in itself serve to accelerate the desperately desired development of the world's poor nations, which, given unchanged growth rates, would not attain—even under optimistic assumptions—a mere third of current (1958) US per capita income for decades (by which time US income would, of course, be much higher). Yet America's response to this issue had been a conservative course aimed at preserving social stability in these lands at all costs by supporting "anachronistic and corrupt [governments] . . . which have a vested interest in *preventing* social advance" and at supplying little if any economic aid to developing nations. In summary, Heilbroner warned Americans that "growth is not simply a process by which we put a magnifying glass over the present." It was instead a wrenching process of change both at home and abroad. The failure of Americans to understand this would result, he feared, in the continued and uncontrolled expansion of private and public bureaucratic power and in the "ideological isolation of the American system" from Europe, and, even more, from the Third World.

Under such circumstances, America's continued optimism was, Heilbroner proposed, both naive and politically dangerous. Americans, a people who had always ignored the forces and limitations of history—a subject never popular in a nation that believed itself unleashed from the bonds of the past—would soon find that although there were "no fixed and immutable limits to what is historically possible," the sphere of freedom in history was not infinite. In fact, Heilbroner saw only three alternatives for

Americans. One was a kind of advanced Luddism in which modern technology and economic structures would be smashed or drastically reduced in scale, an overturning of established institutions through "a degree of historic intervention which is entirely alien to our social philosophy." The second option was a passive acquiescence in the direction of historical change. Yet, since the human impact on history was no less real merely because it was unconscious or unintended, this course was what had helped to produce the present state of affairs to begin with. Understanding the forces of historical change and consciously attempting to direct them within the limits of historical possibility was mankind's only hope, Heilbroner proclaimed. The latter option entailed risks; but so did rejecting it.

In conclusion, Heilbroner proposed that the Enlightenment idea of progress was hopelessly flawed. No one who had any knowledge of the horrors of twentieth-century history could confidently assert the moral, cultural, or aesthetic superiority of the modern era. Nor, despite their undeniable material advantages, could it be shown that average people were happier, more serene, or more creative than their ancestors. The expected utopia had foundered, he believed, on the extraordinary inertia of human ideas, motivations, behavior, and institutions, and on a set of beliefs that "already takes for granted an environment in which rationality, self-control, and dignity are paramount social attributes" and that therefore assumed a benign evolution of desirable human qualities and social structures that presumably already existed—an assumption history did not validate. The Enlightenment concept of progress also failed to deal with the "ambiguity" of scientific, technological, and economic developments as phenomena that provided benefits but also exacted costs and created new difficulties even as they resolved old ones. Heilbroner therefore concluded that if "progress" meant a "fundamental elevation in the human estate, a noticeable movement of society in the direction of the ideals of Western humanism, a qualitative as well as a quantitative betterment of the condition of man," it had to be forgotten for the foreseeable future. In place of that concept, he counseled neither a "black and bitter pessimism" nor a "heroic defiance," but rather a realistic view of past accomplishments and future possibilities.

THE GRIM SPECTER: GLOBAL RESOURCES AND THE HUMAN PROSPECT

The 1960s were a decade that saw many of Heilbroner's fears and prophecies confirmed and in which he further examined problems he had seen as central to current historical trends: economic development in the Third World and internal changes that could be expected in the American economy. As the decade wore on, however, it was the latter issue—the changing face of American capitalism—to which he increasingly turned. In an extended essay entitled *The Limits of American Capitalism*, published in 1966, Heilbroner proposed that America and, indeed, other capitalist societies throughout the world were undergoing a long-term reorientation whose origins were to be found primarily in the nature of modern science and technology. In short, he professed to see in all mature capitalist nations an almost inexorable drift toward the expansion of the welfare state and a slow and sometimes hesitant movement toward planning and the increasing influence of scientific and technical elites in an economy whose dynamics both furthered and depended upon the power of technology. Capitalism, Heilbroner believed, was clearly compatible with planning. Of far greater import for its future were the direct and indirect effects of technology, of which the latter were the more insidious, since unforeseen consequences of technological change such as job displacement and the increasing bureaucratization of economic and social life could not, like the direct impact of technology, be controlled.[11]

Heilbroner continued to elaborate on these views into the late 1960s. Yet while the essential features of this vision would remain unaltered, the phenomena it identified as the driving forces of history would gradually take on a far more sinister character and give his previously sober, but relatively sanguine, outlook a far more pessimistic cast. Until this point, Heilbroner's books and essays seemed to be describing a world that, while not corresponding to the one Americans had anticipated only two decades before, held no real menace to their basic values or the material conditions of life to which they had become accustomed. But in a 1968 essay on the relationship between business and the state, Heilbroner made passing reference to what he termed "the potentially vast regulatory requirements imposed by the ecological problem."[12] And, during the next year, he wrote of "a wholly new problem for all mankind—the problem of maintaining

[11] See Robert L. Heilbroner, *The Limits of American Capitalism* (New York: Harper Torchbooks, 1967); also "Rhetoric and Reality in the Struggle Between Business and the State" and "Technological Determinism" in Robert L. Heilbroner, *Between Capitalism and Socialism: Essays in Political Economics* (New York: Vintage, 1970), pp. 3-31; 147-164.

[12] Robert L. Heilbroner, "Rhetoric and Reality in the Struggle Between Business and the State," p. 29. This was not, however, the first time Heilbroner had called attention to the problem of the environment. See Robert L. Heilbroner, "What Goes Up the Chimney," *Harper's Magazine* (January 1951), pp. 61-69.

the ecological balance, the very viability, of the earth itself." Included in this problem was the environmental deterioration "brought about by enormously enhanced demands for resources, by gigantic scales of physical and chemical transformation of materials, and by the need to dispose of gargantuan quantities of end products, including the peculiarly lethal ones of radioactive wastes."[13] In addition, he noted that increased production itself laid the groundwork for further population increases, which resulted in a still further buildup of environmental waste. This theme would haunt his writings on social and economic problems to an ever more noticeable extent.

Over a period of several months, Heilbroner had "slowly become convinced . . . that the ecological issue is not only of primary and lasting importance, but that it may indeed constitute the most dangerous and difficult challenge that humanity has ever faced."[14] Referring to the relationship among physical and chemical global resources, waste production, and human demand as the "carrying capacity" of "Spaceship Earth," he wrote that "we are well past that capacity, provided that the level of resource intake and waste output represented by the average American or European is taken as a standard to be achieved by all humanity."[15] Citing population growth, the environmental pollution and waste heat generated by the industrial process itself, and the dangers posed by new chemical and nuclear technologies, Heilbroner commented that the cumulative effects of these factors could have drastic implications not only for the industrialized world, but for developing nations as well.

By itself, and without further analysis or integration into a larger interpretive scheme, such expressions of fears of a worsening ecological balance and shortages of various raw materials were no longer unique by the late 1960s among intellectuals and environmental activists. Yet they did not strike a responsive chord with the public until 1973, when food prices began to rise sharply (18 percent within one year) as the result of unfavorable weather conditions. More ominously, in the fall of that year the Arab-Israeli October War led to a cutback in oil supplies to the United States and Europe. Although the reduction amounted to only 10 percent of the world oil supply and the embargo would be lifted within five months, prices rose dramatically as Arab nations arranged for themselves a profit rate and a

[13] Robert L. Heilbroner, "Reflections on the Future of Socialism," in *Between Capitalism and Socialism*, p. 100.

[14] Robert L. Heilbroner, "Ecological Armageddon," in ibid., p. 270.

[15] Ibid., p. 271.

total price six times the size of those that existed before the October War. Objectively, and relative to Europe, the oil shortage was not severe in America, but its psychological effect was enormous.

Nor, despite its extraordinary nature, was this the only dramatic and unsettling event that Americans experienced in the early 1970s. Earlier that year, the United States had formally ended the eight-year Vietnam War, a conflict that had produced bitter social divisions and explosive inflationary pressures that had required the imposition of price controls and had, moreover, presented Americans with the first defeat—though technically a military stalemate—in their history. (The War of 1812 had also ended in a stalemate, but, as a defensive war on the part of the United States, this was tantamount to an American victory.) In addition, a worsening trade balance and the flow of US investment capital overseas had produced continuing declines in the value of the dollar, which until the late 1960s had served as the international reserve currency, as had the British pound during the nineteenth and early twentieth centuries. Meanwhile, the economy was weakening and beginning a slow slide into what would eventually become the worst recession in America since the 1930s (later to be surpassed by the Reagan recession of 1981–1982). On yet another front, the United States was embroiled in one of the most sensational and disturbing political crimes in its history, as President Nixon fought a last-ditch battle to save a presidency wracked for months by the Watergate scandal, an effort that would finally end with his resignation in August of 1974. And— as if this were not enough—India exploded its first nuclear device in May of the latter year, thereby becoming the first Third World nation to possess such a weapon.

This amazing string of events was to have great significance for the reception of Heilbroner's next book. Even more than Galbraith's *The Affluent Society*, Heilbroner's *An Inquiry into the Human Prospect* was to draw popular attention largely (although by no means entirely) because of the fortuitous timing of its publication. Like Galbraith, however, Heilbroner had no way of knowing or predicting the events that were to transpire, the book having been written between July 1972 and August 1973, two months before the October War. Yet, even after taking into account the good fortune of its publication date in early 1974, critics rightly acknowledged it as an important contribution to the debate on the growing world crisis.

''There is a question in the air, more sensed than seen, like the invisible approach of a distant storm,'' Heilbroner began, ''a question that I would hesitate to ask aloud did I not believe it existed unvoiced in the minds of

many: 'Is there hope for man?' '' Referring first to what he termed "topical" events that had brought this question to the fore, among which he
included Vietnam, urban riots, large increases in violent crime, and
marked changes in values and sexual mores, he remarked that they had
produced "a feeling of dismay, often bordering on despair." But there was
also a deeper source of this feeling, one that added to the effect of the
topical events. This was, he suggested, a set of "attitudinal changes,"
among which three were pivotal.

The first change involved the decline of the idea of progress, a belief
that had been originally discredited by World War I, while lingering substitutes for it—a "fortifying belief" in socialism maintained by many and
a later confidence on the part of others in a rational, pragmatic, and managerial approach to social and economic problems in the postwar era—
were gradually eroded by growing doubts concerning the outcome of social
engineering, the continued existence of poverty and racial conflict abroad,
and the persistence of urban decay and poverty in America. Another attitudinal change, the mounting belief that rapid economic growth might no
longer be possible—or even desirable—was considerably more recent.
Observably diminishing natural resources and a growing appreciation of
the "previously unsuspected side effects" of the present rate of economic
expansion had generated grave doubts that mankind's general affluence in
the industrial West could be expanded geographically or even maintained
for those who already possessed it. In addition, Heilbroner identified what
he called a "civilizational malaise" at whose core was a disillusionment
felt by ever greater numbers of people with the fruits of a materialistic
culture. People had become increasingly aware of and puzzled by the fact
that, although they were up to ten times richer than humans of a few generations past, they did not appear to be proportionally more happy, contented, or cultivated than their ancestors. It would not be easy to probe to
the roots of these problems, Heilbroner warned, since uncertainties, personal values, and other difficulties stood in the way. Nevertheless, he believed that a reasonably objective analysis was possible, the more so since
his personal intellectual and political inclinations had led him strongly to
resist his own conclusions.

Heilbroner began his task by considering the chief "external challenges" faced by modern civilizations. The first of these, population
growth, presented a set of alternatives that, in his opinion, were all highly
distasteful. Concerning the monumental difficulties of checking the vast
increases in the number of the earth's inhabitants, he concluded that "For

the next several generations . . . even if effective population policies are introduced or a spontaneous decline in fertility due to urbanization takes effect, the main restraint on population growth in the underdeveloped areas is apt to be the Malthusian check of famine, disease, and the like."[16] Given this probable scenario, he foresaw only two outcomes. One entailed rising social disorder, continued mental and physical deterioration, and the rule of dictatorial governments devoted to advancing the interests of small, privileged elites in poor nations. The other was the rise to power of governments "with dedicated leadership, a well-organized and extensive party structure, and an absence of inhibitions with respect to the exercise of power to bring the population flood to a halt" (*HP*, 38). Such a leadership, he prognosticated, would be of a revolutionary nature and committed to a ruthless restructuring of social and economic institutions. These regimes would also be unlikely to view with equanimity a continuation of the enormous disparities in wealth between the rich nations of the North and the starving nations of the South—a probability that caused Heilbroner to consider the next challenge the world faced: the threat of nuclear weapons.

Reflecting on the popular perception of the danger of nuclear bombs, Heilbroner noted that the average person tended to focus on a single aspect of the peril they posed: the sheer magnitude of the explosive force that would be unleashed by their mass detonation in a full-scale exchange of warheads. This eventuality would result, he acknowledged, in the deaths of between 50 and 135 million Americans. Nonetheless, he felt that the continued proliferation of nuclear arms and technology, combined with the relative ease of obtaining fissionable material, posed a further threat that had been largely overlooked—the possible use of a nuclear explosive as a means of blackmail by Third World nations in an attempt to obtain the foreign aid needed for economic development by holding for ransom the population of an urban center in an industrialized nation. Heilbroner proposed that were such an event to occur it might speed nuclear disarmament, but would not end, and might even increase, the chance of limited wars. The likelihood of war would also strengthen nationalism, which would in turn enhance the prospect of war.

The third external challenge to civilization came from the environment. Of all mankind's problems this, Heilbroner opined, would prove the most unyielding, since "unlike the threats posed by population growth or war,

---

[16] Robert L. Heilbroner, *An Inquiry into the Human Prospect* (New York: W. W. Norton, 1974), p. 35. Subsequently cited parenthetically as *HP*.

there is an ultimate certitude about the problem of environmental deterioration that places it in a different category from the dangers we have previously examined. Nuclear attacks may be indefinitely avoided; population growth may be stabilized; but ultimately there is an absolute limit to the ability of the earth to support or tolerate the process of industrial activity, and there is reason to believe that we are now moving toward that limit very rapidly'' (*HP*, 47). He stressed that precise knowledge of the time span involved was not available; but he also emphasized that industrial production, increasing by 7 percent per year, would at the present rate double every 10 years, requiring at the end of a century an amount of resources more than one thousand times greater than that needed at present. And, although these resources might be made available in sufficient quantities through new technological advances that could capture mineral reserves in presently unattainable forms or develop adequate substitutes, Heilbroner argued that, at the least, future supplies were uncertain. But even if the ''heroic assumption'' were made that such resources would be found in order to ensure economic growth for the next century, he pointed out that an insurmountable obstacle to unlimited growth still remained because ''all industrial production, including, of course, the extraction of resources, requires the use of energy, and . . . all energy, including that generated from natural processes such as wind power or solar radiation, is inextricably involved with the emission of heat.'' The amount of industrial waste heat added to the ''natural'' heat from the sun and earth would at present rates of growth reach 100 percent of solar heat within 250 years, making the earth uninhabitable. What is more, within an even shorter period—150 years—the temperature of the earth would rise by 3 degrees Celsius, a threshold beyond which rapid growth would entail drastic and irreversible damage to the environment; indeed, even the maintenance of the industrial production current at that time might do so once that point were reached. And this did not take into account the effects of expected industrial expansion and population increases in the developing nations.

The point of the latter discussion, Heilbroner hastened to assure his readers, was not that civilization faced ''imminent disaster.'' The increased use of solar energy, for example, would allow more growth without chemical, nuclear, or thermal waste—if, that is, this new power source could be developed in time. Alternatively, the development of these new technologies might itself slow the rate of industrial growth, as would a shift toward a service-oriented economy. The essential fact, Heilbroner declared, was that the problem of thermal waste put an absolute limit on the attainable level of industrial output. Furthermore, the most likely and most immediate limiting factor regarding economic growth was still the side effects of industrial production.

On this point, however, Heilbroner called attention to what he saw as a salient fact: that the motive force of the modern industrial machine was the seemingly autonomous power of an evolving technology. Indeed, he argued that all of the external challenges mentioned thus far "can be seen as an extended and growing crisis induced by the advent of a command over natural processes and forces that far exceeds the reach of our present mechanisms of social control." The central dilemma, then—the root cause of the unease of modern Western civilization—was not the demographic and environmental challenges themselves, but rather the inability of social institutions to harness the disruptive, volatile, and mercurial forces of a technological behemoth that had gradually broken loose from the economic, social, and political moorings that had held it at least tenuously in check until the mid-twentieth century.

With this in mind, Heilbroner considered the viability of the world's dominant socioeconomic systems, capitalism and socialism, stripped of cultural variations and reduced to their barest and most abstract essences— in the case of capitalism, private ownership and the operation of a market economy. Capitalism, he noted, had disappointed both its critics and its admirers. Marxist prophecies of doom clearly had not materialized; but neither had the peace and contentment promised by those who believed that the constant growth of production in a mixed economy under the aegis of government prefigured a post-Keynesian golden age. Regarding the latter disappointment, Heilbroner offered as possible explanations the replacement of absolute by relative poverty, the eventual acceptance of any standard of living—no matter how much higher than those of the past—as natural and deserved, and especially the inability of capitalist society to articulate a satisfying social philosophy. Under such circumstances, socialism might appear almost certain to have a better record. Yet Heilbroner noted a "surprising similarity of outcomes between two otherwise widely differing systems." The critics of socialism had also predicted *its* collapse and had similarly been proved wrong; but it was also true that socialism, like capitalism, had not lived up to *its* promises of rapid economic growth, political freedom, social justice, psychological reorientation, and high morale, as events in Eastern Europe and the Soviet Union testified.

These unexpectedly similar results were not, in Heilbroner's estimation, simply coincidental. For one thing, both systems shared a strikingly similar and dynamic mechanism at the very nucleus of their social structures, since "All the processes of industrial production that are the material end products of scientific technology have one characteristic of overwhelming effect—their capability of enormously magnifying human productivity by endowing men with literally superhuman abilities to control the physical and chemical attributes of nature. Once an industrial system has been established—a historic process that has been as painful for capitalism as for socialism—it truly resembles a gigantic machine that asserts its productive powers despite the sabotage of businessmen or bureaucrats" (*HP*, 76). More than this, both systems exalted efficiency, economic production, and technical skill above all other values and concerns, and as a consequence were societies that "seem dazzlingly rich in every dimension except that of the cultivation of the human person." Some of the most deleterious effects of the industrial mode of production could undoubtedly be mitigated, but there were certain technological "imperatives" that limited these kinds of reforms.

These initial observations having been made, Heilbroner considered the abilities of the respective systems to deal with the challenges mentioned earlier. Regarding relations with the developing countries, he believed that advanced socialist nations had a short-term advantage arising from feelings of solidarity, but that long-term prospects favored neither capitalism nor industrial socialism in their capacities to handle problems arising from a basic and glaring disparity in wealth between rich and poor areas of the globe. Yet with respect to the constraints imposed by industrial wastes and other technological side effects that required an ultimate halting of industrial growth, the outlook was initially far gloomier for capitalism. True, a stationary form of capitalism was theoretically possible; it might even be workable in practice in the short run, since business might well accept this arrangement if market shares could be left as they were and if government spending could be used to prevent the deflationary tendencies of an economy in which new investments were either no longer made or were greatly curtailed or confined to mainly nonindustrial (service) outputs. But Heilbroner doubted that a capitalist society could permanently endure the inevitable, severe conflicts that would almost certainly surround the issues of income distribution that would arise under conditions of a falling per capita output of material goods. The "enormous inflationary pressures" that would result from this kind of struggle would lead, he believed, to the necessity of imposing powerful controls on the economy. At best, life under this kind of capitalism would become quite unpleasant; at worst, the political structures of some capitalist nations, strained beyond the limits of their ability to maintain social control within the boundaries of democratic republicanism, might mutate to other forms. Here again, socialism would appear to possess an advantage, since it had an inherently firmer control over economic and social life.

Yet Heilbroner predicted that an initially democratic socialist regime could be successful on a permanent basis under such conditions only if it too eventually took on an authoritarian cast, making it "virtually indistinguishable from an authoritarian 'capitalism'." And here he admitted that his essentially pessimistic outlook was "based on more than the resistances and inertias of vested interests that we find throughout history when established modes of production become obsolete. It is also founded on a political consideration, namely, whether *any* society can bring about alterations of this magnitude through the conscious intervention of men, rather than by convulsive changes forced upon men" (*HP*, 94-95). This made it necessary to consider the responsiveness of human nature to political authority.

The human personality, Heilbroner observed, was shaped in an environment of prolonged dependency, which led to a ready acquiescence in, and to an easy identification with, authority. He conceded that human development fostered other, offsetting, traits as well, but still submitted that the former tendencies remained powerful and obvious, remarking that "Anyone who has seen the wild excitement of a crowd caught up in the adulation of a political leader cannot fail to recognize the rekindling of childhood feelings of awe and obedience in the behavior of these cheering adults" (*HP*, 105-106). The continuation of hierarchical social and political organization under revolutionary regimes and the persistent inclination of even democratically ruled peoples to move toward centralized authority—especially in times of crisis—suggested to Heilbroner that such a tendency existed at least partly because it found a resonance in the deep emotional structure of human beings that could be traced to their early development.

No less important was the child's capacity, indeed drive, for identification, which made social life itself possible but which also had a negative side: its severely limited scope. Humans had never shown themselves capable of extending the maximum reach of this impulse beyond the boundaries of the nation-state, a fact that led to the persistence and, under conditions of stress, the intensification, of the partly beneficial, partly destructive, phenomenon of nationalism. In addition, given the present-mindedness of modern individuals, it was hardly likely that they could form bonds with future generations and thus be willing to make substantial sacrifices for people few of whom they would ever see or even be aware of. Heilbroner did not subscribe to the conservative belief in the fixity of human nature; human nature could change, he believed. The problem was that genetic traits and the social structures through which they were mediated could not possibly adapt in time to meet the multiple threats that mankind had recently encountered.

The consequences to which the foregoing analysis pointed were bleak. Heilbroner projected that during the next decade the most important issues in Western society would remain the political, economic, and international difficulties to which people had already become accustomed by the early 1970s. During a longer period of fifty years, he prophesied that the central problem before civilization would most probably be the adaptive changes within, and the gradual convergence of, capitalism and industrial socialism. Over the period of a century, however, what loomed largest was "the transformational problem, centered in the reconstruction of the material basis of civilization itself." And here the impetus for civilizational change would not be the persuasiveness of reason and its supposed role in the formation of policy through the discussion and debate of possible alternatives, but instead the crushing force of external events that would compel "convulsive change" on a resisting world. In fact, exhortations to slow industrial growth, if successful, could even make matters worse in the short run, since backward nations needed such growth to avert imminent disaster and its destabilizing consequences for international order, while advanced nations needed technological innovations that would smooth the transition to a new era of scarce natural resources and ecological limits on the generation of heat.

It was possible, Heilbroner suggested, that this relatively short remaining period of growth could be managed in ways that would minimize waste, decentralize industrial life, and thereby "greatly ease" the transition yet to come. What was far more likely, however, was "the risk of 'wars of redistribution' or of 'preemptive seizure,' the rise of social tensions in the industrialized nations over the division of an ever more slow-growing or even diminishing product, and the prospect of a far more coercive exercise of national power as the means by which we will attempt to bring these disruptive processes under control" (*HP*, 135-136). Thus, he could only conclude that there was, in fact, no hope for humanity, if by that was meant the continued existence—in its present form—of the industrial civilization humans had created.

Still, this did not mean, Heilbroner emphasized, that the human race would necessarily perish or that no civilization could survive in the world that emerged from the great wave of change ahead. A new and greatly different civilization would simply replace the present one. But this new culture, he reasoned, would not be the ''Promethian'' type he had foreseen in *The Limits of American Capitalism*. An obsessive preoccupation with science, technology, and industrial production would give way, he now felt, to an orientation based on tradition, ''the exploration of inner states of experience,'' and ''the acceptance of communally organized and ordained roles.'' From this future, Heilbroner sadly concluded, there was no escape. Nonetheless, to the degree that mankind could come to resign itself to the arduous tasks and sacrifices that were in any case unavoidable, it could at least, like the anti-Promethian figure of Atlas, muster the courage to bear its burden.

Chapter 9   *The New Right*

An Inquiry into the Human Prospect enjoyed a favorable critical response (even by most of those who took issue with some of the book's conclusions) and a wide circulation. Heilbroner had long since become one of the most successful economics authors of all time, rivaled only by John Kenneth Galbraith and Paul Samuelson, and, despite his reluctance to identify with the economics profession, a respected figure within his discipline. A full professor and chairman of the economics department at the New School for Social Research, he had been appointed to the Norman Thomas Chair in Economics in 1971 and elected to the executive committee of the American Economic Association in 1972. Having also lectured widely before business, military, and college audiences, he was seen as one who had analyzed with great skill and persuasiveness many of the crucial problems of American and world capitalism.

THE CONSERVATIVE REBUTTAL: THE NEW RIGHT AND THE REBIRTH OF CAPITALIST IDEOLOGY

And yet within the mid-1970s there emerged the rapidly growing nucleus of a political and intellectual movement that would strongly challenge Heilbroner's major conclusions concerning the present problems and the future evolution of capitalism. As this movement gained substantial political influence by the late 1970s, it would also challenge the institutional foundations and philosophical premises on which the New Deal and the Great Society had been built, thus seeming to cast doubt particularly on Heilbroner's prediction of a continuing movement toward state intervention in economic and social affairs. Perhaps most extraordinary of all was the fact that, of the three major "ideal types" of American conservatism—social (based on a concern for social and political continuity), cold war (centered on a philosophical commitment to a powerful national defense establishment and an interventionist foreign policy), and libertarian (devoted to the ideals of classical economic liberalism and therefore to the minimization of government control over the economy)—it was the third, long believed by most analysts to be functionally extinct, that along with the second led the political coalition dubbed by many the "New Right" and that largely defined its intellectual positions and political programs.[1]

Indeed, in the view of many, a more unlikely candidate for an important role in the resurgence of conservative influence in America could hardly be imagined. Laissez-faire ideology, battered throughout the twentieth century in both Europe and America by the centralizing tendencies of total war and rapid economic and social change, by the political need to ameliorate economic downturns, and by the general demand and support for social-welfare policies, had certainly sunk to its lowest level of prestige during the generation following World War II. If 1946 had been a year of anxiety for new liberals, for old liberals with libertarian views it was beyond any question a time of despair. Despite the uncertainty that would plague America's new capitalism until the early 1950s, on the intellectual and political fronts American conservatism, except for its significant contribution to the origins of the cold war, was able to stage only a defensive reaction against the ideas and *faits accomplis* of the new liberal establishment. The quiescence of the Eisenhower years notwithstanding, economic and political thought was in practice constrained by the conceptual framework of an ascendant new liberalism that had been the legacy of Keynes and of the cadres who had forged the political alliance of the New Deal. On all fronts, the initiative clearly lay with the latter forces.

But the old faith had not completely disappeared. Even as the war against the Axis moved to its expected conclusion, a small counterattack was launched against the new liberals by an Austrian emigre living in London. *The Road to Serfdom*, published in 1944, caused a mild sensation among conservative American intellectuals who feared the evolution of a state-regulated capitalism in the United States. The book's author, Friedrich A. Hayek, saw—as did the American writer James Burnham—a dangerous trend in the twentieth century toward an increasing centralization and extension of government power that posed a threat to the liberties that he believed were ensured by the decentralized institutions of capitalism. Hayek went so far as to suggest that nazism had little to do with "a capitalist reaction against the advance of socialism. On the contrary, the support which brought these ideas to power came precisely from the socialist camp."[2] Another Austrian economist, Ludwig von Mises, advanced sim-

---

[1] I have taken this tripartite division from George H. Nash, *The Conservative Intellectual Movement in America: Since 1945* (New York: Basic, 1976).

[2] Friedrich A. Hayek, *The Road to Serfdom* (Chicago: University of Chicago Press, Phoenix, 1944), p. 168.

ilar ideas in a series of works, writing, for example, in 1944: "The essential teaching of liberalism is that social cooperation and the division of labor can be achieved only in a system of private ownership of the means of production, i.e., within a market society, or capitalism. All the other principles of liberalism—democracy, personal freedom of the individual, freedom of speech and of the press, religious tolerance, peace among the nations—are consequences of this basic postulate. They can be realized only within a society based on private property."[3]

It was no mere coincidence that the staunchest remaining supporters of classical liberal ideas were of Austrian descent. In the early twentieth century Austria had given birth to the most prestigious group of economists in Europe. Founded by Carl Menger in 1883, the Austrian School of economics was launched with an assault on the German Historical School, which emphasized—as did the American institutionalists, who were greatly influenced by its teachings—the evolutionary nature of economic institutions. The Austrians insisted on the universality of economic laws and feared that the relativism of the Germans could be used to justify state interference in the economy. Ironically, the ahistorical bias of the Austrians was itself at least partly a consequence of the historical, cultural, and political peculiarities of the Austro-Hungarian Empire. Ethnically fragmented and prone to constant disorder, the empire was held together by a dictatorial monarchy that felt compelled to rule through a rigid and repressive bureaucracy (one of whose employees was, significantly, Franz Kafka) that imposed numerous constraints on the intellectual and political freedoms of its citizens and tolerated open discrimination against minorities, particularly Jews. Although matters improved somewhat after World War I, the exodus of Austrian economists such as Hayek, Mises, Gottfried von Haberler, and others (one of them, Joseph Schumpeter, though a supporter of capitalism, was a relativist, and therefore a maverick) to Europe and the United States in the 1930s and 1940s after the rise of nazism was quite understandable.

Not surprisingly, the arrival of these men had a substantial impact on conservative economic thought in America in the mid-1940s, then engaged in a weak and fruitless attack against the New Deal and the enhanced power of the federal government. Writers like Albert Nock (whose libertarian ideas were deeply to influence a family friend, the young William F. Buckley, Jr.), Frank Chodorov, Henry Hazlitt, and John Chamberlain were to add their own contributions to the anti-statist, libertarian literature

---

[3] Quoted in Nash, *The Conservative Intellectual Movement in America*, p. 11.

of these years. But it was at the University of Chicago (where Hayek became a professor in 1950) that American economic libertarianism became gradually institutionalized under the influence of Henry C. Simons and Frank H. Knight, who founded the Chicago School of economics in the late 1940s. In these years, too, there arrived as a faculty member one of their former graduate students, a man who would one day become the preeminent member of the Chicago School—Milton Friedman. An advocate of modified laissez-faire economics (serving as an adviser to Barry Goldwater in 1964 and to presidents Nixon and Ford), Friedman would also eventually become the premier economic theorist of the American New Right and the propagator of a set of ideas fundamentally opposed to those of Heilbroner.

Friedman's assault on the Broker State, no less vehement than those of Galbraith and Harrington, proceeded from radically different premises and was built on two parallel and connected planes. First, Friedman accepted, predictably, the arguments of Hayek concerning what he perceived as an intimate connection between economic and political liberty. Friedman, himself a victim of anti-Semitism and bureaucratic harassment in his academic career, came to believe, as did the Austrians, that institutions not connected to the marketplace could not be trusted to ensure freedom. The only reliable protection of minority rights was, he affirmed, the maintenance of a free market in a largely unrestricted private economy, a point he made forcefully in his 1962 book *Capitalism and Freedom*. On the basis of this argument, Friedman reasoned that the extension of the regulatory and welfare functions of the American government since World War II was by its very nature destructive of personal and political freedom.

There was, however, another and equally important dimension to Friedman's thought, which involved the development of a new economic theory—an indispensable requirement for the revitalization of a floundering American conservatism. By the mid-1950s, he had led the way toward the restructuring and reinvigoration of the old and largely discredited quantity theory of money. Briefly stated, Friedman's theory proposed that government fiscal policy did not have the effects assumed by Keynesians. A believer in the basic validity of Say's Law, Friedman argued that, since by assumption GNP was always at or near its maximum potential level, additional government spending could have no lasting effect on output, other than to displace private expenditures by public ones, leading to economic inefficiencies, the proliferation of huge and unwieldy government bureaucracies, and, because of the crowding out of private investments by funds used to supply public services, to a decrease in productivity and a burgeoning inflation. Secondly, unlike Keynes, he believed that the growth of the total supply of money in the economy acted to increase the rate of spending not only through a lowering of interest rates, but also through the direct route of adding to a fixed proportion of cash that he assumed people held, thereby encouraging any sum accumulated beyond that to be spent. The effect of the large increases in the money supply by the Federal Reserve System since World War II had therefore been, he proposed, a further addition to the inflation which was already created by excessive government spending.[4]

Friedman's policy recommendations followed directly from his theory. Since he believed that government could do little or nothing to increase output and employment (attempts to do so, he declared, were doomed to failure: imperfect knowledge and legislative inertia made such policies ineffective even during times of recession, because they were never synchronized with actual conditions), it should confine its activities to the prevention of a too-rapid growth in the money supply. This could be done, he suggested, by removing control over the money supply from the Federal Reserve System—and thus, ultimately, from political influence—and placing it under a fixed rule allowing its growth to proceed no faster than the natural rate of increase in productivity in an unfettered economy, that is, from 3 to 5 percent per year. Such a change needed to be accompanied by the deregulation of most facets of economic activity, the replacement of present forms of government aid to the poor by a negative income tax, and constant annual decreases in federal taxation with concomitant decreases in federal spending. Friedman predicted that these policies, if carried out, would soon end America's economic woes.

It long seemed that Friedman's theory would not receive an actual test. After the disastrous Goldwater campaign, libertarian social and economic philosophy appeared again to be what it had been considered for decades— an anachronistic remnant of a bygone age. But the apparent failures of Keynesianism after the late 1960s gave new credibility to Friedman and his followers, many of whom had identified themselves by the late 1970s with what had been christened "supply-side economics"—the popular term for a variety of Friedman-like approaches that distinguished them from the "demand-side" Keynesian view, which stressed the primacy of

[4] For a more technical discussion of Friedman's monetarist views, see Milton Friedman and Anna Jacobson Schwartz, *A Monetary History of the United States, 1867–1960* (Princeton: Princeton University Press, 1963).

demand over business investment and capital formation. Furthermore, the revival of neoclassical economic thought was merely one part of what would become a flood of literature and oracular pronouncements extolling the virtues of American capitalism. Taking their cue from Friedman and other conservative economists, journalists, and political activists, authors and media personalities sought to demonstrate that the market system, if freed from the weight of tax and regulatory burdens, could cure inflation, end energy shortages, rebuild inner-city slums, dramatically increase economic efficiency, create full employment, and generally bring unprecedented prosperity. Moreover, the conservative shift in American politics would result in the rise to power of the most business-oriented administration since that of Calvin Coolidge. Ronald Reagan, elected president in 1980, promised to implement the central features of Friedman's program, having employed him as an economic adviser before his election. The nation, it now seemed to many, was reversing what had previously appeared as an inexorable trend toward the political guidance of the economy—the very trend that Robert Heilbroner had noted and analyzed with such evident acuity. Had Heilbroner's analysis been mistaken?

HEILBRONER'S REJOINDER: THE THEORY OF INFLATIONARY CAPITALISM

Heilbroner believed that neither his arguments nor his conclusions were unsound. On the contrary, he submitted that the New Right—and not it alone—labored under a fundamental misapprehension regarding the nature of the economic difficulties that had plagued the nation to an ever greater degree since the end of the 1960s. Much of Heilbroner's work from 1978 to the early 1980s was in fact devoted to a searching—and often searing—critique of conservative economic and social thought. In this effort, one of his prime targets was Friedman's theory of modern capitalism.

Friedman's espousal of free-market economic theory was based, in Heilbroner's view, on a tendentious, ahistorical, and often culturally naive perception of capitalist economic development and activity, a fact that he felt was evident, for example, in Friedman's comparison of the relative economic success of free-market Japan vis-à-vis the travails of socialist-inclined India. Friedman, Heilbroner noted, conveniently left out the disorienting effects of British imperialism and "linguistic fragmentation" when attempting to account for the comparative economic stagnation of the latter nation. Similarly, Friedman's discussion of the remarkable economic performance of postwar Japan ignored that nation's cultural homogeneity, its dictatorial government from the 1930s to 1945, its receipt of massive amounts of US capital after the war, and its highly organized system of indicative economic planning. Calling attention to many other shaky comparisons and propositions, Heilbroner contended that Friedman's ideas were "to serious economic and political debate what fundamentalist preaching is to Bible scholarship."[5]

Beyond this, Heilbroner strongly challenged the views of Friedman and the "supply-siders" concerning what they saw as the "naturalness" of capitalism, its vaunted ability to supply goods that satisfied needs and wants and thereby maximized human happiness, and its tendency to achieve a maximum and stable level of output and employment. The market system in the West, he observed, was "the product of a violent process of social displacement during the seventeenth and eighteenth centuries that culminated in an unstable and unwelcome structure of social and economic relationships."[6] Heilbroner also scored conservatives for what he considered their simplistic view of human nature. The New Right's concept of human motivation, he maintained, was often a "most vulgar materialist reductionism, in which capitalism is presented as embodying a primordial and unchanging 'economic man.' " He was certain that such a model of human psychology "would be treated with the scorn it deserves if it were adduced as a defense of, say, the Marxian view of history," yet it was routinely accepted by even sophisticated theorists on the right.[7] Concerning the superior ability of capitalism to meet economic needs and wants, Heilbroner wrote:

> No one denies that the forces of capitalism can give rise to dramatic economic growth. [Friedman is] entirely right in pointing to Hong Kong—or to Japan or West Germany or Israel—as monuments to the capital-accumulating capacities of such systems, and perhaps to their

[5] Robert L. Heilbroner, "The Road to Selfdom," *The New York Review of Books*, 17 April 1980, p. 4.

[6] Ibid., 6. George Lichtheim has emphatically and repeatedly made this same point, noting that most European peasants neither wanted nor welcomed the rise of industrial capitalism. What they did want, he writes, was "the continuation, and if possible the improvement, of their customary way of life—one based upon the economic independence of small farmers and urban craftsmen." He adds that it was, of course, the latter strata which were the ones virtually swept away by the rise of a market economy and the Industrial Revolution. Lichtheim, *A Short History of Socialism*, p. 5.

[7] Robert L. Heilbroner, "The Demand for the Supply Side," *The New York Review of Books*, 11 June 1981, p. 40.

ability to create and nurture democratic political processes. That is not however the entire picture. Capitalism builds and it also undermines. It satisfies wants but creates new ones even more rapidly, so that capitalist societies are marked by a perpetual craving, not a sense of contentment. Capitalist societies create political freedoms and simultaneously fear the implications of applying the democratic creed to the economic sphere.

Thus capitalism is far more dynamic, more restive, more self-contradictory than [Friedman] would have us believe. [His] view of the market system is naive, grasping one part of its nature, blind to others.[8]

Finally, Heilbroner questioned the monetarist/supply-side picture of capitalism as a harmonious, self-correcting institutional mechanism that guaranteed steady growth with only minor interruptions in production and employment as long as state intervention in the market was kept to a minimum. This, he argued, was a grossly distorted view of the actual operation of a system whose dysfunctions were paradoxically "brought about by the *success*—not the failure—of capitalist processes." Far from inclining automatically toward equilibrium, "The system tends naturally toward economic disequilibrium and toward social and political tension." In reality, "Economic strains or crises are the unavoidable, 'natural,' consequences" of capitalist production, a problem that stemmed from the "continuing difficulty in accumulating surplus successfully. There are potential disruptions and mismatches at every stage of the process, from engaging a labor force, through assuring its disciplined performance, to selling its output. These difficulties are also recognized by conventional economists, but a radical view stresses the self-generated nature of these problems, largely rooted in the wage-labor relationship. Capital is thus seen as the source of its own economic crises, rather than as the victim of crises thrust upon it from outside forces, such as government 'intrusions.' "[9]

These misrepresentations and misconceptions were, in Heilbroner's opinion, bad enough in themselves. But their worst consequence was their cumulative harm in misleading both policymakers and the public with respect to an issue that was seemingly at the center of the myriad economic problems of advanced capitalist societies—inflation. As noted previously, inflation was viewed by the New Right as a problem rooted in the growth of government spending and in the government-supported expansion of the money supply since the New Deal, and particularly since the 1960s. The

---

[8] Heilbroner, "The Road to Selfdom," p. 6.
[9] Heilbroner, "The Demand for the Supply Side," p. 38.

New Right thus averred that the inflationary surge of recent years could be ended by cutting government spending, bringing the money supply under control, and eliminating the large budget deficits that they believed were a powerful factor in fueling the Great Inflation of the 1970s.

The apparent plausibility of these propositions notwithstanding, Heilbroner maintained that they were all misleading, unproven, or totally lacking in explanatory power. There was no doubt, he admitted, that government spending could (although it need not) in itself add to inflationary pressures, as could deficits. He pointed out, however, that the supposedly damaging federal deficit existed only because state and local governments during the decade of the 1970s had been receiving constantly greater amounts of grants-in-aid and other subsidies from federal sources. State governments therefore had increasing surpluses while the federal government had an increasing debt. But, since the latter was more than canceled out by the former, there was not, nor had there been, any *total* government deficit to eliminate! Secondly, while it was true that spending at all levels of government had increased during the past two decades, Heilbroner noted that the real per capita federal debt had not risen during this period, and that federal employment as a proportion of the total work force had actually *declined by a quarter* over the preceding generation. (Heilbroner observed that state and local governments accounted for more of GNP than the federal government.) Also, no empirical evidence had been adduced by monetarists to show that government spending "crowded out" private investments that would otherwise have been made.[10] Lastly, the charge of the New Right concerning the ballooning money supply contained, Heilbroner believed, both a minor insight and a major obfuscation. There could be no doubt, he conceded, that the unwillingness and/or the inability of the federal government acting through the Federal Reserve to slow the growth of money prevented the retrenchment in spending that Friedman and others affirmed would end inflation. The action of the federal government in underwriting the constant accumulation of private debt (far more massive than its public counterpart) was, to be sure, a sine qua non for sustained inflation. But this "explanation" was merely a means of begging the question. What the Friedmanites could not provide was a convincing explanation of precisely *why* the federal government could not readily cease, and possibly could not even control, its expansionary monetary policy, and

[10] See Robert L. Heilbroner and Lester C. Thurow, *Five Economic Challenges* (Englewood Cliffs, New Jersey: Prentice-Hall, 1981), chapters 1 and 3.

was instead only able to effect an alternate tightening and loosening of monetary controls—the "stop-go" policy that had shown no signs of being successful.

Heilbroner, it seemed, had effectively disposed of the conservative view of the causes of inflation. He was no more satisfied with liberal interpretations, however, which stressed the upward "shocks" given to the economy by astronomical price increases in specific sectors of the economy, such as health care, food, housing, and especially energy supplies, or which sought the origins of inflation in wage increases, interest rates, or military spending for the Vietnam War. The dramatic increases in the prices of certain services and commodities, whether internally or externally induced, were probably indeed *proximate* causes of rising price levels in the general economy, as were the other factors cited. Yet this account of the emergence of inflation was also deeply flawed, for it could not elucidate the reasons for the continued and unrelenting upward movement of prices. A sudden, drastic jump in the price of coal during the nineteenth century, Heilbroner noted, would not have "touched off a widespread, self-feeding chain reaction of rising prices throughout the economy." "Instead," he explained, "a coal OPEC would have resulted in the wholesale shutting down of coal mines unable to sell their product; in the drastic curtailment of steel output as plant managers cut back their unprofitable operations; in a decline of purchasing from the businesses and households affected by this turn of events; and thereafter in a fall in 'carloadings,' the index of general economic activity we used before GNP was invented."[11] Why, if such events would have transpired in an earlier period, were the consequences of increasingly expensive energy so enormously different in the 1970s? Again it was obvious that the proffered "explanation" turned out, on closer examination, to explain very little.

Where had these interpretations gone wrong? Heilbroner proposed that what lay beneath the failure of both conservative and liberal attempts to explain inflation was their critical neglect of an indispensable consideration: the social, political, and perceptional contexts in which economic forces operated. The continuous inflationary bias of modern capitalism could only be understood, he argued, as the result of deep structural changes within advanced market systems. His strongly affirmed view was that inflation was not a kind of economic "sickness" or "ailment," as it

[11] Robert L. Heilbroner, "The Inflation in Your Future," *The New York Review of Books*, 1 May 1980, p. 6.

had often been portrayed; he objected, in fact, to the very metaphor of illness, because it "suggests that there exists such a thing as a 'healthy' economy in which there are no problems, just as there are healthy persons who have no ills or disorders."[12] Inflation, Heilbroner contended, was not a disease, but rather the functional adaptation of an extraordinarily dynamic and resilient economic system to new conditions. Indeed, he explained that industrial capitalism had undergone three major crises before, all of which were preceded and caused by, and/or followed and "resolved" by, basic structural change.

The central problem of capitalism at the time of the Industrial Revolution was, Heilbroner pointed out, the widespread urban poverty that accompanied the economic and demographic dislocations of industrialization—a problem that was greatly ameliorated, but not eradicated, by the tremendous growth of productive capacity in the fourth quarter of the nineteenth century. By the turn of the century, the most widely discussed issue in market societies was the rapid increase in the size of business organizations and the resultant concentration of economic power, a systemic transformation induced by the impact of technological changes that arose along with the "Second Industrial Revolution." No "solution" was found to the perceived dangers of this development, which was, in fact, still a major topic of debate and controversy in the early 1930s, when a new dilemma quickly overshadowed it: the catastrophic collapse of capitalism into a seemingly permanent state of economic stagnation. The Great Depression, after all, was itself the product of great changes such as the increased complexity, scale, and interdependence of economic activity in an increasingly urban—and therefore socially and politically volatile—society in which the severity of routine economic downturns constantly intensified and eventually became politically explosive. Yet Heilbroner reminded readers that this depression, like others in the past, was initially seen as a temporary malady affecting an otherwise "healthy" economic system. "Given the prevailing diagnosis," he wrote, "the condition remained intractable. Vigorous government intervention was ruled out as worse than the 'disease.' "[13] The "sickness" of depression, however, was finally "cured"—though again, not completely—by fundamental institutional change. And, again, this "solution" was to have a major bearing on the nature of the next "ailment" the system would suffer.

[12] Robert L. Heilbroner, "Inflationary Capitalism," in Mark Green and Robert Massie, Jr., eds., *The Big Business Reader* (New York: Pilgrim, 1980), p. 511.

[13] Ibid., p. 518.

The necessary preconditions for the inflation-wracked era that began in the late 1960s were established, Heilbroner maintained, over the period of the preceding eighty years. The long-term and still active process of business concentration and the eventual evolution of large trade unions that followed in its wake in exactly this concentrated part of the economy had led, as Galbraith had pointed out, to the increasing bureaucratization of capitalist economies and thus to the inevitable curtailment of competitive, self-adjusting economic forces. In itself, this made the system neither depression- nor inflation-prone: it simply gave it greater inertia in any direction it began to move. Thus, the "pervasive insecurity and instability" that had always characterized capitalism and had been the bane of both entrepreneur and worker had gradually given way, under the influence of new technologies and techniques of organization, to a social order in which those threats had been reduced for a major section of the economy.

It was this constant movement toward an interconnected and interdependent system—one that lessened the resistance of the structure to shocks so that it resembled a "rickety architecture of frames and beams and spans" rather than, as before, a "great heap of sand"—that was both further to enhance this drive for security by well-organized interests and—paradoxically—to simultaneously make its attainment for the general economy less certain. The experience of the Great Depression revealed that the vulnerability of the market economy by the 1930s was such that its uncertain and unreliable features had to be reduced to a still greater degree for a large number of groups and for the system as a whole. Again, therefore, the system would change. The upshot of this change was that "floors [were] placed under a multitude of economic activities, shoring up purchasing power, protecting most households against severe reversal, ensuring a degree of economic safety totally unknown in the era of pregovernmental capitalism."[14] It was this development, he observed, that gave modern capitalism its inflationary bias.

Yet even this did not by itself produce inflation. The most immediate general cause of continued price increases was, Heilbroner proposed, a dramatic and widespread change in the beliefs of the public concerning the future. Contemporary economic fears and apprehensions notwithstanding, many people had forgotten "how much more secure is the outlook of 1980 than that of 1880. Most of us expect, for example, that our pay will be increased each year, whether we work harder or more successfully or not.

[14] Heilbroner, "The Inflation in Your Future," p. 6.

We expect that the nation's economic ills will be the object of vigorous government action, not left to work themselves out. We expect that our personal futures will be somehow provided for, so that we can indulge in large consumption spending in good conscience." The result was that "today's economic structure propagates, magnifies, and sustains increases in costs or demand, instead of blocking, damping, or eliminating them."[15] No one, in other words, believed that a major contraction could occur and, as a consequence, everyone behaved accordingly, fueling by their very attitudes and actions the propensity toward rising costs and prices inherent in governmental capitalism. The "floor" that had been placed under the system had thus "solved" the problem of depression, but only through structural change and at the cost of inflation, which rose from average annual rates of about 2.5 percent in the 1950s to 3.5 percent by the 1960s, 6 percent by the 1970s, and to well over 10 percent by the late 1970s.

On the effects of inflation, Heilbroner revealed that, by available means of measurement, they were surprisingly mild for the average person. Despite a ten-year price rise of approximately 100 percent, real per capita disposable income rose by 28 percent from 1969 to 1979. And, since GNP grew from 1970 to 1980 by $324 billion (1972 dollars) while the distribution of that income had not changed, it could not be shown that anyone was worse off. Indeed, the opposite could be shown. Why, then, did people feel harmed?

Because, Heilbroner said, *money* incomes had risen 134 percent during the same period, causing people to feel cheated as the vast bulk of that money evaporated away. Also, because individuals in a capitalist society are always moving up and down the economic ladder (although *relative* positions, as just noted, often remain the same) and because inflation, unlike depression, does permit many to benefit by the income losses of others, the losers in an inflationary period tend to blame inflation instead of other factors (for example bad luck) for their slippage. Rising money incomes for all make such persons feel that, while they only *appeared* to be advancing economically with higher incomes, they would be *in fact* advancing were it not for inflation.

Heilbroner nevertheless noted that inflation presented three real threats and one real cost for society as a whole. Inflation threatened, if not checked, to become *hyper*inflation, which would shatter the nation's economy as it had done to Germany's in the 1920s; it menaced assets in mon-

---

[15] Ibid.

etary form and led many people to shift their funds to various physical commodities; it endangered the economic system as a whole by forcing banks to accept large amounts of short-term debt at high interest rates from businesses and municipalities, thereby making the financial structure highly susceptible to even localized defaults or bank failures; and finally, inflation led to fiscal and monetary policies that, by slowing down economic growth, produced an income loss for society in general and caused high unemployment and economic suffering, especially among minorities and the poor.[16]

Heilbroner believed that sooner or later—probably within a decade—inflation, like depression, would come to be seen as an unacceptable feature of modern capitalism. He also believed that this problem could be largely eliminated in only one way in a society that could not afford (or, more precisely, would not accept) depressions, permanently high unemployment, the radical decentralization of the American economy, or a ripping apart of the fabric of advanced capitalism through the removal of the "floor" that had now been placed under the economy. Inflation could only be brought under control, he argued, by putting a "ceiling" on the economy through the imposition of a steep tax on all increases in money incomes from one year to the next and the establishment of a comprehensive incomes policy. A bureaucratic mechanism would also be needed in order to deal with increases not resulting from inflation and also to adjudicate individual cases that were troublesome or involved. This bureaucracy would not be popular, nor would the entire policy expunge inflation from the economy. In addition, these actions would lead to slower economic growth and probably to a proliferation of black and gray markets. But chronic and severe inflation would cease to be a threat.

Capitalism, however, would continue to be threatened, as would industrial society itself, by a series of immediate, medium-range, and long-range problems. Inflation was of the first variety and one of the least serious, but nonetheless illustrative of the forces likely to change the workings of Western market systems within coming decades. Of these, some, like inflation, were generated largely by internal pressures; others, such as the side effects of industrial output and technology, were created mainly by external stresses and constraints, the last, most immovable, and ultimately most decisive of which was the ability of the earth's atmosphere to absorb the thermal refuse that was the inevitable by-product of industrial produc-

---

[16] Heilbroner and Thurow, *Five Economic Challenges*, pp. 20-30.

tion. Inflation, like the other dangers that threatened or would threaten industrial capitalism, could only yield to greater planning and more conscious control over the economy. Could a planned capitalism work? ''That depends,'' Heilbroner replied, ''on what one means by 'work.' As I see it, *no organizational system can smoothly combine the explosive technology, restless polity, and deadening work experience of contemporary industrial society* [Heilbroner's emphasis]. This is as true for self-styled socialist societies as for capitalist ones. Hence I do not expect state capitalism to 'work' particularly well, but I expect it to survive and to continue the function that is the driving force of capitalism—the accumulation of capital by means of wage labor.''[17]

[17] Heilbroner, ''The Demand for the Supply Side,'' p. 41.

Chapter 10   *Heilbroner and Corporate Society*

It is obvious that if Heilbroner's ideas and interpretations are valid, the implications are staggering for every area of social life. It would mean that the prospects for social democracy in America—a development desired by Heilbroner—are considerably more bleak than they would otherwise be, and it is therefore especially vital to come to a reasoned judgment concerning his views. To some extent, an evaluation of Heilbroner's thought must remain tentative, since much of his work has been of a speculative or predictive nature. This is clearly true of the four specific and closely interrelated problems he sees at the base of the monumental difficulties before mankind: the issues of energy and resource limitations, thermal pollution, the aspirations of the Third World, and Western economic growth. Nevertheless, an attempt must be made. Is Heilbroner's gloomy scenario, most fully outlined in *An Inquiry into the Human Prospect*, one that will become a reality?

ECONOMIC CYCLES AND HISTORY: THE HUMAN PROSPECT REEXAMINED

The study that appears to have provided the immediate inspiration for Heilbroner's book was a computer-based project by a research association called the Club of Rome, whose report was titled *The Limits to Growth*. Published in 1972, one of its main conclusions was the following proposition: "If the present growth trends in world population, industrialization, pollution, food production, and resource depletion continue unchanged, the limits to growth on this planet will be reached sometime within the next one hundred years. The most probable result will be a rather sudden and uncontrollable decline in both population and industrial capacity."[1] The best result that could be hoped for, in the authors' opinion, was a state of "global equilibrium" in which capital and population were held con-

---

[1] Donella H. Meadows, Dennis L. Meadows, Jørgen Randers, and William W. Behrens III, *The Limits to Growth: A Report for the Club of Rome's Project on the Predicament of Mankind* (New York: Signet, 1972), p. 29.

stant, all input and output rates (demographic and economic) were kept to a minimum, and the levels of capital and population as well as the ratio between the two were determined consciously and "revised and slowly adjusted as the advance of technology creates new options," although the attainment of this state was viewed as a far more benign occurrence than the one prophesied by Heilbroner.[2] The study suggested that, although technological progress in the past had "resulted in crowding, deterioration of the environment, and greater social inequality because greater productivity has been absorbed by population and capital growth," a new zero-growth society could ensure, if it had the political will and social consent, an order that used a putatively rising productivity to allow higher material standards of living or greater equality, more leisure, and the freedom to pursue other goals in life. This difference in outlook aside, the fundamental assumptions regarding energy, resources, world economics, and the severe limits imposed by an inflexible set of physical circumstances were quite similar to those of Heilbroner.

These were not, of course, the first predictions of a "steady-state" economy in the age of industrial capitalism. Malthus' dismal forebodings of a food supply that could not keep pace with geometric increases in population cast the first shadow of doubt on the hopeful vision of Adam Smith. Limits on the availability and productivity of land would lead, Malthus thought, to an inevitable shortage of agricultural sustenance for the expanding multitudes, the natural increases of whose numbers could only be checked by disease, famine, and war. David Ricardo, only slightly more optimistic, foresaw a social order in which a persistent shortage of land would lead to the ascendancy of the landowning class, who drew off the benefits of a rising economic surplus to themselves through ruinously high rates of rent that in turn would cause profit rates in industry to fall to nothing.

Nor did this idea disappear as the nineteenth century progressed. John Stuart Mill also proposed that profit rates would someday approach infinitesimal levels, causing an end to additional net investment and the arrival of a no-growth economy—what he called a "stationary state." In Mill's formulation, however, this condition would arise not because of a capital shortage, but because of a general capital *abundance* and the placing of a voluntary limit on population growth by the working class. Once a certain level of material comfort were reached, Mill assumed that people would

[2] Ibid., pp. 178-179.

not want to strive endlessly for more production and income, thus enduring the "trampling, crushing, elbowing, and treading on each other's heels, which form the existing type of social life," but would instead want, as soon as possible, to voluntarily terminate increases in both population and material wealth.

This was not a belief confined to the last century. Keynes, like Mill, believed that capitalism would eventually reach a steady state; moreover, he reckoned that it would have the productive capacity to do so within a single century. Thus capitalist society could, if it wished, "attain the conditions of a quasi-stationary community where change and progress would result only from changes in technique, taste, population and institutions, with the products of capital selling at a price proportioned to the labor, etc., embodied in them on just the same principles as govern the prices of consumption-goods into which capital-charges enter in an insignificant degree."[3] Again, like Mill, Keynes suggested that the achievement of such a state might "be the most sensible way of gradually getting rid of many of the objectionable features of capitalism," and that the end of continuous growth would work no great hardship on mankind, since the satisfaction of "absolute needs" would free humans to pursue "non-economic purposes."[4]

And British economists were not the only ones who doubted, for one reason or another, the ability of capitalism to sustain its forward drive toward ever greater production. Alvin Hansen, one of Keynes's first American converts, adopted the view in the late 1930s that, as a result of the enormous, unused industrial capacity then extant (created by a trailing off of the investment needs of the past for the development of railroads, electric power, and eventually the automobile industry, a trend exacerbated by a declining birth rate and the closing of the Western frontier), the American economy had fallen into a permanent condition of "relative stagnation of technical progress." Under such a hypothesis, the expected rate of return on capital would be so small that, no matter how low interest rates could be pushed, business could not be induced to borrow and invest idle funds. The only possible resolution of this dilemma lay in the permanent and massive use of government spending to prevent an unending economic lethargy. Hansen, in other words, did not think, as did Keynes, that stationary capitalism was one hundred years away: he believed it already ex-

---

[3] Keynes, *The General Theory of Employment, Interest, and Money*, pp. 220-221.

[4] Ibid., p. 221. Also see J. M. Keynes, "Economic Possibilities for Our Grandchildren," in J. M. Keynes, *Essays in Persuasion*, pp. 358-373.

isted, but not by choice. A perspective far more pessimistic than Keynes's, the view of the Stagnationist School appeared for a while to be borne out by the continued discouraging performance of the economy during the latter years of the Great Depression until the remarkable expansion that followed World War II. (It was the stagnationist thesis that was a main target of attack in Joseph Schumpeter's 1942 classic work *Capitalism, Socialism, and Democracy*.)[5]

Such concerns almost completely disappeared—as did the interest in, and the fear of, depression—in the 1950s and 1960s, only to reappear in the 1970s. Heilbroner's contribution to the rekindled debate is distinguished by its eloquence, coherence, and persuasiveness, but it remains only one part of a chorus of disillusion and dire warnings.[6] Moreover, it seems only fair to say that at least some of the chiliastic pessimism of Heilbroner and those who might be called the "neo-Malthusians" was ill-founded.

The first cracks in Heilbroner's own Malthusian edifice appeared in an article written by him a year after the publication of his disturbing appraisal of the "human prospect." Here Heilbroner, while reaffirming the validity of his main arguments, reevaluated his prediction of a relatively rapid disappearance of certain key minerals essential to the functioning of industrial society and of the extreme consequences that would ensue by suggesting that it might be possible to mine the oceans for such minerals, thereby forestalling the problem, a solution he had not been aware of a year before.[7] He could well be commended for his honesty and his willingness to modify his thinking as new facts arose or became known to him. And it is certainly true that he had allowed for the possibility of new technological developments lessening the burden of the adjustment to a steady-state economy.

But beyond this, it was not made clear by Heilbroner why the increased scarcity of other mineral resources should not generally lead, as with any scarce commodity, to higher prices in the short run followed by reduced demand and in the long run by the progressive substitution for existing

[5] See Herbert Stein, *The Fiscal Revolution in America* (Chicago: University of Chicago Press, 1969), pp. 160-176.

[6] This chorus has not yet entirely ceased. For two of the more sober and persuasive recent works of this genre, see Herman E. Daly, *Steady-State Economics: The Economics of Biophysical Equilibrium and Moral Growth* (San Francisco: W. H. Freeman, 1977) and Jeremy Rifkin (with Ted Howard), *Entropy: A New World View* (New York: Bantam, 1981).

[7] See Robert L. Heilbroner, "Second Thoughts on The Human Prospect," *Challenge* (May–June 1975), 21-28.

minerals by acceptable replacements found through various means and in various places. Indeed, with some qualifications, this same basic mechanism ought to work with equal efficiency with respect to the problem of energy itself, and there is evidence that it has done so in the period since Heilbroner's work appeared. The problem, therefore, is not the physical exhaustion of resources or an absolute scarcity of energy, but rather the increasingly high prices that will prevail at least until alternative sources are found, together with the psychological, social, and political costs the development of new technologies and forms of organization may entail.

Regarding the ultimate threat to economic growth, the limit to the amount of thermal waste that can be safely released into the atmosphere, Heilbroner admitted the existence of an alternative source of energy that would solve much of the problem—solar power—but then dismissed this solution with the suggestion that this and other new technologies "may not arrive 'on time.' " They may not; but there is no reason to assume this. New technologies have typically been developed since the dawn of the industrial era with great rapidity once economic pressures exerted themselves.[8] Nor, it seems, did Heilbroner take sufficient account of the possibility of substantial increases in the efficiency of energy use predicted by some experts—increases that have actually taken place since the mid-1970s. The fact that new and more efficient technologies were not in general use earlier proves only that there had not been—in a period of cheap energy—an incentive to invest in such projects, with the consequence that their development was given a low priority in a market system. This was particularly true in America, where the state minimized its influence in the market generally, while in the 1950s and 1960s actually subsidizing the profligate use of fossil fuels and of large, inefficient automobiles.

An additional problem with Heilbroner's predictions is that he used the recent annual growth rate of the industrialized world (7 percent) and the annual rate of increase in energy use since World War II (4 percent) as his model of future growth, extrapolating on the basis of these assumptions a quintupling of demand for resources within 50 years and a doubling of energy use every 18 years. Yet it is unlikely that the developed nations can in the near future again match the extraordinary rates of expansion that characterized the first decades of the postwar era, which, because of the impact of the Great Depression and World War II, were highly atypical in

---

[8] On the prospects for the development of solar power, see Modesto A. Maidique, "Solar America," in Robert Stobaugh and Daniel Yergin, eds., *Energy Future: Report of the Energy Project at the Harvard Business School* (New York: Ballantine, 1980), pp. 231-269.

terms of the magnitude of demand for capital investment to rebuild anti-
quated, atrophied, or physically destroyed industrial bases in Western societies. Subsequent growth figures have been markedly lower and are
likely to remain so at least until a transition to new forms of energy is
completed. Heilbroner was correct in pointing out that exponential growth
certainly cannot continue (that is, not at a rapid rate), but there is no evidence that it will do so. He was indeed aware that slower growth and a
service economy could affect his predictions, but tended to brush such
factors aside with the comment that these trends might slow, but could not
prevent, the ringing down of the ecological curtain on industrial society.

Finally, it does seem clear that conflict will continue between wealthy
Northern and impoverished Southern nations, but for reasons more complex than those given by Heilbroner. The Third World, it is becoming ever
more obvious, is far from homogeneous. The industrialized North is indeed at odds with the nonindustrialized South, but many groups within the
former region are increasingly in conflict both with newly industrializing
regions of the South and with elites in their own nations that benefit greatly
from massive investments in some regions of the South at the cost of investment in the North. Nonetheless, it is quite clear that capitalism is continuing the process it began four centuries ago—the integration of the
world into an interconnected economy. It has been a fitful endeavor, one
that has progressed at times rapidly, at times slowly, having been retarded
during the first three-quarters of the twentieth century by global warfare,
revolutionary turmoil, and colonial struggles. Here the somewhat aberrant
nature of the recent past has served to obscure rather than clarify the dominant trend.[9]

Heilbroner's Malthusian predictions, it should now be clear, may well
be premature and are at least open to serious doubt. Heilbroner, however,
was not the first to foretell the inevitable and impending end of capitalist
growth. The belief that capitalism cannot grow further or even survive,
either for endogenous economic reasons or for exogenous physical/envi-
ronmental reasons, has been a recurrent, almost constant feature of Western social thought during the last two centuries. The question is how so
many great intellects could arrive at prophecies of what, to paraphrase
Mark Twain, has turned out to be the greatly exaggerated death of capital-

---

[9] For critical reviews of Heilbroner's *An Inquiry into the Human Prospect*, see *The New York
Times Book Review*, May 12 1974, p. 5; *The New York Review of Books*, 27 June 1974, pp. 14a-
20b; *Commentary* 58, no. 2 (August 1974), 84-86; and *Contemporary Sociology* 4, no. 5 (September 1975), 555-556.

ism. So persistent an error is obviously not to be found in any psychological or philosophical structures common to so varied a group of thinkers. Its origins must lie instead in the peculiar nature of capitalism itself.

As the great economist Joseph Schumpeter (who himself predicted the decay of capitalist institutions, but for social and cultural reasons) recognized, the central feature of capitalist economic growth has been what he called the "process of creative destruction" through which old firms, capital, products, and techniques have constantly been replaced by new ones in a cyclical process of investment, expansion, and contraction in which innovation played a key role in the approximately fifty-year cycles of boom and bust characteristic of capitalist evolution (see above, Chapter 7). The spasmodic and frightening retching, gasping, and wheezing typical of the twenty-five-year downswings of the business cycle have repeatedly led pessimistic thinkers to believe that the system was approaching either senility or extinction, while twenty-five-year upswings have encouraged optimists to expect an earthly nirvana of increasing and unending material abundance produced by what is then viewed as an eternally vital and dynamic economic engine. It is indeed a tribute to the power of the manic-depressive psychology engendered by this roller-coaster motion that Heilbroner, who understands the *modus operandi* of business civilization so well and has traced its activities so perceptively, should have failed to consider an obvious possibility: namely, that the present crisis engulfing capitalism will lead it not to a moribund state, but instead merely to the kind of transformation he himself has chronicled and analyzed, one that will allow this extraordinary economic machine to rise again, phoenix-like, from its own ashes.

Indeed, the latter outcome seems the more probable as one considers a historical peculiarity of major business cycles that supports a richly suggestive hypothesis concerning not only the origins of these cycles in general, but also of neo-Malthusian theories of ecological constraints on capitalist growth. Economic historian W. W. Rostow has proposed that what has caused the universally recognized Kondratiev cycles of industrial capitalism "are periods of relative shortage and relative abundance of food and raw materials. Changes in relative prices underlie the shifts in income distribution, the directions of investment, trends in interest rates, real wages, and the overall price level which are the hallmarks of a Kondratiev cycle." The lengths of major upturns and downturns relative to conventional business cycles was explained, Rostow theorized, by the fact that the opening up of new sources of food and raw materials required substantial periods of time—much more time than it takes to build a new factory or house. The lags involved in responding to a relative rise in food or raw material prices, and the fact that the response often required the development of whole new regions, led to an overshooting of world requirements and a period of surplus. A relative fall in the prices of food and raw materials then followed. This trend persisted, gradually slowing down, until expanding world requirements caught up with the excess capacity and stocks generated in a Kondratiev upswing.[10]

Rostow has noted that the descending part of each major cycle was accompanied by higher prices and interest rates, by pressure on real wages, and by greater incomes for producers of food and raw materials, the ascending part by the opposite features.

The first major Kondratiev collapse from 1790 to 1815 (the period during which Malthus and Ricardo expounded their theories) was, Rostow reveals, a time when an increasing strain was placed on the supply of food and raw materials in Europe in response to the shortages induced in the wake of the French Revolution and the Napoleonic Wars. The resultant need to expand agricultural production in Britain retarded the development of England's leading industry, cotton textiles, while at the same time redounding to the benefit of a major food producer and raw material exporter across the sea—the United States (that is, until Jefferson's Embargo of 1807). The subsequent era from 1815 to 1848 (the time of John Stuart Mill's intellectual development) was one of explosive industrial growth in Europe and Northeastern America as well as one of cheap food and resource prices.

Again, however, pressure on food supplies resulting from a historically unprecedented, continuous rise in Western population caused a steep upward movement in grain and cotton prices together with lower wages, as British and American capital poured into railroad construction and agricultural development in the United States aimed at opening up new lands in the South and the Midwest to cotton and grain production, respectively. These conditions did not halt Europe's tremendous thrust toward industrial

---

[10] W. W. Rostow, *Getting from Here to There* (New York: McGraw-Hill, 1978), p. 22. The following section is taken from pages 25-37. Also see W. W. Rostow, *Why the Poor Get Richer and the Rich Slow Down: Essays in the Marshallian Long Period* (Austin, Texas: University of Texas Press, 1980), chapter 1.

expansion, although this did occur temporarily in the United States because of the Civil War. A "transient energy crisis" occurred in the 1870s, as coal production lagged behind demand; but mining capacity was rapidly expanded and prices dropped. Also, the phenomenal investments made to establish transportation networks in the American West had by this time led to vast increases in US grain exports. Thus, by 1873 another economically favorable period began that would be "marked by strong downward trends in the prices of grain, coal, cotton, and most other raw materials."

Until 1896 Western economies plowed resolutely toward a completion of the work begun early in the nineteenth century: the laying out of the basic economic infrastructure of modern Western civilization. The preeminent component of this new wave of growth was, Rostow explains, cheap steel, whose production had first been stimulated by the building of the railroads, but which was now the basis for the creation of new capital goods and urban construction projects. Electricity and chemicals also formed an integral part of the Second Industrial Revolution, which sputtered into low gear as demands generated by urbanization and population increases in America pressed ever more tightly against a closing frontier and current grain production, and as "relative shortages of foodstuffs and raw materials again emerged in an environment of small wars, enlarged military outlays, and then a great war." Profits climbed and wages dropped during the next two decades, which saw the rise of labor unrest and of opposition and socialist political parties in Europe and America. Again resources were channeled into agriculture and minerals, this time in Canada, Argentina, Australia, and the Ukraine, and now also into armaments. And, although new industries (for example the one based on the internal combustion engine) arose to absorb capital investment, they could not take up the slack created by the decline of old sectors such as railroads and steel.

The year 1920 opened a new phase of lower prices (relatively and absolutely) for agricultural goods and raw materials coupled with high employment and production rates as mass consumption goods like the automobile propelled industrial growth forward. Europe's export markets, however, which had not recovered from the disruption of war, produced, in conjunction with a relatively low per capita income compared to the United States, "a situation where the new leading sectors of high mass-consumption did not move forward rapidly enough to bring the major economies back to sustained full employment. Then came the Great Depression, with catastrophic consequences in both industrial and basic commodity sectors.'' As a result, the years 1933-1951 again saw increased relative prices of commodities, which followed the monumental distortions of the Great Depression and the massive military spending and havoc of war. They also witnessed, not surprisingly, the rise of stagnationist theory and general economic pessimism.

It was, of course, the next generation—that of the fourth Kondratiev upswing—that experienced the extraordinary economic performance associated with capitalism in the 1950s and 1960s when, Rostow writes, the ''leading sectors of high mass-consumption moved forward rapidly in North America, Western Europe, and Japan, strengthened by cheap energy, food, and raw materials,'' simultaneously allowing modernization to proceed for the first time in many parts of the Third World. As the initial postwar boom in consumer goods slackened first in America and then in other countries, the gap was closed by private and state expenditures on education, health care, and travel. But, like all periods of capitalist expansion, this one could not continue indefinitely. Nor were the seeds of this new period of difficulties completely atypical or mysterious. ''As the 1960s wore on,'' Rostow explains, ''it was also evident, beneath the surface, that the rapid global expansion in food and energy requirements was altering the balance which had existed since the downward price turn in 1951.'' Just as the closing of the American West in the 1890s and ''the end of [America's] agricultural frontier, given existing agricultural prices and technologies,'' had terminated the second Kondratiev upswing, Rostow argues that the fourth was ended ''by the United States reaching the end of its gas and oil frontier, given existing energy prices and technologies.'' Historically, as he points out, the primary economic effect of a downswing has been to redirect investment in order to increase the supply of scarce commodities or make their use more efficient until they could be replaced. The chief difference now was that, whereas past business cycles had witnessed shortages primarily in grain and cotton, at present ''the list has extended to energy production and conservation, the supply of clean air and water, the supply of water itself, and, quite probably, to the supply of a wide range of raw materials.''

These same problems have drawn the comments of Barry Commoner, who, in determining their origins, has arrived at broadly similar conclusions. ''Energy production,'' Commoner explains, ''is extraordinarily capital-intensive.'' This means that energy use becomes progressively more expensive, while the marginal returns on expenditures for producing increasingly scarce nonrenewable energy constantly diminish. This fact, together with the increasing costs of agricultural production (modern agriculture is energy-intensive and therefore capital-intensive) and the often unacknowledged, but no less real, costs of environmental pollution, has caused a growing diversion of economic resources to energy production and the control of its by-products. In short, the other sectors of the economy are being cannibalized to produce energy, grow food, and fight pollution![11]

CAPITALISM IN TRANSITION: ROBERT HEILBRONER AND THE WANING OF ECONOMIC LIBERALISM

In light of the foregoing analysis, the economic doldrums of the 1970s become more understandable and at the same time take on new meaning and significance. Their existence does not necessarily imply, as Heilbroner believed, the beginning of the end for capitalism, since, as we have seen, the world market economy has periodically undergone major readjustments lasting for extended periods of time. There is therefore no empirically discovered reason why capitalism or industrial society itself should come to a relatively sudden end. Heilbroner, it might well seem, had seriously miscalculated the consequences of recent historical events and trends.

Yet, although the latter proposition undoubtedly contains some truth, I do not believe that Heilbroner has misperceived the general direction in which capitalism is moving and will, in all probability, continue to move in the near future. In spite of the relative implausibility of his apocalyptic vision, it is certainly obvious that the system is in a state of turmoil that has not only economic, but also social, political, and philosophical dimensions. Indeed, if the present condition of capitalism is neither wholly unprecedented nor mortal, it does bear, as previously noted, certain unique characteristics that make its substantial amelioration through the medium of past policies and ideologies extremely difficult, if not impossible. For the central fact of the present crisis of capitalism in the West is that it

[11] See Barry Commoner, *The Politics of Energy* (New York: Knopf, 1979), chapter 4. It is also important to remember that the world experienced energy crises long before the Industrial Revolution. Carlo Cipolla has pointed out, for example, that there arose a serious shortage of wood in late-fifteenth-century Europe. England reacted to this shortage by expanding shipbuilding, navigation, and trade, and by increasing iron and coal production—the very course that set that nation on the path that would eventually lead to the Industrial Revolution. See Carlo N. Cipolla, *Before the Industrial Revolution: European Society and Economy, 1000–1700* (New York: W. W. Norton, 1976), pp. 228-230; 265-273.

almost certainly cannot be surmounted without recourse to a marked increase in the extent of state intervention in the private economy. Because
of the nature of the current problems and the institutional and international
contexts in which they occur, government funds are required to an ever
greater degree to provide sufficient capital for the huge and not immediately profitable investments that are needed for the development of renew-
able energy resources, increased agricultural production, pollution control, research and development projects, and effective competition with
other advanced and industrializing nations. Furthermore, state guidance
and subsidization of investment undertaken in cooperation with business
and labor has become an ever more common adaptive measure in an increasingly interconnected domestic and world economy.[12] Such policies
already exist to a greater or lesser degree in many capitalist nations, but
the events of the 1970s and 1980s have extended and reinforced them.

This, however, raises an important issue. Assuming the general validity
of the preceding statements, we are still left with an unresolved problem:
the emergence of the New Right in America, a phenomenon that apparently flies in the face of Heilbroner's predictions (and my own). In a 1968
essay Heilbroner had written that "the very diminution of political controversy over the business-state issue implies that the ideological battle is
already won and that big business is slowly making its peace with big
government. The acceptance of planning by businessmen in Western Europe indicates, I would suggest, the direction of business thought in America tomorrow."[13] Yet the New Right has directly challenged the philosophical basis of the Broker-Welfare State and the regulatory and social-service
bureaucracies that have grown up since the New Deal, and has in addition
seemed to garner public support for its views and policies. Again Heilbroner appears to have made a fundamental error. Was his hypothesis,
after all, mistaken? Again I think not, and to understand why, one must
consider the reasons for the somewhat puzzling rise of conservative
thought and political power in recent years.

At first glance, the appearance of New Right ideology in America is an
anomaly and a wonderment. How could forces thought to be long since
buried still exert a powerful influence in American life? The most popular
explanation has directed attention to a rightward drift in a number of advanced capitalist nations since the mid-1970s, which has been interpreted

---

[12] Rostow and Commoner both advocate variants of this kind of policy, although their specific
prescriptions for remedies and political structures to implement them do not usually coincide.

[13] Heilbroner, "Rhetoric and Reality in the Struggle Between Business and the State," p. 30.

as a backlash against the growth of government regulation and especially taxation. But, leaving aside the fact that the programs of these new rightist governments have not been notably successful and are not likely to be in the future, the most important fact to note about the rise of these new regimes in Europe is the limited, cautious, even pusillanimous nature of their general approach to changes in the structure of governmental capitalism. No European government has attacked the welfare state per se, rightists in general having moved only toward a partial reversal or halting of some labor-socialist policies (for example, extensive nationalization and increasingly high marginal tax rates) that had proceeded far beyond anything established or even proposed in the United States. In addition, the fact that some nations (for example, Sweden) have undoubtedly reached the fiscal limits to the growth of social services does not imply any reluctance to provide those services that already exist, and no major non-American conservative party has suggested this.[14] Nor have many politicians touted laissez-faire economics even during electoral campaigns.

A somewhat more helpful explanation is that conservative parties have been able to capitalize on the social and economic discontents of recent years that have brought some social democratic parties into disrepute. In the broadest perspective the conservative attack on the welfare state in America was certainly born of the frustrations attendant on the most recent downturn in the world economy. The end of cheap energy and the consequent need to channel resources into the development of new supplies combined with the absence of capital-intensive technological breakthroughs of the kind that powered the great period of prosperity from 1950 to 1972 led in the 1970s to slower growth, smaller increases in real income, less employment, diminished opportunity for upward mobility for the new middle class, and, in the new context of governmental capitalism, relative economic stagnation, and the political deadlock produced by groups struggling to maintain their share of national income, to a high and continuing rate of inflation. (Heilbroner was mistaken when he claimed that no one was worse off in 1980 than in 1970. While it is true that real per capita income rose during that decade and that the distribution of family incomes remained about the same, families were able to keep their relative positions on the income scale only by sending more of their members into the work force.) This environment could not fail to alter the per-

---

[14] Britain's Margaret Thatcher has not, for instance, threatened to dismantle the National Health Service (although she has quietly done much damage to it as well as to other parts of the British welfare state).

ception of the new middle class concerning the success of welfare Keynesianism.

The natural beneficiary of this altered view, especially in a nation like
the United States, which lacks a strong and independent social democratic
political alternative, was business conservatism (an odd, indeed oxymo-
ronic concept, given the distinctly *un*conservative economic and social
philosophy of the vast majority of the American upper class, in contrast to
that of its European counterpart, which stresses caution, continuity, and
the need for social justice). A political force long out of direct power, it
was thus not tarnished as a purveyor of policies that appeared wanting in
time of great economic stress and strain. But rightist parties prospered not
merely by offering the comforting view that economic pain and readjust-
ment were unnecessary and the result of incompetent leadership and discredited ideas. They also benefited (despite their own position as representatives of private bureaucratic power) from the perceptibly growing
alienation of broad masses of people from the central institutions of urban
life—the huge public and private bureaucracies whose workings had come
to influence their lives to an ever more extensive and obvious degree. Finally, but by no means least in importance, conservatives in America and
elsewhere have profited from the accumulated fears and uncertainties produced by a generation of rapid, complex, and wrenching domestic and
international changes (again, paradoxically, given the fact that capitalism
and business were largely responsible for these changes) that frequently
challenged and sometimes shattered people's images of themselves and of
their nation's—and the West's—role in the world, the very theme of which
Heilbroner has written so perceptively.

But while most of the latter discontents apply particularly to the previously optimistic United States, they also extend to Western nations in general, and therefore cannot in themselves account for the specific features
of the New Right in America, particularly its vehemence and radical nature. Reduced growth and a disillusionment with certain aspects of the
welfare state can help to explain the unwillingness to fund increased social
expenditures, but not the massive cuts proposed by Ronald Reagan. Similarly, a popular distaste for expanded bureaucracy makes understandable
the inevitable complaints that regulations and red tape bring forth. But this
in no way explains what in the late 1970s purported to be a virtual rejection
of governmental capitalism by much of the American public and business.

Had this rejection actually taken place? Such a perception of popular
and business attitudes and ideology contains an important element of truth.

While sophisticated conservatives and businessmen in America have long recognized that a modern capitalist society cannot be operated according to the principles of nineteenth- (or eighteenth-) century economic theory, the American public and particularly the American business class have retained a strong, though usually latent, opposition to the ideological legacy of the New Deal, whose institutional legitimacy was largely established—contrary to widely held views—not in the 1940s, but in the 1960s. This in itself explains much of the tenuousness of governmental capitalism in America. Nonetheless, another and more significant factor must also be considered: the specific form Keynesian policy has taken in the United States.

Galbraith, Harrington, and Heilbroner have all rightly emphasized that stimulative fiscal policy in postwar America has had a predominantly military character (that is, except for one recent decade), and herein lies an important key for understanding the rise of the New Right, its ideas, and its actions. What has become quite clear is that the majority of the New Right—an uneasy and conflict-ridden coalition catapulted to power on the slogans of libertarian conservatism, but containing social conservatives and dominated by cold-war conservatives—does not reject Keynesianism and the Broker State *in general*. What it does oppose is a certain *kind* of Keynesianism and *type* of Broker State.

After World War II military spending comprised the bulk of federal expenditures for well over fifteen years (see above, Chapter 3), but this spending gradually declined as a percentage of GNP until the late 1950s. It was at this time, as Rostow explained, that the first phase of the postwar expansion began seriously to weaken in America. Rostow also mentioned that private and public service outlays increased and therefore maintained the forward momentum of the economy. What he did not mention was the massive boost in military expenditures that accompanied the Kennedy-Johnson tax program. After the Berlin Crisis in 1961, President Kennedy increased defense spending by 15 percent within eighteen months. This was followed after 1965 by the great military buildup associated with the Vietnam War. There is no evidence that this extraordinary expansion of the military sector was undertaken mainly for economic reasons; nevertheless, the impact of this increased spending, as Alfred Eichner has explained, was a major force behind the prosperity of the 1960s.[15]

Military spending, however, declined at a real average rate of 2.1 per-

---

[15] Alfred S. Eichner, "Reagan's Doubtful Game Plan," *Challenge* (May–June 1981), 21.

cent per year during the decade 1969–1979 (it declined by 2.5 percent from 1953 to 1960, and rose by 3.1 percent from 1960 to 1969), while federal expenditures as a whole grew significantly. Where did the money go? Two researchers have pointed out that

> Between 1965 and 1981, the federal budget grew from 18 percent of GNP to 23 percent, doubling in real terms from $330 to $660 billion in 1981 prices. These aggregates, however, mask an important shift in priorities. Income security expenditures (Social Security, Unemployment Insurance, Aid to Families with Dependent Children (AFDC), and other programs that provide cash transfers or access to essentials) increased from 22 to 35 percent of the budget. In percentage terms, the growth in health expenditures—now largely Medicare and Medicaid—was even more rapid, from 1.4 to 10 percent of the budget. Similarly, the share of the budget devoted to education, training, employment, and social services increased from 1.9 to nearly 5 percent. Taken together, the budget share of these three categories of social programs doubled from 25 to 50 percent.
>
> While the budget in 1965 could have been characterized as defense-oriented, by 1981 it was clearly oriented toward social welfare. The budget share devoted to national defense, international affairs, and veterans' benefits and services declined from 50 to 29 percent.[16]

Thus, for all the criticism directed at them from the left, the Nixon, Ford, and Carter administrations presided over and acquiesced in the continued real growth of the welfare state during the 1970s. What therefore exercised the American right, it is reasonable to deduce, was not primarily the growth of federal spending (its increase as a percentage of GNP was, after all, quite modest), but the shift from military Keynesianism to social-welfare Keynesianism—partly reversed in the 1980s by the Reagan administration—and, what is more, the implications of this shift for the future structure of American capitalism. As Galbraith, Harrington, and Heilbroner have remarked, the replacement of military spending by social-welfare spending is not economically damaging (or militarily damaging, given legitimate defense needs and the gargantuan power of conventional and nuclear arsenals). On the contrary, most European nations spent far more for social purposes during the 1950s and 1960s, and yet their economies

---

[16] Sheldon Danziger and Robert Haveman, "The Reagan Budget: A Sharp Break with the Past," in ibid., 5.

grew much more rapidly than America's. But the change in budgetary emphasis did remove tax funds from a noncompetitive segment of the private sector, where they functioned as government subsidies under the control of business, and placed their investment under direct public control, with consequences the latter deeply resented. This shift in the composition of government spending occurred, of course, in virtually every other advanced capitalist nation during the years immediately after World War II, while in the United States it began to take place only in the mid-1960s, and continued until the late 1970s. However, it neither reached the stage of development in America that it did in Europe nor acquired the full legitimacy accorded it by the middle and upper classes on the latter continent—the result of lingering American traditions, slow economic growth, and the new strength of conservative politics. There can be little doubt that the ''Europeanization'' of American capitalism was—and remains—an unsettling fear among a large segment of the American business class and is a powerful motivating force behind its political arm, the New Right.

Yet I do not think that it was even the expanded size of the federal, state, and local social-service bureaucracies and their increased funding that was the chief cause of the estrangement of the New Right from the policies that have evolved since the New Deal. There is something more basic involved here, and even a cursory examination of New Right ideology and political actions reveals what it is. If there can be said to be a primary issue for the new conservative movement in America, it can be summed up in the ubiquitous refrain of the New Right and its economic and intellectual allies throughout the 1970s concerning the ''burden'' of government regulation and the general interference of the state in economic and social life.

At first glance, the grumblings of American business regarding government regulation seem exaggerated and unjustified, even though, as Lester Thurow has remarked, there was a ''burst of regulatory activity [that] occurred during the late 1960s and early 1970s'' and that mainly concerned the problem of the social costs of economic production and income security. (The first surge of regulation, aimed largely at monopoly power, took place at the turn of the century; the second, in the 1930s, primarily involved the legitimation of labor unions.)[17] There is, after all, much more general regulation in the nations of Europe and Japan, yet most of those countries have made dramatic economic strides since 1945, often leaving

---

[17] Lester C. Thurow, *The Zero-Sum Society: Distribution and the Possibilities for Economic Change* (New York: Basic, 1980), p. 124.

the United States behind. On closer inspection, however, it becomes clear, as Thurow and others have conceded, that the business view of regulation in America has some merit. For it is true that, while there is less *total* government control over the American economy than over those of other capitalist nations, there is in America far more regulation of a particular, and largely ineffectual kind, such as antitrust laws, production quotas, price supports, and detailed directions concerning the production of goods or their operation after they are manufactured or sold.[18]

Yet it seldom occurs to most Americans—especially businessmen—to reflect on the reason why this kind of regulation has predominated in the United States. Thus, they have never considered the strong possibility that this state of affairs may exist primarily because, unlike those in other advanced capitalist nations responsible for economic performance and its domestic and international consequences, public officials in America have had no overall capacity to steer investment, establish economic priorities, and directly affect levels of employment and income *within the market system itself*. While highly sophisticated forms of indicative planning—often utilizing strong nationalized industries as leading economic sectors—are employed in many countries abroad, Americans have accumulated, by way of a long, piecemeal process of forced responses to immediate economic malfunctions and social discontent, a collection of myriad detailed, limited, and uncoordinated ad hoc rules and adjustment procedures. The persistent refusal of most of America's corporate elite to draw the obvious inference from these facts, conditions, trends, and comparisons has therefore produced tremendous costs and inefficiencies. Moreover, it has led to a major irony: namely, that American business, which pioneered managerial capitalism from the late nineteenth to the early twentieth centuries, has been the least willing of any corporate elite to recognize and accept the implications of the transformation it has wrought. Indeed, what has especially disturbed and frightened many business leaders since the early 1970s was not simply the growing weight of state intervention in the economy, but also their perception—largely correct—that the shape of that intervention was threatening to undergo a basic qualitative change.

Signs and symptoms of the apparently inexorable movement of American capitalism toward planning since World War II have continued to multiply and have generally shown a striking independence of supposed policy shifts under different political administrations. The era beginning in the

[18] Ibid., pp. 150-151.

late 1960s, however, ushered in a new and enhanced concern for measures to coordinate national economic and social policies, especially in the aftermath of the substantial expansion of federal power in the executive branch that followed the establishment of Lyndon Johnson's Great Society. Under the administrations of Nixon, Ford, and Carter, this process quietly continued, rarely surfacing in relatively open terms until the striking proposals for explicit planning in the proposed energy and economic policies of the Carter administration and the similar proposals found in the ideology underlying the surprisingly powerful candidacy of Senator Gary Hart.

Such developments clearly have an important bearing on Heilbroner's debate with the New Right and his entire view of the future of American capitalism. In *The Limits of American Capitalism* Heilbroner had argued that there existed a three-way split in American business ideology. There was, he hypothesized, a dominant, centrist wing of business opinion. This group, drawn mainly from the professional managers and directors of big business, represented a "new capitalism," and above all sought stability, order, good public relations, and a general environment that would allow them to give undivided attention to their jobs. They were also willing to grant, although "only grudgingly," "the legitimacy of labor and government as centers of economic power." There was even, Heilbroner remarked, a group somewhat to the left of the centrists, which accepted this legitimacy completely. But he also noted that the moderates were flanked to their right by an "older vintage" of business thought, found most often among those who ran small and middle-sized firms, who were represented by Chambers of Commerce and who "participat[ed] in the middle-class culture of lodges, sales conventions, and lower-echelon community organizations." Unlike the first two segments of the business world, which were "trying to make [their] peace with the realities of the twentieth century," the latter sector, he reported, was characterized by an unyielding opposition to unions, government regulation, social-welfare spending, and economic planning.[19]

It could be argued that Heilbroner somewhat underestimated the continuing influence of an older business ideology in American life. Yet his main conclusions on this issue cannot be easily overturned. The mainstream of American business, for all its lingering laissez-faire rhetoric and despite the undoubted cultural power that ideology still retains, is not willing to go to the barricades—or even to the legislature—to fight for an economic order that it knows cannot be restored. It will, given a special opportunity

---

[19] Heilbroner, *The Limits of American Capitalism*, pp. 38-41.

(for example a markedly conservative political climate), push for policies and short-term advantages that Europeans would shun as inimical to their long-term interests; but it will also, given a more typical or reformist environment, ''grudgingly'' acquiesce in policies far less immediately beneficial to it, such as those of the Great Society. The mascot of American business is not the tiger, but the chameleon.

There is, in addition, compelling evidence of a widening division among the main groups that comprise the business class. An increasing, though still minor, part of the business community has in recent years not only come to accept much of the welfare state, but has also begun to accept, or even advocate, the concept of economic planning. This phenomenon, together with the constant movement toward planned capitalism by even conservative governments faced with the realities of managing and taking ultimate responsibility for the productive machinery of an advanced industrial society has led, quite understandably, to a feeling of betrayal and a sense of apocalyptic alarm on the part of the New Right wing of American conservatism. If the policies of the latter forces fail—a highly probable occurrence—business and government will have no choice but to proceed at an accelerated pace on the course mapped for corporate capitalism since the days of Theodore Roosevelt. The flowering of old-style conservative thought in modern America would in such an event be comparable to the publication in the late fifteenth century of Thomas Malory's *Le Morte D'Arthur*, the classic epic that glorified knighthood and chivalry precisely at a time when they were already in irreversible decline. Heilbroner was caught off guard by the resurgent power of the right wing in America— strong enough to break the political deadlock in its favor, sending the forces of labor reeling and thereby dampening inflationary pressures—but he did not, I believe, misperceive the forces to which capitalism is now subject or the basic nature of the changes that lie ahead.

Indeed, capitalism has already modified its workings to a degree that would not have been believed a scant fifty years ago. The state in capitalist nations has acquired a basic responsibility not only for the level of economic output and employment, but also for the general welfare of its citizens, an obligation even the Progressive Herbert Hoover refused to accept or even consider in the 1930s. Government today routinely transfers incomes, engages in and massively subsidizes scientific and social research, eliminates, moderates, and sometimes deliberately *causes* economic downturns, provides insurance against numerous kinds of economic insecurity, and alters the outcomes of the market in countless other ways. In short, economic liberalism, the philosophy that proposed maximum freedom for those in the private economy, is at the end of its tether, attempting to describe an industrial capitalism that is in reality radically different and confronting mounting crises it cannot manage or even explain. Having survived in a still-influential—though weakened—form until World War II, it had largely ceased to exist as a viable option during the succeeding generation. What has replaced it to an ever greater extent in country after country is *corporatism*, the formal, joint public-private control of the economy and society by organized economic interest groups that include, most prominently, major labor unions, a big business sector most of whose firms are still "privately" owned, and the state itself, which acts to mediate demands and to press its own views and interests. A form of industrial and social organization least developed in the United States, corporatism holds the promise of allowing industrial capitalism to continue its workings into the indefinite future, although possibly at increasing psychological, political, and ecological costs.

But the effects of this change have extended far beyond the issue of industrial production. Its repercussions have in both obvious and subtle ways altered behavior and institutions that were born in a very different age. Moreover, it has shaken the very principles on which that behavior and those institutions were based. It is this fact, as Heilbroner has understood, that underlies much of the confusion, turmoil, and alienation that has typified the history of modern capitalism. What he misunderstood is the probable ability of Promethean Man to continue his mode of existence *if he so desires.*[20] Nonetheless, he has raised, even if in a somewhat indirect way, the critical question that now haunts the world. In an age in which technological and economic changes have proceeded much more rapidly than changes in ideas, perceptions, and ideologies, Western civilization has arrived at a new crossroads in the 1980s—a long-term legacy of the trends that began in the nineteenth century and continue to the present day. What is consequently most uncertain is not whether capitalism or industrial society itself can survive, but instead in what *form* they can do so, and what this will mean for the remaining elements of liberalism and for the possibility of the evolution of what Heilbroner hopes will be a humane and democratic socialism. If his work has helped to focus attention on this crucial issue, he has indeed earned an important place in American social thought.

[20] Putting new emphasis on the influence of economic cycles on capitalist development, Heilbroner has now stated flatly: "I do not believe that we can predict the life span of capitalism." Robert L. Heilbroner, *The Nature and Logic of Capitalism* (New York: W. W. Norton, 1985), p. 179.

THE UNRESOLVED DILEMMAS

David Hume

After [the] convention concerning abstinence from the possessions of others is entered into, and every one has acquired a stability in his possessions, there immediately arise the ideas of justice and injustice; as also those of *property, right,* and *obligation.* The latter are altogether unintelligible without first understanding the former. Our property is nothing but those goods whose constant possession is established by the laws of society—that is, by the laws of justice. Those, therefore, who make use of the words *property,* or *right,* or *obligation,* before they have explained the origin of justice, or even make use of them in that explication, are guilty of a very gross fallacy, and can never reason upon any solid foundation. A man's property is some object related to him. This relation is not natural, but moral, and founded on justice. It is very preposterous, therefore, to imagine that we can have any idea of property without fully comprehending the nature of justice, and showing its origin in the artifice and contrivance of men. The origin of justice explains that of property. The same artifice gives rise to both.

Louis Hartz

Surely, then, it is a remarkable force: this fixed, dogmatic liberalism of a liberal way of life. It is the secret root from which have sprung many of the most puzzling of American cultural phenomena. Take the unusual power of the Supreme Court and the cult of constitution worship on which it rests. Federal factors apart, judicial review as it has worked in America would be inconceivable without the national acceptance of the Lockian creed, ultimately enshrined in the Constitution, since the removal of high policy to the realm of adjudication implies a prior recognition of the principles to be legally interpreted.

Chapter 11   *Economics, Power, Justice: American Liberalism and Democracy*

Since the last quarter of the nineteenth century, Americans have confronted a series of critical issues that arose as a direct result of the rapid evolution of a mass industrial society and that challenged the economic, social, and political principles that had guided the nation as a semi-rural society. Since that time they have actively and continually strained to deal not only with the structural changes occurring over the last century, but also with the deeper meanings of those changes for a social order pulled loose to an ever greater extent from its philosophical moorings. Yet because the nation continues to define its central concern—freedom—in a narrow, peculiar, and unsatisfying way, their idiosyncratic world view has caused Americans to misperceive an economic transformation whose broadest political meaning seems to have eluded them. Moreover, the resulting confusions and errors have clearly made more difficult the development of an honest approach to the central questions that cry out for resolution, including the one that, lying at the ideological basis of society, has proved the most intractable and yet the most important—the legitimacy of governmental capitalism and the welfare state it supports. While they have adopted, although in weakened form, the social democratic policies that have evolved elsewhere in the West, Americans have not been able to accept the welfare state in theory, just as they have not been able to reject its substantial establishment in practice, with all of the disastrous economic, social, and fiscal consequences this inability has produced.

The three thinkers whose work we have examined thus far have each analyzed the central institutions and policies on which the American welfare state is based and have tried to explain the origins of the present crisis. There are, however, important differences of perception, emphasis, and interpretation in their writings, as well as a number of similarities, including one that is of fundamental importance. What are these differences and similarities? Moreover, how do their evaluations of the malady that now afflicts us compare with that of the American public? Finally, how have

Americans' beliefs shaped present policies, and how have these beliefs promoted or hindered the development of viable alternatives?

JOHN KENNETH GALBRAITH has argued that America's troubles stem mainly from the fact that the dominant sector of the US economy operates according to principles entirely different from those that underlay the more freely competitive economy of an earlier era. Indeed, he has proposed that this powerful segment of the private economy, controlled by big business, actually bears in some respects a striking resemblance to the *public* sector that has always been the main focus of American fears. Managerial capitalism, he demonstrates, involves the administrative control of huge amounts of capital, not by countless small firms whose activities are strictly constrained by market forces beyond their control, but by gigantic economic organizations ruled by faceless technocrats. The American welfare state is so minimal, he maintains, because the interests of those technocrats revolve about a narrowly circumscribed agenda whose key features embody the economic preferences as well as the cultural and political values typical of private bureaucracies. The last crucial link in Galbraith's analytical chain is the role of the state, whose drive to promote stability, economic growth, technological innovation, education, and public spending (of a particular kind) meshes perfectly with that of the "planning system." Together, they form a powerful union of interdependent bureaucracies whose effective symbiosis has fostered economic irrationality and a social imbalance exacerbated by massive military spending which, in turn, drains resources desperately needed for social purposes. Such wasteful government spending concomitantly fuels an arms race that conveniently justifies the very policy that gives rise to it. The end result, Galbraith concludes, is a schizophrenic, unstable, dual economy, part of which is planned and well funded while the other part is unregulated and exploited. This, while the public sphere is starved for resources (except for military purposes) and lacks the ability to coordinate the two disparate halves of the private sector. The remedy, according to Galbraith is obvious: the assertion of strong—yet democratic—public authority over the planning system to break its stranglehold on the commonweal and rearrange national priorities.

Yet Michael Harrington and Robert Heilbroner, while not denying the dramatic changes that have occurred in the economy or the skewing of national policies to more closely match the desires of those who manage large corporations, have found a significantly different explanation for some of the phenomena to which Galbraith refers. They have both called attention to what they see as a crucial fact generally missing from the latter's portrait of the "mature corporation": namely, that great enterprises are not simply repositories of economic power and political influence in their own right, but are also *reflections of class structure in society at large*. Like Galbraith, they see capitalism as an economic system that has been transformed; unlike Galbraith, they do not see it as one that has been transcended, even as it approaches the end of the twentieth century. They emphasize that the origins of the shriveled American welfare state are therefore connected not only to a potent combination of bureaucratic and technocratic interests, but additionally, and vitally, to power relations between and among important social groups whose relative strength is largely a complex function of traditions, institutions, values, ethnic and racial composition, and, perhaps most significantly, history. Harrington in particular has suggested that meaningful change can come about, but only if broad social coalitions can be formed that can effectively challenge the true locus of power in the United States—the upper strata who benefit most greatly from the status quo. Such a coalition, he believes, is possible even within the constraints of American social structure. Moreover, a decent society—that is, one in which no persons fall below minimally adequate levels of income or are denied access to health care, affordable housing, or social services comparable in quality to those of the middle class—in his view (and Galbraith's) can be achieved before, and maintained even without, radical social change.

Heilbroner, on the other hand, is now less certain about this possibility, just as he has become less sure of other matters. He accepts Harrington's analysis in general outline, but has increasingly tended toward an even more tentative, and generally rather pessimistic, appraisal of prospects for greatly enhanced economic and social equality, since the constraints he perceives are more formidable and unyielding, the course of history even more unpredictable. Having become an agnostic on the issue of impending ecological disaster, he nevertheless maintains a deeply skeptical attitude regarding the malleability of a badly flawed human nature and finds a disturbing tendency for social institutions to assume a self-interested and partly parasitic character, thus leading both people and their social works most often to take the path of least resistance and self-aggrandizement. Paradoxically, Heilbroner sees a greater likelihood of economic, social, and political reconstruction than Galbraith or Harrington, but, to an even greater extent than the latter, he remains doubtful that it will evolve in a desirable, or at least a benign, direction. Impressed by the durability of capitalist institutions and their earth-rending drive for an accumulation of profits and wealth together with the reproduction and extension of their social relations on a global scale, Heilbroner harbors a barely suppressed anxiety that the most likely path for market economies lies along a route both he and Harrington abhor—that is, toward a creeping, inexorable statism of the left or right that would offer to maintain the momentum of industrial growth at the cost of truncated liberties, curtailed personal autonomy, lessened intellectual creativity, and an abandonment of the egalitarian and democratic goals cherished in the West for so many generations.

On one fundamental point, however, all three men agree. All of them are convinced that the shape of the new social order will be determined not through the relatively impersonal, even unconscious, mechanisms that have usually predominated in the past history of market systems, but rather in the course of a highly politicized process of conflict and accommodation that will center not primarily on tactical economic issues, but on the control of the state itself—a struggle that they see as virtually unavoidable. To understand why they hold this view, we must, of course, review the changes that have overtaken the American economy during the last century. But we must also do more, since of equal importance to future developments is the reaction to these changes by the dominant mode of thought in American culture, one that has been unable to recognize the true character of the conundrum slowly building for generations. For it is the essential nature of the long-held values and ideals of that culture that has allowed Americans to avoid until relatively recently—albeit at an increasingly intolerable cost—the dilemmas that they must now face squarely.

The essential fact, as Galbraith, Harrington, and Heilbroner all apprehend, is that modern industrial society functions through the medium of large, complex institutions that by their very nature possess substantial power. The logical inference is inescapable. Since power in a democracy is not self-justifying and is incapable of being rationalized as a delegated extension of a Divine Will, it must either trace its origins to a public consensus or contract or else risk being denounced as illegitimate. The problem therefore confronting modern American capitalism, the above theorists affirm, is that it is under the effective control of elites who have arrogated to themselves quasi-public powers (largely, it must be admitted, through the default, or with the actual collaboration, of public authority) that were never constitutionally granted and are not subject to the check of democratic political institutions. How well have Americans dealt with this issue?

Neither American response to this reality—regulation or the perennial and increasingly ritualistic pursuit of antitrust action—has provided an effective or democratic means of dealing with corporate capitalism. Yet the pattern of their ebb and flow has been useful as a kind of Rorschach test for the insecurities experienced by Americans at various times during the last century, their actual results often being not at all those intended or supposed. Indeed, the Sherman Act from its very inception has been a prime example of how America's liberal mystique has repeatedly brought about paradoxical results. As Alfred Chandler has observed, by disallowing the formation of cartels composed of small, family-owned businesses, the law ran the latter out of the market. Unable to cooperate and to coordinate output and the allocation of resources as did similar firms in Europe, family firms in America were forced "to consolidate their operations into a single, centrally operated enterprise administered by salaried managers."[1] The act thus served not to reverse, but actually to accelerate, the trend toward bureaucratic capitalism in the United States.

Nor were its subsequent effects generally more beneficial. If anything, they were less so as time wore on, antitrust law at best producing little additional competition, at worst leading to wasteful and futile attempts to restore a condition that, as scholars have reminded us, was not an unmixed blessing, but an idealized arrangement whose enshrinement in American folklore has masked a past reality that included uncertainties, risks, losses, and pain.[2] Oddly enough, some competition has been preserved, as Lester Thurow has noted, not through the free play of market forces or by antitrust suits, but instead because of what Galbraith has correctly seen as the useless, trivial, or nonessential nature of much that is produced in modern market economies. Because most consumer goods are purchased largely or entirely for the psychic utility derived therefrom, the oligopolistic manufacturers who might dominate the production of one particular good must often compete not only with each other, but also with those who produce a wide variety of other goods that no one needs but almost everyone wants.[3] Indeed, the Gordian knot for Americans does not mainly involve the issues of competition or regulation, but rather the more fundamental, Herculean task of bringing under control and into the realm of democratic

---

[1] Chandler, *The Visible Hand*, p. 499.

[2] See Thurow, *The Zero-Sum Society*, p. 126.

[3] See ibid., pp. 146-150.

choice the gigantic and volatile forces unleashed by a modern market economy.

A crucial aspect of such choice is the balance between public and private goods. And it is here that the social democratic perspective of theorists such as Galbraith has without a doubt produced a most telling critique of the bias of American liberalism against social spending. Hoisting the advocates of free-market choice on their own petard, they have observed with perfect logic that the only fundamental difference between the "products" of government and those of private firms is that the former are necessarily purchased by the public at large rather than by individuals. If Americans wish collectively to buy more (or less) clean air or water, more (or fewer) public parks, more (or fewer) public health services, more (or less) armaments, more (or less) occupational safety, and larger (or smaller) quantities of other public goods and services, there are no economic reasons why they should not.

And, in fact, the embarrassing reality for conservatives has been the pronounced desire on the part of the public to maintain, and often increase, the level of these purchases, a circumstance rooted again in the changed nature of modern economies. General affluence has shifted consumer preferences in favor of more public and other nonmaterial goods, a result not at all surprising with the rise since World War II of a new middle class all of whose physical needs and many of whose psychological wants have long been satisfied, and whose pleasure from additional material acquisitions has clearly reached a point of diminishing returns.[4] Despite the results of the 1980 and 1984 elections, there is no support for a general roll-back of government services or of consumer and environmental regulations (something made quite obvious by the results of the 1986 election), an intriguing example of changed practical attitudes and needs racing ahead of established ideas and traditions that still treat the sums expended for those services and regulations only as economic costs, not as benefits.[5] Social democratic ideology, on the other hand, has seen the growth of the public sector not as a strange, deviant, or incomprehensible occurrence, but as a consequence following both from the greatest success of the market—the generation of unprecedented material abundance—and from its signal failure—its inherent inability to check its own accumulations of power and guide its own overall workings. Finally, in spite of their railings

---

[4] Thurow also makes this point in ibid., pp. 104-105.

[5] Robert Kuttner, *Revolt of the Haves: Tax Rebellions and Hard Times* (New York: Simon and Schuster, 1980), pp. 24-25.

against government spending in the abstract and especially against "welfare"—the only specific kind of public spending to receive widespread condemnation—Americans have been and are willing, as Harrington has noted, to support such things as Social Security, urban aid, national health care, full employment, and aid to the *working* poor. They have opposed, however, at least in principle, and to a significant degree in practice, some of the policies that have characterized most other advanced capitalist nations—the result of a number of historical and recent developments and, by no means least, the interplay of these factors with American liberal ideology.

On this point it is, first of all, certainly true that the slower economic growth and inflation experienced during the 1970s made Americans less willing to support the new social programs launched in the 1960s. Adverse economic conditions always augur ill for social reform, and it is largely for this reason that the Democratic party—in effect the ruling political coalition since World War II, even after the 1980 election—has pursued for almost four decades a policy of rapid economic growth at home and open markets abroad, knowing that such growth permitted the evolving American welfare state that they were creating to be financed with a minimum of conflict over the relative distribution of shares, all of which were rapidly increasing in size. Another important reason for the stunted welfare state in America is the fact that a progressively larger proportion of its direct beneficiaries since the mid-1960s have come from the lower classes and from minority groups (although the most numerous and most favored recipients of aid are actually from the middle class, and most lower-class people are white). The constituency of the New Deal, whose programs and concepts formed the core of the later welfare state, was the nascent middle class that emerged in the years after World War II. It therefore followed that the major social issues of the 1930s were workers' issues geared to the concerns of the lower to lower-middle classes to which the vast majority of Americans then belonged: unemployment, unions, wages, Social Security and other forms of income insurance, and the distribution of income and wealth. The entry of the large majority of these people into the new middle class of the postwar period naturally meant a shift in the political center of gravity toward that class and *its* concerns: namely, inflation, environmental quality, occupational safety, job satisfaction, and women's rights. Clearly, the poor today have problems that generally correspond more closely to the former issues than to the latter. The new middle class has obviously not lost interest in the first set of issues, but has generally taken their resolution for granted in its own case—an assumption that may well be mistaken.[6]

This, however, only *begins* to unravel the puzzle since, contrary to popular belief, the largest increase in government taxation from the mid-1960s to the late 1970s was not levied to benefit the lower class per se. As Robert Kuttner has explained, the poor did benefit, at least marginally, from poverty programs and social spending since the Great Society and from a transfer of income from the middle class. Nonetheless, the prime recipients of these monies from middle-class taxpayers were not members of the lower class proper, but rather those taxpayers' own aging parents! "The steepest tax hike of all," he writes, "the eightfold increase in social security taxes since 1964, resulted from the aging of the population, the falling birth rate, the ability of the enlarged millions of pensioners to lobby successfully for more benefits, and the early failure of the social security system to build up sufficient reserves to pay benefits out of earnings from past premiums. But this tax increase was certainly not the result of government 'waste' or excessive solicitude for the hard-core poor. Social security is essentially an intergenerational transfer, not an interclass transfer." Yet if this were so, why did the middle class complain? Because, unlike other government services which that class could directly perceive and enjoy, most of the newer expenditures and services went either to the invisible poor of whom Harrington has written or to aging retirees, with the result

---

[6] Indeed, a number of researchers have demonstrated that the commitment of American voters to New Deal issues remains strong, and that since the late 1970s they have become increasingly worried that policies to promote such things as full employment are not being adequately implemented. Assembling impressive statistical data, they have argued that, to the extent that Democratic candidates lost voter support in the 1980 and 1984 elections, it was mainly due to their party's failure to identify itself with the policies and goals associated with the New Deal—precisely at a time when Republicans were seemingly embracing them. Moreover, as Thomas Ferguson and Joel Rogers have pointed out, it was the Republican party that was increasingly seen as embodying them most concretely, noting that Jimmy Carter "became the first President since Herbert Hoover to run for re-election at a moment when the national income was actually shrinking, and the first elected incumbent since Hoover to lose a bid for re-election. Ronald Reagan did not make this mistake. His Administration chose to have a long and exceptionally deep recession early in its term and then (helped along by the collapse of OPEC and other factors) staged one of the greatest political business cycles in modern history, producing a 5.8 percent increase in real per capita disposable income in 1984—the largest election-year increase since 1936." Calling attention to Walter Mondale's refusal in 1984 to advocate or endorse policies long associated with Democratic candidates, Ferguson and Rogers conclude that Democratic losses in 1980 and 1984 "coincided with the party's move away from its traditional commitment to promoting employment gains and growth." Thomas Ferguson and Joel Rogers, "The Myth of America's Turn to the Right," *The Atlantic* 257, no. 5, (May 1986), 52-53.

that "ordinary working taxpayers found themselves increasingly taxed to pay for services they couldn't see and didn't use."[7]

In addition to feeling that it was bearing an unfair burden of taxation (it was), the new middle class came to believe in the 1970s that anti-poverty programs and government bureaucracies in general were not efficiently run, a distortion that contains an important element of truth. For, although many reformers have been unwilling to concede the point, it is true that many social programs seem to have accomplished far less than they should have, while others are what Kuttner has called "costly failures." He recognizes, however, that the reason for the ineffectiveness of much public spending is not any inherent inefficiency of government bureaucracy, but instead the very structure and operating principles of American government—especially its peculiar relationship to the private sector—and it is here that Americans again stumble badly over their own ideology and its institutional progeny.

By turning over "block grants" to the states (even with restrictions imposed), the federal government loses effective control over the distribution of funds, with the consequence that those groups and areas most in need do not receive the bulk of the expenditures, a large proportion of which is spent by communities on civic projects such as recreational facilities and luxury items for the middle class. Public spending is also exceptionally wasteful in America, Kuttner writes, "simply because the American system has more layers of government," meaning that "it takes more bureaucrats per capita than in other nations to spend the same amount of public money." An even more powerful factor, producing much the same effect and arising similarly out of a fear of centralized authority and the liberal belief in the effectiveness of the market has been the need in America to "deal in" private economic interests that are actually used to provide the good or service that the government is called upon to deliver. Public housing and health care in the United States have been disasters, Kuttner notes, while providing enormous subsidies and profits for building contractors and private health organizations.[8]

---

[7] Kuttner, *Revolt of the Haves*, pp. 22-23.

[8] See ibid., pp. 333-335. Foreign observers have long remarked on these problems and their cause. Well over half a century ago, Johan Huizinga wrote that in America "Each branch of government forms a small specialized and autonomous organization. The whole system of administration is an extension of the principle of local self-government." He went on to explain that "As a result, private business interests have been able to intrude unhindered into city and state government. The entire system of private understandings, mutual favoritism, concession and job hunting, and intrigues, can arise because government, having been deliberately created with weak

Lastly, Americans' antipathy to "welfare"—by which they mean getting paid for doing nothing—is not a major concern in most European countries, since "welfare" in this sense is rarely necessary. A full-employment economy such as exists in Sweden minimizes the need for this despised category of payments, while at the same time enhancing tax revenues in order to pay for social programs that *are* needed. Indeed, it was the assumption of those who laid the intellectual foundations of the welfare state that full-employment policies would be permanently in place. High unemployment rates—and, of course, the political dominance of groups that benefit from them—thus underlie the "fiscal crisis of the state" and fuel further the hostility to social democracy.

What thus appears to be the ultimate paradox of the American welfare state is that, while it operates through a fragmented and partially privatized state apparatus designed to minimize government size and intrusiveness and to maximize efficiency, this very weakness of public authority inevitably produces both inefficiency and a much larger government presence than would otherwise be necessary. But it is here that the third central issue of modern American liberalism emerges. For the problem of social justice and the debate on the proper relation between private and public power in contemporary America are closely bound up with a consideration that forms the very essence of all liberal, but especially *American* liberal thought—the concern for freedom.

It would, I think, be readily conceded that capitalism in America derives its legitimacy from two main sources. One has clearly been its widely acknowledged and acclaimed ability to satisfy the economic needs and wants of the great majority of citizens. The other has been a perceived complementarity between its workings in the economic sphere and the procedural rights and personal liberties of the political sphere. Nevertheless, it has become increasingly evident since the late nineteenth century that market sovereignty and its political reflection in the splintered structure of public

---

powers, can offer no resistance to the penetration of private interests. Once people become accustomed to seeing the public authority working frequently in the interest of individuals, the resistance to energetic activity of government can only increase. Out of fear of abuse of power, the power of government has been shackled wherever possible. . . . Because of the limited extent of government activity, private organizations with public functions have been developed. The government gave little police protection, so that citizens got into the habit of protecting themselves. Private bodyguards, under European notions of public law, belong to the Middle Ages; in America, they have developed as a form of modern business. . . ." Johan Huizinga, *America: A Dutch Historian's Vision from Afar and Near* [1928] (New York: Harper Torchbooks, 1972), pp. 126-127.

power—the supposed guarantors of liberal freedoms—have themselves created under the conditions of advancing capitalism growing barriers to the attainment of other ends of liberal society: social welfare, social justice, and acceptable political authority. The precipitous decline in public confidence in almost all American institutions in the 1970s, but particularly government and business, undoubtedly has several specific causes. But the primary cause of much of this alienation and disaffection surely lies in the palpable sense of incompatibility between the oldest and most crucial liberal goal sought by Americans—freedom—and the other aims that were once thought to issue naturally from its attainment. Americans have seemingly arrived at the conclusion that this disjunction cannot be narrowed and that, regrettably, either freedom and economic efficiency must be sacrificed or the welfare state must not grow beyond a minimal size.

Yet we have seen that economic success has not been the exclusive hallmark of American capitalism. Indeed, the welfare states of Europe have been far more generous to their citizens and have nonetheless achieved generally higher rates of economic growth and productivity and lower levels of unemployment.[9] Furthermore, the latter capitalist nations have not experienced any demonstrable or perceptible loss of either personal freedom or representative democracy. Such facts can only lead to the conclusion that the present crisis of the American welfare state involves a flaw not in social democratic principles and policies, but in some of the fundamental ideas of American liberalism. Further, they reveal a fallacy that has long shadowed social democratic proposals in the United States.

Classical liberal thought has always emphasized the close interconnection between what are really two quite different concepts of freedom that are historically, but not logically, related: economic freedom and political liberty. Those who, like Milton Friedman, have seen capitalism as a necessary, though not a sufficient, prerequisite for the establishment of fundamental political freedoms have undeniably uncovered an important, if somewhat distorted, truth. There is undoubtedly an intimate relationship between the economic rights associated with capitalism (the right to engage in trade, to buy and sell land, to rent labor, to enforce contracts, and to keep one's property and earnings) and the political rights enshrined in liberal political philosophy (the right to freely express ideas and opinions,

---

[9] See Robert Kuttner, *The Economic Illusion: False Choices Between Prosperity and Social Justice* (Boston: Houghton Mifflin, 1984).

to assemble, to travel, to form political organizations, and to choose political representatives through a reasonably open competition for public support).

But Friedman and his followers have failed to perceive that this connection is not one of direct causality. Capitalism quite obviously required the
existence of the aforementioned economic rights because, as Charles Lindblom has pointed out, they were necessary and central to the interests of
the rising middle classes of early modern history. Moreover, it is no mere
coincidence that the economic and political freedoms associated with liberalism were historically related and mutually supportive, and that they
were defined in negative terms. For, although the economic rights associated with free markets did not ensure political freedoms, they were both
consequences of the broader and longer-term evolution of constitutional
liberalism. Its origins traceable to the Magna Carta, constitutional liberalism was, as Lindblom remarks, "a movement to enlarge and protect the
liberties first of nobles and then of a merchant middle class, incorporating
as a means of so doing constitutional restrictions on the prerogatives of
government."[10] It is, of course, this concept of liberty that has remained
the only one to achieve broad ideological support in America.

It is a concept, however, that in both practical and philosophical terms
has become increasingly unsatisfactory to Americans since the rise of managerial, oligopolistic capitalism in the late nineteenth century. The economic rights granted to the emerging bourgeoisie and eventually to the
general population of liberal society could easily be defended and welcomed in earlier times by those who saw them as measures that freed merchants, artisans, journeymen, and serfs from the stifling constraints of feudal society and unleashed the tremendous productive power of capitalism.
Indeed, the right to engage in voluntary market exchange is defended today
even by the majority of the left as a necessary concession to economic
efficiency and, just as important, as a bulwark against the accumulation of
decisive economic power in the hands of state bureaucrats and tyrants, a
lesson painfully learned by examining the extreme economic centralization
of authoritarian socialist regimes of the twentieth century.

But it would be increasingly seen as eccentric to maintain that the economic freedoms given to downtrodden serfs were producing the same beneficial results when they began to be bestowed on large and powerful pri-

[10] Charles E. Lindblom, *Politics and Markets: The World's Political-Economic Systems* (New
York: Basic, 1977), p. 163.

vate organizations. Nor, since it was not true that economic liberty was an absolute end in itself, was it clear that the continued expansion of market liberties into more and more areas of life under industrial capitalism was always liberating or that their curtailment always entailed the loss of valuable economic or political assets. Child labor laws deprived employers of the right to hire ten-year-olds to work twelve-hour days; but it was difficult to argue that employers were less ''free'' in any meaningful political sense because of this, that their essential economic freedoms had been trampled, or that children and society did not gain far more important benefits than those lost by businessmen. Social Security taxes deprived both employers and employees of the economic right to keep all of their profits and earnings; but they granted the elderly the right to live the remainder of their lives in less fear of poverty. Democratic ownership and control of industry would deprive private bureaucrats of the right to dispose of the social capital they manage in any way they see fit; but it has been increasingly argued that this would give the public the freedom to choose not merely among various consumer goods, but among alternative economic futures. Not only did it appear to be true, however, that other freedoms and rights were at least as important as those that were strictly economic (some, of course, were widely acknowledged even by classical liberals to be far *more* important, hence the prohibition against selling one's vote or selling oneself into servitude, acts that cannot be faulted from an economic standpoint): as the twentieth century wore on, the potential though latent conflict between economic and political rights and freedoms became progressively more manifest as greater numbers of citizens called for the abridgement of market prerogatives.

The possibility of increased social and economic demands on the part of a fully enfranchised and politically aware and active electorate whose relative affluence had released it from an immediate struggle to survive had long been recognized—and feared. Lindblom, for example, explains that as constitutional liberalism ''came gradually to be associated with ideas of popular rule in the late eighteenth century, it maintained its preoccupation with liberty, to which popular rule was, however, never more than a means, and a disputed means at that.''[11] It is therefore not surprising that many great liberal theorists of the past, including most of the founders of the American republic, favored a system of government that buffered the demands and pressures of the citizenry through a diffuse set of political

[11] Ibid.

institutions specifically designed to weaken popular influence and participation. Indeed, Peter Steinfels has noted that "democracy, in this sense,
could coexist with a limited franchise, deference to aristocracy, extreme
class differences, infrequent elections, and—most important for the modern situation—a passive citizenry marked by a low level of political consciousness."[12] Such "democracies" have, of course, existed in the past,
and are in fact today characteristic of noncommunist nations outside Europe and North America.

Concrete and disturbing evidence of the conflict between economic and
political liberalism is seen in the open hostility to active democratic participation and even to basic political equality and freedoms evinced by the
remarks of many business executives in interviews and discussions.[13] Heilbroner has also commented on this phenomenon, thereby illuminating
what would otherwise appear to be an anomalous lacuna in the allegedly
interwoven threads of economic and political freedom: namely, the fact
that

> political and intellectual freedom, the freedoms that are most immedi-
> ately in jeopardy in bourgeois societies, have seldom been actively sup-
> ported by the "private," i.e., the business, institutions of the capitalist
> order. Intellectual and political freedoms are only indirectly connected
> with the institution of wage labor on which the capitalist system rests.
> Indeed, to the elements of the upper class immediately engaged in pro-
> duction, these liberties are likely to seem inimical to the stability of the
> capitalist order, the province of troublemakers and agitators. These free-
> doms, it must be recognized, have for the most part been the concern of
> those political, cultural, and professional elites who oversee, not those
> who themselves directly carry on, the capitalist process of accumula-
> tion.[14]

Capitalism thus provided a necessary precondition for political freedom by
establishing one form of a decentralized economy (although not the only
possible form). Nonetheless, while "punching holes" in authoritarian social and political structures in which this freedom might develop, capital-

---

[12] Peter Steinfels, *The Neoconservatives: The Men Who Are Changing America's Politics* (New
York: Touchstone, 1980), p. 250.

[13] See, for example, Leonard Silk and David Vogel, *Ethics and Profits: The Crisis of Confidence in American Business* (New York: Touchstone, 1976), chapter 7.

[14] Heilbroner, "The Demand for the Supply Side," p. 40.

ism by no means ensured its development, and in fact contains features and tendencies positively opposed to liberal democracy.

Another fundamental issue confronting American economic liberalism is the distribution of income and wealth, a problem rooted in moral and philosophical values, but possessing consequences that spill over into almost every area of life. The continuing advance of formal democracy together with a surfeit of material goods has increasingly led to a struggle not only for these goods, which can, at least in theory, be supplied in greater quantities to all, but also for public goods and especially for what Fred Hirsch has called *positional goods*, which lose their value or become unattainable, or both, as their possession becomes widespread. Neither of these kinds of goods can be provided without intense and destructive conflicts unless an agreement can be reached concerning a just basis for their distribution.[15] The inability to arrive at a workable consensus concerning what quantities of each of these goods will be produced and how they will be divided is central to the dilemmas of modern American liberalism. What, for example, is an acceptable balance between public and market goods, and thus the proper relation between public and private power? What is a warrantable trade-off among various kinds of freedoms and rights? What, in other words, is an appropriate standard of social justice? The failure to reach a general agreement on these matters has produced a mass of confusions, contradictions, frustrations, and inefficiencies obvious to anyone who picks up a newspaper or views a TV news program.

The signal characteristic that these problems have in common is that they are fundamentally political in nature. But this is not in itself what makes the critical, distributive issues involved specifically different from those that were encountered in the past, for, although the actual workings of the market were not explicitly politicized during an earlier stage of capitalism, the decision to accept the results of the market was always political—and moral. As Daniel Bell has recognized, ''Without a public philosophy, explicitly stated, we lack the fundamental condition whereby a modern polity can live by consensus (and without it there is only continuing conflict) and justice.''[16]

The establishment and internalization of social norms and ethics became increasingly important in industrial civilization, whose sheer scale and impersonality made it impossible to rely mainly on the mutual restraints of

---

[15] See Fred Hirsch, *Social Limits to Growth* (Cambridge: Harvard University Press, 1976); also above, chapter 6.

[16] Daniel Bell, *The Cultural Contradictions of Capitalism* (New York: Basic, 1978), p. 250.

face-to-face encounters, which had acted as effective cohesive elements in past social orders. Modern market societies were therefore in special need of an autonomous and independent ethical principle that did not rely on the market for validation. And no market system could internally generate such a self-supporting principle (even though—particularly in America— it was generally thought to do so), since the system is itself dependent, as Hirsch and others have pointed out, on prior assumptions and principles: namely, that people will tell the truth, that they can trust each other, that they will exercise restraint in their behavior and desires, that they will accept others as equal participants in social life, and that they will feel obliged to adhere to social rules and constraints. Religion, Hirsch has observed, once helped to provide these necessary a priori values and conventions, but this agency was undermined by the individualism and rationalism of the market itself. At present, he notes,

> Society is in turmoil because the only legitimacy it has is social justice; and the transition to a just society is an uncertain road strewn with injustice. This is the awkward stage that has been reached through the working out of the modern western enlightenment. The central fact of the modern situation is the need to justify. That is its moral triumph and its unsolved technical problem. The need to justify imposes drastic limits on the set of feasible solutions. Solutions that work have traditionally dominated solutions that have ethical appeal. The distinction is now blurred: to work it must be ethically defensible.[17]

It is in fact the present condition that has produced what Heilbroner has justifiably referred to as the "hollowness at the center of a business civilization—a hollowness from which the pursuit of material goods diverts our attention for a time, but that in the end insistently asserts itself."[18] He has proposed that the glorification of consumption and pecuniary values ("the mindless commercialization of life"), the devaluation of work, egregious social inequality, an indifference to the side effects of economic production, and a self-interested and present-minded insensitivity to moral and altruistic goals thus form "the basis for that vitiation of the spirit that is sapping business civilization from within." This "vitiation of the spirit" may apply, as Heilbroner believes, to capitalism in general; it certainly applies to that system in America.

[17] Hirsch, *Social Limits to Growth*, p. 190.
[18] Robert L. Heilbroner, *Business Civilization in Decline* (New York: W. W. Norton, 1976), p. 113.

Given these facts, a declaration of desirable ethics is not enough. A social order must *embody* them to a sufficient degree that adherence to them is based not on a fear of punishment, but rather, as Christopher Lasch has written, "on the more solid emotional foundation of loyalty and gratitude," which political authority can establish only by "provid[ing] the security and protection that inspire confidence, respect, and admiration," and by "hold[ing] out the rewards formerly associated with observance of social rules."[19] What has clearly become necessary, therefore, is the replacement of the radically individualistic Lockian liberalism still dominant in America with another social code. Many proposals have been made, most centering on a broadening of the central tenets of liberal theory by granting not merely the equal *procedural* rights associated with formal democracy, but also *substantive* rights to fair shares of economic goods, prestige, and authority derived from the use as well as the intrinsic nature of labor, creativity, and knowledge, not from the extrinsic power of money to buy rewards and influence unconnected to the merit of the purchaser.[20]

Yet, however great might be the economic and social benefits of adopting such a system of values and policies, are Americans likely to reject their Lockian heritage? To a significant degree they have already done so, accepting key social democratic principles and programs on a de facto basis while retaining an ideological hostility to their philosophical underpinnings—a dissonance whose cacophonous harmonies have strangely gone unheeded by most citizens, but whose strains have roared with ever more fury in the ears of legislators who must confront the practical consequences of this contradiction. Nevertheless, it may well be true that the budgetary and fiscal crises of the Reagan Presidency—surely one of its chief future legacies to the nation—are slowly forcing Americans to recognize the truth about themselves.

Should this recognition turn out to be painful, Americans might well be reminded that the social philosophy they have absorbed through cultural osmosis is not the one that the first colonists brought with them to the rocky shores of New England. The views of these first European immigrants on social and moral obligation would indeed sound strange were they to fall

---

[19] Christopher Lasch, *The Minimal Self: Psychic Survival in Troubled Times* (New York: W. W. Norton, 1984), pp. 203, 204.

[20] See John Rawls, *A Theory of Justice* (Cambridge: Harvard University Press, Belknap, 1971); Peter Singer, *Practical Ethics* (Cambridge: Cambridge University Press, 1979), chapters 2 and 3; and especially Michael Walzer, *Spheres of Justice: A Defense of Pluralism and Equality* (New York: Basic, 1983).

on the ears of the country's modern inhabitants. But, then, so would those of Thomas Jefferson, who, almost certainly influenced as much by the moral philosophers of the Scottish Enlightenment (a group that included David Hume and a man named Adam Smith) as by John Locke, retained a view of man more as *homo communis* than as *homo oeconomicus*. Jefferson, a transitional figure in American social thought, defined man not as an autonomous entity joined to a bundle of property rights, but as an inherently social being whose propensity for cooperation with his fellows and whose pleasure in observing and wishing to extend a harmonious social order led him to spontaneous acts of benevolence.[21] The supremacy of Lockian liberalism was fully attained only in the latter part of the nineteenth century, as earlier traditions and ideas were suppressed or bent to the purposes of the developing commercial and industrial order.

This analysis of American liberalism has examined some of the historical and philosophical roots of its modern dilemma, and in that sense has been literally radical (from the Latin *radix*, meaning "root"). The tree of liberalism has been found to have grown from an organic structure far different from its present form, having undergone mutations and prunings that would have made it almost unrecognizable to its advocates of the last century and earlier. Indeed, it has many roots and a number of branches, which are being nourished and cultivated by various groups with diverse goals in mind. Using this analogy, the tree is far from dead.

Yet the matter is still not resolved, and the analogy may be inappropriate, since the most fundamental dilemma has not been mentioned. In the end, after all, it does not matter how satisfactory proposed solutions to the problems of economic policy and social justice appear to be if at the same time economic liberalism cannot provide the institutional and ideological means of implementing those solutions. Here the prognosis is not at all encouraging.

The most glaring blind spot of American liberalism has been an ideological myopia concerning power, a phenomenon abhorred for the loss of liberty it presumably entailed. Thus it was that the founders of the American republic, although themselves acutely aware of the reality of power and the need to check it, sought an answer in the Balkanization of the political structure, not realizing that their scheme of force and counterforce, checks and balances, could operate roughly as intended only in the rural society

---

[21] Indeed, Garry Wills has argued forcefully that Americans have had a distorted image not only of Thomas Jefferson, but also of Adam Smith. See Garry Wills, *Inventing America: Jefferson's Declaration of Independence* (Garden City, New York: Doubleday, 1978), p. 232.

America was until the early nineteenth century and the rural-commercial society it was until the late nineteenth century. Yet most modern Americans have not abandoned, and have certainly not rethought or reworked, the key elements of their philosophy. Having long since ceased to inhabit this kind of social order, they have nonetheless resolutely refused to deal with the monumental reality of private economic power, let alone plumb the deeper meanings of its existence. On the contrary, they have continued to look to *government* power as the main threat to their freedom, oblivious to the main source of their unease—their inability to control the economic and technological forces at work in the private sector. The reason for this lack of understanding is not hard to find. It stems from the same all-pervasive and culturally specific liberalism that has blinded Americans to so many obvious realities both at home and abroad. Convinced that the reign of a free-market economy and liberal republicanism is "natural," they have never understood that such institutions are cultural and historical peculiarities that are not, and have never been, the common lot of mankind. Indeed, they were not the ones American colonists themselves established when they first settled the Northeastern corner of the country.

Such beliefs nevertheless served a number of important functions in bygone years. At the most obvious and superficial level, they provided what all peoples need in one form or another: a reasonably consistent and coherent world view that presents native ideas and social forms as natural and therefore closed to rational and critical inquiry. But the doctrinaire liberalism to which Americans adhered was especially comforting to a people who, for historically conditioned and understandable reasons, feared the need to confront the universal problem of power. And, obligingly, the American theory of economic liberalism reassured them that they would never be forced to do so.

The market, Americans believed, could relieve them of the need to make political decisions concerning the production of economic goods or the distribution of the income and wealth that issued forth from that process. Such a view was to have extraordinary ramifications. It implied, for instance, that social justice was not a problem to be addressed in a conscious and explicit manner as long as the market was open to all comers. Justice, in fact, could best be served by removing constraints on economic freedom from both private and, especially, public sources. Public authority was rarely, if ever, allowed to limit economic freedom since, to the extent it did, it not only deprived citizens of their right to a fair share of the nation's wealth: it also arbitrarily, and thus unjustly, misallocated resources, leading to both economic inefficiency and an unjustified denial of the fruits of one's labor. What is more, economic freedom was not simply connected to justice: it was also directly responsible for what Americans perceived as a coequal good—*political* freedom. Thus defined by the absence of all economic, social, and political constraints beyond the minimum needed to avert anarchy and enforce contracts, a liberal order was seen as attainable only if, in effect, the bounds of substantive political discourse were sufficiently circumscribed to include only a few instrumental issues.

But these beliefs—however sociologically naive, economically questionable, philosophically dubious, and politically stultifying—had more to recommend them than the mere fact that they filled the ideological vacuum abhorred by all civilizations and that they contained the satisfying tenets of the particular strain of social thought embraced by Americans. Above all, the American system seemed to rest on firm values and institutions—something that, despite the superficial optimism of the Reagan years, is no longer believed at a deeper level. We have already observed how the great economic, social, and technological changes of the past century have continually battered the fortress of American liberal thought and, moreover, how this merciless bombardment has intensified since 1945 and particularly since the late 1960s. Its redoubts, it is true, have undergone constant repairs and redesign, but these can no longer suffice: the walls are crumbling. New Deal liberals are confused and disoriented; the right wing openly advocates reaction and repression; so-called "neoliberal" political leaders and candidates have periodically raised an ever louder chorus of support for what must be termed corporatist solutions that effectively nullify, albeit in a veiled manner, the essence of both classical and reformed liberalism (the Reagan victories of 1980 and 1984 temporarily squelched this tune, but as the depth of the fiscal and economic fiasco now nearing fruition is coming to be understood, it has already resumed and will certainly increase in vigor, even without the major recession that seems almost inevitable); the left wishes partly to maintain, partly to alter and go beyond, the legacy of the New Deal.

Like it or not, Americans are confronted with a present that is far more collectivist than their past, and with a future that will be even more—and more explicitly—so. Given the Faustian bargain the West has made with industrialism and its close ally, modern technology, there is only one remaining question: Will the new order be one in which public *and* private power are brought under democratic control, or one in which they are placed ever more firmly in the hands of a financial-managerial-technical elite that rules at best by plebiscite? The issues of economic growth, freedom, and social welfare have not disappeared and cannot be banned from the arena of political conflict any more than can the issue of power, for they are themselves political in essence. In vain have Americans sought a new Keynes or a new economic philosopher's stone to solve with a simple technical mechanism or theory the difficulties that now surround them. There will, I suggest, be no such mechanism or theory, for the dysfunctions of America's market society lie much deeper. If Americans wish to preserve—indeed restore and rebuild—a free and democratic society, they must first reexamine the foundations on which their ideology and institutions are built, and thus discover what is still valuable—and what is not—in the principles that Lincoln fought to preserve.

Select Bibliography

Andrain, Charles F. *Politics and Economic Policy in Western Democracies*. North Scituate, Massachusetts: Duxbury, 1980.

Aron, Raymond. *The Industrial Society: Three Essays on Ideology and Development*. New York: Clarion, 1967.

Bailyn, Bernard. *The Ideological Origins of the American Revolution*. Cambridge: Harvard University Press, Belknap, 1967.

Baumol, William J. *Business Behavior, Value and Growth*. New York: Macmillan, 1959.

Bell, Daniel. *The Cultural Contradictions of Capitalism*. New York: Basic, 1978.

Bell, Daniel, and Irving Kristol, eds. *Capitalism Today*. New York: Mentor, 1971.

Berle, Adolf A., Jr. *Power without Property: A New Development in American Political Economy*. New York: Harvest, 1959.

————. "The Impact of the Corporation on Classical Economic Theory." *The Quarterly Journal of Economics* 79 (February 1965), 25-40.

Berle, Adolf A., Jr., and Gardiner C. Means. *The Modern Corporation and Private Property*. New York: Macmillan, 1932.

Boulding, Kenneth E. *The Organizational Revolution: A Study in the Ethics of Economic Organization*. New York: Harper & Brothers, 1953. Rpt. Chicago: Quadrangle, 1968.

Bremner, Robert H. *From the Depths: The Discovery of Poverty in the United States*. New York: New York University Press, 1956.

Burch, Philip H., Jr. *The Managerial Revolution Reassessed: Family Control in America's Large Corporations*. Lexington, Massachusetts: Lexington, 1972.

Burnham, James. *The Managerial Revolution: What Is Happening in the World*. New York: John Day, 1941.

Caves, Richard. *American Industry: Structure, Conduct, Performance*. Englewood Cliffs, New Jersey: Prentice-Hall, 1964.

Chamberlin, Edward. *The Theory of Monopolistic Competition*. Cambridge: Harvard University Press, 1935.

Chandler, Alfred D., Jr. *The Visible Hand: The Managerial Revolution in American Business*. Cambridge: Harvard University Press, Belknap, 1977.

Clark, John Maurice. *Strategic Factors in Business Cycles*. New York: National Bureau of Economic Research, 1935.

Cochran, Thomas C. *200 Years of American Business*. New York: Delta, 1977.

Cohen, Stephen S. *Modern Capitalist Planning: The French Model*. Berkeley: University of California Press, 1977.

Commoner, Barry. *The Politics of Energy*. New York: Knopf, 1979.

Croly, Herbert. *The Promise of American Life*. Macmillan, 1909. Rpt. Archon, 1963.

Daly, Herman E. *Steady-State Economics: The Economics of Biophysical Equilibrium and Moral Growth.* San Francisco: W. H. Freeman, 1977.

Dennison, H. S., and J. K. Galbraith. *Modern Competition and Business Policy.* Oxford: Oxford University Press, 1938.

Domhoff, G. William. *The Powers That Be: Processes of Ruling-Class Domination in America.* New York: Vintage, 1979.

Dorrien, Gary J. *The Democratic Socialist Vision.* Totowa, New Jersey: Rowman & Littlefield, 1986.

Drucker, Peter F. *Concept of the Corporation,* rev. ed. New York: Mentor, 1975.

————. *The New Society: The Anatomy of the Industrial Order.* New York: Harper & Brothers, 1950.

Foner, Eric. *Free Soil, Free Labor, Free Men: The Ideology of the Republican Party before the Civil War.* 1970. Rpt. Oxford: Oxford University Press, 1976.

————. *Tom Paine and Revolutionary America.* Oxford: Oxford University Press, 1977.

Forcey, Charles. *The Crossroads of Liberalism: Croly, Weyl, Lippmann and the Progressive Era, 1900–1925.* Oxford: Oxford University Press, 1961.

Freeman, Roger A. *The Growth of American Government: A Morphology of the Welfare State.* Stanford: Hoover Institution Press, 1975.

Friedman, Milton. *Capitalism and Freedom.* Chicago: University of Chicago Press, 1962.

Friedman, Milton, and Anna Jacobson Schwartz. *A Monetary History of the United States, 1867–1960.* Princeton: Princeton University Press, 1963.

Galbraith, J. K. *The Affluent Society.* Boston: Houghton Mifflin, 1958.

————. *Ambassador's Journal: A Personal Account of the Kennedy Years.* Houghton Mifflin, 1969. Rpt. New York: Signet, 1970.

————. *American Capitalism: The Concept of Countervailing Power.* Boston: Houghton Mifflin, 1952.

————. *Annals of an Abiding Liberal.* Edited by Andrea D. Williams. Boston: Houghton Mifflin, 1979.

————. *A Contemporary Guide to Economics, Peace and Laughter.* Edited by Andrea D. Williams. Boston: Houghton Mifflin, 1971. Rpt. New York: Signet, 1972.

————. *Economics and the Public Purpose.* Boston: Houghton Mifflin, 1973. Rpt. New York: Signet, 1975.

————. *A Life in Our Times: Memoirs.* Boston: Houghton Mifflin, 1981. Rpt. New York: Ballantine, 1982.

————. *The New Industrial State.* Boston: Houghton Mifflin, 1967. Rpt. New York: Signet, 1968.

————. *A Theory of Price Control.* Cambridge: Harvard University Press, 1952.

————. ''Monopoly and the Concentration of Economic Power.'' In Howard S. Ellis, ed. *A Survey of Contemporary Economics.* Vol. 1. Homewood, Illinois: Richard D. Irwin, 1948.

————. ''Monopoly Power and Price Rigidities.'' *The Quarterly Journal of Economics,* 50 (May 1936), 456-475.

Gambs, John S. *Beyond Supply and Demand: A Reappraisal of Institutional Economics*. New York: Columbia University Press, 1946.

Goldsmith, Raymond. *Institutional Investors and Corporate Stock: A Background Study*. New York: Columbia University Press, 1973.

Goodwyn, Lawrence. *The Populist Moment: A Short History of the Agrarian Revolt in America*. Oxford: Oxford University Press, 1978.

Gouldner, Alvin W. *The Future of Intellectuals and the Rise of the New Class*. New York: Seabury, 1979.

Graham, Otis L., Jr. *Toward a Planned Society: From Roosevelt to Nixon*. Oxford: Oxford University Press, 1977.

Green, Mark, and Robert Massie, Jr., eds. *The Big Business Reader*. New York: Pilgrim, 1980.

Hansen, Alvin H. *A Guide to Keynes*. New York: McGraw-Hill, 1953.

Harrington, Michael. *The Accidental Century*. New York: Macmillan, 1965. Rpt. Baltimore: Penguin, 1966.

———. *Decade of Decision: The Crisis of the American System*. New York: Simon and Schuster, 1980.

———. *Fragments of the Century*. New York: Saturday Review Press/E. P. Dutton, 1973.

———. *The New American Poverty*. New York: Holt, Rinehart and Winston, 1984.

———. *The Next Left: The History of a Future*. New York: Henry Holt, 1987.

———. *The Other America: Poverty in the United States*. 1962. Rpt. New York: Macmillan, 1963.

———. *Socialism*. New York: Saturday Review Press, 1972. Rpt. New York: Bantam, 1973.

———. *Toward a Democratic Left: A Radical Program for a New Majority*. New York: Macmillan, 1968. Rpt. Baltimore: Penguin, 1969.

———. *The Twilight of Capitalism*. New York: Simon and Schuster, 1976.

———. "Our Fifty Million Poor: Forgotten Men of the Affluent Society." *Commentary* 28, no. 1 (July 1959), 19-27.

———. "Slums, Old and New." *Commentary* 30, no. 2 (August 1960), 118-124.

———. "The Welfare State and its Neoconservative Critics." *Dissent* (Fall 1973), 435-454.

Harris, Seymour E. *Economics of the Kennedy Years*. New York: Harper & Row, 1964.

———, ed. *Postwar Economic Problems*. New York: McGraw-Hill, 1943.

———, ed. *Saving American Capitalism: A Liberal Economic Program*. New York: Knopf, 1950.

Hartz, Louis. *The Founding of New Societies: Studies in the History of the United States, Latin America, South Africa, Canada, and Australia*. New York: Harbinger, 1964.

———. *The Liberal Tradition in America: An Interpretation of American Political Thought since the Revolution*. New York: Harcourt, Brace & World, 1955.

Hawley, Ellis W. *The New Deal and the Problem of Monopoly: A Study in Economic Ambivalence*. Princeton: Princeton University Press, 1966.

Hayek, Friedrich A. *The Road to Serfdom*. Chicago: University of Chicago Press, Phoenix, 1944.

Heilbroner, Robert L. *Between Capitalism and Socialism: Essays in Political Economics*. New York: Vintage, 1970.

———. *Beyond Boom and Crash*. New York: W. W. Norton, 1978.

———. *Business Civilization in Decline*. New York: W. W. Norton, 1976.

———. *The Future as History: The Historic Currents of Our Time and the Direction in Which They Are Taking America*. New York: Harper & Row, 1960.

———. *The Great Ascent: The Struggle for Economic Development in Our Time*. New York: Harper & Row, 1963.

———. *An Inquiry into the Human Prospect*. New York: W. W. Norton, 1974.

———. *The Limits of American Capitalism*. New York: Harper & Row, 1966. Rpt. Harper Torchbooks, 1967.

———. *The Nature and Logic of Capitalism*. New York: W. W. Norton, 1985.

———. *The Worldly Philosophers: The Lives, Times, and Ideas of the Great Economic Thinkers*. 5th ed. New York: Touchstone, 1980.

———. "The Demand for the Supply Side." *The New York Review of Books*, 11 June 1981, pp. 37-41.

———. "The Inflation in Your Future." *The New York Review of Books*, 1 May 1980, pp. 6-10.

———. "The Road to Selfdom." *The New York Review of Books*, 17 April 1980, pp. 3-8.

Heilbroner, Robert L., and Lester C. Thurow. *Five Economic Challenges*. Englewood Cliffs, New Jersey: Prentice-Hall, 1981.

Herman, Edward S. *Corporate Control, Corporate Power*. Cambridge: Cambridge University Press, 1982.

Hession, Charles H. *John Kenneth Galbraith and His Critics*. New York: New American Library, 1972.

Hirsch, Fred. *Social Limits to Growth*. Cambridge: Harvard University Press, 1976.

Hofstadter, Richard. *The Age of Reform: From Bryan to FDR*. New York: Vintage, 1955.

———. *The American Political Tradition: And the Men Who Made It*. New York, Knopf, 1948. Rpt. New York: Vintage, 1974.

Hunter, Robert. *Poverty*. New York: Macmillan, 1904.

Jaher, Frederic Cople, ed. *The Rich, the Well Born, and the Powerful: Elites and Upper Classes in History*. Secaucus, New Jersey: Citadel, 1975.

Johnson, Lyndon Baines. *The Vantage Point: Perspectives of the Presidency, 1963–1969*. New York: Popular Library, 1971.

Kaysen, Carl. "Another View of Corporate Capitalism." *The Quarterly Journal of Economics* 79 (February 1965), 41-51.

———. "The Social Significance of the Modern Corporation." *The American Economic Review* 47 (May 1957), 311-319.

Keynes, J. M. *Essays in Persuasion*. London: Macmillan, 1931. Rpt. New York: W. W. Norton, 1963.

———. *The General Theory of Employment, Interest, and Money*. New York: Harcourt, Brace, 1936. Rpt. New York: Harbinger, 1964.

Kotz, David M. *Bank Control of Large Corporations in the United States*. Berkeley: University of California Press, 1978.

Kuhn, Thomas S. *The Structure of Scientific Revolutions*. 2d ed. Chicago: University of Chicago Press, 1970.

Kuttner, Robert. *The Economic Illusion: False Choices Between Prosperity and Social Justice*. Boston: Houghton Mifflin, 1984.

———. *Revolt of the Haves: Tax Rebellions and Hard Times*. New York: Simon and Schuster, 1980.

Ladd, Everett Carll, Jr., and Charles D. Hadley. *Transformations of the American Party System: Political Coalitions from the New Deal to the 1970s*. New York: W. W. Norton, 1975.

Larner, Jeremy, and Irving Howe, eds. *Poverty: Views from the Left*. New York: William Morrow, 1968.

Larner, Robert J. *Management Control and the Large Corporation*. New York: Dunellen, 1970.

Lasch, Christopher. *Haven in a Heartless World: The Family Besieged*. New York: Basic, 1979.

———. *The Minimal Self: Psychic Survival in Troubled Times*. New York: W. W. Norton, 1984.

Laslett, John H. M., and Seymour Martin Lipset, eds. *Failure of a Dream? Essays in the History of American Socialism*. Garden City, New York: Anchor/Doubleday, 1974.

Lekachman, Robert. *The Age of Keynes*. New York: Random House, 1966. Rpt. New York: McGraw-Hill, 1975.

Lichtheim, George. *A Short History of Socialism*. New York: Praeger, 1970.

Lindblom, Charles E. *Politics and Markets: The World's Political-Economic Systems*. New York: Basic, 1977.

Lippmann, Walter. *Drift and Mastery: An Attempt to Diagnose the Current Unrest*. Mitchell Kennerly, 1914. Rpt. Englewood Cliffs, New Jersey: Spectrum, 1961.

Marris, Robin. *The Economic Theory of "Managerial" Capitalism*. New York: The Free Press of Glencoe, 1964.

Meadows, Donella H., Dennis L. Meadows, Jørgen Randers, and William W. Behrens III. *The Limits to Growth: A Report for the Club of Rome's Project on the Predicament of Mankind*. New York: Signet, 1972.

Melman, Seymour. *Pentagon Capitalism: The Political Economy of War*. New York: McGraw-Hill, 1970.

———. *The Permanent War Economy: American Capitalism in Decline*. New York: Simon and Schuster, 1974.

Nash, George H. *The Conservative Intellectual Movement in America: Since 1945*. New York: Basic, 1976.

Noble, David F. *America by Design: Science, Technology, and the Rise of Corporate Capitalism*. New York: Knopf, 1977.

Piven, Frances Fox, and Richard A. Cloward. *Regulating the Poor: The Functions of Public Welfare*. New York: Vintage, 1972.

Rawls, John. *A Theory of Justice*. Cambridge: Harvard University Press, Belknap, 1971.

Rifkin, Jeremy, with Ted Howard. *Entropy: A New World View*. New York: Bantam, 1981.

Rifkin, Jeremy, and Randy Barber. *The North Will Rise Again: Pensions, Politics and Power in the 1980s*. Boston: Beacon, 1978.

Rostow, W. W. *Getting from Here to There*. New York: McGraw-Hill, 1978.

———. *Why the Poor Get Richer and the Rich Slow Down: Essays in the Marshallian Long Period*. Austin, Texas: University of Texas Press, 1980.

Routh, Guy. *The Origin of Economic Ideas*. New York: Vintage, 1977.

Samuelson, Paul A. *Economics*. 10th ed. New York: McGraw-Hill, 1976.

Schumpeter, Joseph A. *Capitalism, Socialism and Democracy*. 3d ed. 1950. Rpt. New York: Harper Torchbooks, 1962.

Seckler, David. *Thorstein Veblen and the Institutionalists: A Study in the Social Philosophy of Economics*. Boulder, Colorado: Colorado Associated University Press, 1975.

Sharpe, Myron E. *John Kenneth Galbraith and the Lower Economics*. 2d ed. White Plains, New York: International Arts and Sciences Press, 1974.

Shonfield, Andrew. *Modern Capitalism: The Changing Balance of Public and Private Power*. Oxford: Oxford University Press, 1965.

Silk, Leonard. *The Economists*. New York: Basic, 1976.

Silk, Leonard, and David Vogel. *Ethics and Profits: The Crisis of Confidence in American Business*. New York: Touchstone, 1976.

Singer, Peter. *Marx*. New York: Hill and Wang, 1980.

———. *Practical Ethics*. Cambridge: Cambridge University Press, 1979.

Sobel, Robert. *The Last Bull Market: Wall Street in the 1960s*. New York: W. W. Norton, 1980.

Sombart, Werner. *Why Is There No Socialism in the United States?* [1906] Translated by Patricia M. Hocking and C. T. Husbands. White Plains, New York: International Arts and Sciences Press, 1976.

Stein, Herbert. *The Fiscal Revolution in America*. Chicago: University of Chicago Press, 1969.

Steinfels, Peter. *The Neoconservatives: The Men Who Are Changing America's Politics*. New York: Touchstone, 1980.

Stobaugh, Robert, and Daniel Yergin, eds. *Energy Future: Report of the Energy Project at the Harvard Business School*. New York: Ballantine, 1980.

Thurow, Lester C. *The Zero-Sum Society: Distribution and the Possibilities for Economic Change*. New York: Basic, 1980.

Vatter, Harold G. *The U.S. Economy in the 1950s: An Economic History*. New York: W. W. Norton, 1963.

Veblen, Thorstein. *The Portable Veblen*. Edited by Max Lerner. New York: Penguin, 1976.

Walzer, Michael. *Spheres of Justice: A Defense of Pluralism and Equality.* New York: Basic, 1983.

Wills, Garry. *Inventing America: Jefferson's Declaration of Independence.* Garden City, New York: Doubleday, 1978.

Wood, Gordon S. *The Creation of the American Republic, 1776–1787.* Chapel Hill, North Carolina: University of North Carolina Press, 1969. Rpt. New York: W. W. Norton, 1972.

Yergin, Daniel. *Shattered Peace: The Origins of the Cold War and the National Security State.* Boston: Houghton Mifflin, 1977.

Index

LIBRARY OF CONGRESS CATALOGING-IN-PUBLICATION
DATA

Okroi, Loren J., 1950–
    Galbraith, Harrington, Heilbroner: economics and dissent
in an age of optimism / by Loren J. Okroi.
      p.   cm.
    Revision of the author's thesis (Ph.D.)—University of
California, Irvine, 1982.
    Bibliography: p.
    Includes index.
    ISBN 0-691-07771-1 (alk. paper)
    1. Economics—United States. 2. Distributive justice.
3. Wealth, Ethics of. 4. Liberalism—United States. 5. Capitalism—United States—Moral and ethical aspects. 6. Galbraith, John Kenneth, 1908– . 7. Harrington, Michael,
1928– . 8. Heilbroner, Robert L. I. Title.
HB119.A2049 1988   87-35416
330'.0973—dc19   CIP